KATE GIBBS is a Sydney-based food and travel writer whose work has appeared in *The Wall Street Journal, The Sydney Morning Herald, Australian Gourmet Traveller, delicious.* magazine and many other publications. She writes a weekly food trends column in the *Sunday Style* magazine in *The Sunday Telegraph*, as well as a popular blog, kategibbs.com. Kate is the granddaughter of Australian food writer and National Living Treasure, Margaret Fulton. This is her third book.

MARGARET and ME

KATE GIBBS

FOREWORD BY MARGARET FULTON

MURDOCH BOOKS

FOREWORD

I've been interviewed by a lot of journalists. They want to know this and that about my life, what I eat, whether it's a whole egg or an egg yolk in mayonnaise, or how to make the perfect sponge cake. As a writer myself, I always knew what they wanted, and could give them a pithy something. But these interviews with my granddaughter were different.

Writing a book in my family is always celebrated with a jolly cheer and perhaps a glass of champagne. This book was different.

'It's called *Margaret and Me*, Grandma,' Kate told me when breaking the news that she would write a memoir with recipes.

'Margaret who?' I replied.

But Kate's memoir – she calls it a foodoir, which makes me laugh – is my story, too. Her ongoing career and her passion for food are entwined in the tales of what I did, what I ate, and how I gave food and cooking my all. But Kate's story is her own – different to mine yet as exciting. Woven within these pages are the adventures, fantastic fun and lives of two very strong, very independent women.

Our tales are different. Kate, so far, has not had to hitch a ride during a Great Depression. She has not won a job on the quality of her brown bread rolls. And I didn't learn about the magic of a home-cooked meal while I was bedraggled and blistered in faraway China. I've spent the last thirty-odd years listening to Kate's stories, hearing about her escapades, her ups and downs. And it's so exciting to read them in book form.

I've had a marvellous time doing this food thing. I learned early on that breakfast can be a bit of a rush and lunch can pass by in a whirl. But all my life I have sat down with the family and friends I love for the evening meal, gathered to share not only the food but the day's happenings. It's the people that keep you going. As Kate and I sat down for yet another interview for this book, what joy it was sitting with her, reliving it all, and sharing it yet again with someone I love.

This is my legacy. I could not be more proud that my granddaughter Kate has embraced it with all the love, energy and sparkle that she uses, also, to take on the world.

Much love,
Margaret (Grandma)
December 2014

CONTENTS

INTRODUCTION

Margaret Fulton looked up from her cup of tea and breakfast and met my eyes.

'Is there salt in this, darling?'

I shook my head. I'd been watching her arteries.

'Kate. There are three ingredients in porridge. Use all of them.'

I've been telling stories about my grandmother for a long time. When I was growing up, people asked what it was like to have the National Living Treasure, the indomitable Margaret, as a grandmother. They wanted detail. So I started telling stories. I told about the time she made my mother eat the maggots in the cooked cabbage, and when the butcher delivered a whole lamb to her house as payment for work, or how impressed she was when I returned from school camp one year and had finally figured out that it was polite to help clear the table (never mind that I stacked the plates at the table at first, it was a start).

As I grew older, gradually my grandmother slipped out of the tales of what-was-eaten, and I forged a career around writing stories for newspapers and magazines instead. As a journalist, my own experiences, the food and the remarkable chefs who cooked, the gastronomic world, became the fascinating centre of my epicurean scribblings.

But what Margaret ate, how she taught middle Australia how to cook, how she travelled and brought recipes for nasi goreng and rice pilaf back from overseas, and drew the majority of households away from a diet of boiled veg and chops and meals delivered with names so unromantically literal that they were hardly a cause of national pride, remains one of the most important stories of my life.

Food is important. My view on it echoes the 200-year-old words of the French lawyer and politician, Jean Anthelme Brillat-Savarin, who famously wrote in *The Physiology of Taste*, 'Tell me what you eat and I will tell you who you are'. Maybe if we could get a better grip on what we eat, where it comes from, and how we eat it, we could better understand ourselves.

Food can be the marker of our lives, too, a culinary pointer to what we did and how we did it, and who we did it with. These are the stories of all our lives, of holidays and the daily grind. For me, my father's oyster fritters for breakfast on holidays a few hours north of Sydney, staying near the beach, remains one of my strongest memories. He'd wake us up by whistling Brahms, brewing pots of plunger coffee and tumbling these fried, crunchy morsels studded with whole oysters that tasted of the sea onto plates, lemon wedges for squeezing over. Then there were my mother's hot Indian curries, mountains of pappadams and homemade chutneys, each of us serving and being served, talking over each other, spooning mango pickle from a jar, a sip of Dad's beer. It helps me better understand myself, somehow.

Cooking for your people makes life better. Few of us like to cook for professional cooks and chefs for fear of being judged or, worse, berated. Better to bow to the experts and just bring dessert in a box. Usually, though, cooks are the most generous, gracious diners, who heap praise on those of us who bother to take to the saucepan or the whisk for them at all. Margaret is no exception. She once swore my Korean beef tacos were the best things she's ever eaten. The saltless porridge though, not so much.

My grandmother talks about growing up at the table, singing for her supper. Everyone helped and pitched in, stirred the pots and set the table, cleared up. The kitchen was the centre of the house for her, as a child. And she made it so for us, too. I grew up the way many do, at the table, surrounded by family and friends. It's the stories from these tables that I now share. This is my inheritance.

IT STARTS WITH FOOD

AN INTRODUCTION TO FOOD AND COOKERY

'They taught us the daftest things,' Grandma tells me. 'Goodness only knows why I ever took up a career in food. I might have run away, gone into fashion or become a stage actor or a Bluebell girl, and never made a sponge cake at all.'

My grandmother, Margaret Fulton, was making her way through the Leaving Certificate exam of her final year domestic science class. The girls-only class incorporated a bit of cooking and sewing; it was about lining the fairer sex up to do the domestic arts that would be required of them later in life.

'I learned how to make awful food, and to cook it badly.'

She knew it was bad. She'd tried the potted meat and sloppy stews, overhauled lumpy custard and cloying puddings.

She had taken one recipe on as a homework assignment in her mother's kitchen. Margaret bought the ingredients herself on the way home from her local school in Glen Innes, in country New South Wales, pulled out her mother Isabella's pots and pans, and set a single place at the kitchen table for the designated tester. Her father Alexander unfolded a napkin on his lap and prepared for the youngest of his six children's foray into food.

'Brains in white sauce, Father,' she announced.

The brains were soft under the pressure of his knife, slightly grainy, the white sauce watery and a little lumpy: too much flour, not enough seasoning.

'Father looked up at Mother and appealed with his eyes, as if to say "save me",' Margaret remembers. 'Mother knew how to do brains in black butter sauce, a touch of vinegar for acidity – brains noisette.'

Isabella washed the plates and saucepans clean, then showed her how to make the dish properly: browning the butter for a nutty sauce, the brains just done.

Margaret entered the linoleum-clad classroom, her black hair in long plaits, pleated tunic with a fabric belt around her waist, white socks folded over twice, and prepared to cook more food badly, and be judged on it. But when she sat at her place in the classroom, she was presented with a twelve-foot damask tablecloth. Her task was to iron the fabric using a flat iron – the kind you need to heat over an actual fuel stove – even though electric irons were widely available then.

She says now: 'Of course, to iron damask you need the fabric damp and the iron hot, so I did that. But what a ridiculous thing to test. I think they were just being cruel.'

Ironing damask, soggy brains and talentless teachers were not going to deter her from success, however. She had ambitions and nothing would stop her pursuing the career she really wanted: to be a leading Australian concert pianist. Or, failing that, a music teacher.

Andrew Denton, Australian interviewer and host of the long-running television show *Enough Rope*, asked Margaret in 2008 what she dreamed of doing when she was a child, knowing she never planned to be a cook.

'When you decided to head into cooking as a career, you said that this wasn't what nice young women did at that time,' Denton pressed her in front of an audience.

'No, I didn't want to be a cook. I wanted to be a Bluebell Girl because...'

'Which is?'

'I had visions of me in Paris, you know, dancing across the stage, Andrew, and then I was going to marry a duke,' Margaret said.

'Mmm.'

My mother and I sat front row, hearing these aspirations for the first time. But we knew her, we knew she was going somewhere with this. The audience laughed.

Margaret continued: 'And then he was going to run away with a younger girl and I was going to be left homeless.'

The audience laughed again, and Denton latched onto their thinking.

'Not many people think through their fantasies to an unhappy ending, Margaret.'

'Well, that's why I didn't do it.'

While the teenager was still working it all out, Margaret's mother raised the subject of her daughter's future career over dinner one night.

'When Miss Scott gets married, Margaret will take over as the local piano teacher. I think it's perfect,' her mother announced, as if saying it made it so.

'I loved piano and I knew everyone liked Miss Scott, so I thought I would be lucky to take her place,' remembers Margaret.

Isabella would never push Margaret into something she didn't want to do, but if Margaret wanted it, then she knew her girl well enough to know she could get it. She placed her napkin on the table and stood up to clear away the meal; the matter was sorted.

Margaret did want to be a pianist; her nimble fingers and joints from practising eight hours a day were proof. She had dreams of great concert halls and, perhaps one day, crossing paths with an orchestra in Sydney. Meanwhile her mother might have had her teaching school children until a wedding took her away from her career, just like it did Miss Scott. But they agreed on the piano at least.

'Mother and Father had faith in me,' she tells me now. 'As a school student I wasn't brilliant, but they kept me on, believing it was good for me. Like a lot of Scots, Mother used to say: "Margaret, you put it between here and here" – pointing between her temples – "and nobody can take that away from you. The Scots and the Jews know that." '

With a final exam at the Conservatorium of Music just days away, Margaret tied her hair in plaits and put on her sports tunic at school. She picked up her hockey stick and ran across the grass to compete with her classmates in a practice match to prepare for the finals. She'd just got going, barely warmed up, when she found the ball in her possession. She moved it across the field as fast as she could and had steadied herself to pass it to her teammate when she heard a cry from across the pitch.

'Attack Margaret Fulton!'

In a bid to incite a bit of competition, the sports mistress had unwittingly unleashed the school bully onto Margaret.

'I looked into her eyes and I could see what was coming next,' she tells me. '"Whack" went the hockey stick on my unprotected thumb, and "whack" again. And bang went my brilliant career; my thumb was pulverised. That's one way of looking at it, anyway. The world lost a second-rate pianist, a piano teacher at worst. I had to find something else I felt passionate about.'

THIRD-GENERATION FOODIE

The first thing I remember eating, ever, was a mussel. This was the first time I consciously put something in my mouth, chewed it, and actively swallowed it. Really *ate* it.

I was eight, just, by a matter of days. I'd persuaded my grandmother and her partner Michael that I could handle it. They argued with me for a bit, pointing to the cheese soufflé and the onion tarte tatin on the menu, but could see it was futile. We were on holidays in America, at this moment in Hawaii on the way to Los Angeles. I'd seen moules marinières listed on the fold-out pleather menu, with its slip-in paper rundown of the day's specials, and there was no going back. My recent birthday and new age brought with them a sense of wanting to do something a bit daring. The next day for breakfast I could gorge myself on plate-sized waffles and whipped cream from a can at the hotel restaurant, but tonight – wearing my jumper with Donald Duck on the front and my crepe navy skirt, with clean hair and a bangle – tonight, I'd do something grown-up. Mussels seemed as grown-up as anything else.

Michael's steak arrived, pommes frites on the side, and I envied his melting disc of butter with chopped chives. Grandma's roast 'baby chicken' came as half a chicken. Mussels! I felt so clever ordering this smart dish, all black and shiny and adult-appropriate. But inside they were more quivery, pink, opening in distorted rippling mouths, than I remembered my parents making for themselves at home. I braved the first mussel but it wouldn't go down. I chewed it a bit and tried again: no. I was embarrassed for myself.

Grandma moved swiftly, shifting portions onto side plates, rearranging the table. My mussels became a shared plate between the adults. And I had a predictable quarter baby chicken.

You remember well the first time food transports you. You are a kid, you've been under the weather all week, and your mum brings a bowl of homemade chicken broth to the table. With every slurp from the hot spoon, you feel it rescuing you from the grey cloud of your head. Steam flushes over your cheeks and it lifts you.

Or maybe it's the wedge of baklava, eaten in your bikini on the beach in Greece as a nineteen-year-old, your first boyfriend lying tanned beside you. You bite into the pastry, flaky, laden with pistachios and dripping with sweet aromatic golden honey.

Or, maybe, it's the crackling shell of takeaway deep-fried chicken that you eat in your first dorm room, independent at last.

Food that you remember – food that stays with you all your life, no matter how rumpled the tablecloths or how convoluted the map to get there, no matter what it cost you (or someone else) – is the most powerful of all. These gastronomic markers of our lives take us back to places and moments, and allow us to recall our adventures, when everything else turns to dust.

Grandma's New Year's Eve parties: watching boats make their fairy-lit processions around the harbour, neighbours popping corks and lighting barbecues, cheering at ferries overloaded with people, rocking on the busy harbour as they progress under Sydney Harbour Bridge.

New Year's Eve is like Christmas for us, a family gathering that encompasses as many friends as we've collected through the year, hope to reconnect with next year. It's important to Grandma – a Hogmanay tradition brought from Scotland to Sydney Harbour. Each year we put in orders in for Guinness-glazed ham, a side of homemade gravlax cured with vodka, sugar and salt, a cucumber salad, steamed potatoes with mint, a roast fillet of beef, Mum's béarnaise sauce and, for me, piroshki and little potato scones for the gravlax. The potato scones are whipped morsels of potato and egg whites, cooked in a frying pan so they have a golden pikelet quality, but lighter (see recipe on page 21).

These last two dishes are, to me, the culinary epitome of New Year's Eve, a necessary family custom that began when I was five or six, when I ate my canapés under the table with my labrador, Winnie. Together, we shared piroshki (see recipe on page 22), those doughy bites filled with soft, sweet onions, speck and sometimes sauerkraut.

'One for me, Winnie, one for you.' Labradors are good like that.

We balanced glasses and bottles of beer, cheese gougères, still hot from the oven, in our free hands. I always made my way to Grandma's good friend Lewis Morley, a gentle, talented photographer who took portraits of me in my teens. He told me stories of photographing Charlotte Rampling, the Beatles, Salvador Dali. I swooned. My sister Louise, two years younger than me, and I would chase each other in circles with other kids, playing tip into the summer evening. Years later, we'd sneak a bottle of champagne, with other friends, and lie down on the cool grass into the night.

Bursts of laughter rose towards the darkening sky, a picture from one of the Great Gatsby's parties. We waited for Sydney's nine-o'clock fireworks to start, working up a steam and through the canapés, the champagne. The air smelled of summer gardenias and perfume – as it had done every year before.

Guests teetered on heels, navigating the decking and balancing plates piled with Guinness-glazed ham carved from the bone, dill-flecked potato salad, and Mum's roasted tomatoes with charred capsicum (see recipe on page 24). That dish *is* New Year's Eve. Barely a week goes by in summer when I don't have another batch of large red capsicums charring on my gas burner. I spoon it onto toast for breakfast, pack it for lunch with a tin of tuna, and every year I request it for another New Year's Eve banquet.

Year after year these dishes returned. I did too, in slightly more bizarre outfits as I approached my teens, then with attempts at sophistication since then – more lace, less tulle, more legs, less cleavage, more cleavage, less makeup, tamed hair – but the food stayed the same.

When my dad was a boy, some over-powdered, tweed-wearing New Zealand relative asked him if he was going to get married when he grew up. Instead of skipping the hell out of there as most boys might, he replied, with the assurance of a kid who knew what he wanted:

'I'm going to marry a Cordon Bleu cook'.

I can picture the ruddy matron now, squeezing his adorable cheeks and ruffling the little head so full of fanciful romantic dreams. Except, when he grew up, he did.

He knew what was good for him. My mother, my grandmother's only child, took on food as wholeheartedly as her famous mum. And her cooking changed his life. It changed all of our lives. The daily fare that might have turned up on the table, had he chosen another girl in 1969, was instead inventive and extraordinary food. Delicately lifting sheets of homemade shortcrust from a well-floured bench with the hands of a master, my mother kept us all entranced.

As a child and teen, my cooking was akin to taming a lion. I'd nervously throw ingredients together prod mixtures with a wooden spoon, and the results had the few survivors running away screaming. Mum knew that a soufflé wouldn't rise even before I'd put it in oven, before I'd placed it in the dish or folded its two 'halves' together. She'd step in with a whisk, beat the whites a little more, and deftly pull it together to achieve the desired awed applause.

Sometimes I dreamed up things to eat as a kind of dare to her aptitude. After dinner, dishes all packed away, I'd pose: 'Wouldn't a lemon delicious pudding go down well?'

Far from being a slave to our desires, Mum saw it as an opportunity to teach us how to cook. If we wanted something, we'd be there while she made it, zesting lemon rind and adding the milky lemony mixture to the egg whites, buttering the dish.

'Profiteroles!' I suggested one morning, hoping she'd get to it as she prepared the evening meal.

'Uh-huh,' she replied, getting into the car in her nightie to drive Louise and me to the bus stop for school. But that evening, when I got home, she had laid out a dish of butter cut into cubes, a pot of sugar, a dozen eggs, and an assortment of flours on the kitchen bench.

'Really?' I said, disappointed.

'Prop yourself up there,' she said, pointing to the corner of the kitchen bench, 'and just watch.'

Now I can do it. I couldn't straight away; it took years of not bothering, or ordering in from some French patisserie, or cajoling Mum herself before I finally invested in a pastry bag and a clatter of nozzles. But the image of Mum's profiteroles that evening has kept me deeply vested in the dish. Arranged on a platter, each choux pastry ball is filled with thick vanilla custard, almost gelatinous and velvety at once, and the lot is drizzled with dark, bitter-sweet chocolate sauce (see recipe on page 26).

I have Dad's wisest possible choice in a future wife and the mother of his children to thank for it.

POTATO SCONES *with* SALMON CAVIAR

See story on page 17

MAKES 35
PREPARATION 25 minutes
COOKING 25 minutes

250 g (9 oz) all-purpose
   potatoes (such as sebago),
   peeled and halved
25 g (1 oz) butter, softened
   plus extra for frying
45 ml (1½ fl oz) milk
125 g (4½ oz) self-raising
   (self-rising) flour
4 free-range eggs, separated
45 g (1½ oz) sour cream,
   plus extra, to serve
sea salt and freshly ground
   black pepper
salmon caviar, to serve
snipped chives, to serve

Cover the potatoes with cold water in a large saucepan and cook over medium heat for 10–15 minutes, or until easily pierced with a fork. Drain, then push the potatoes through a ricer, or mash them. Return the potato to the saucepan, add the butter and milk, and mix together well while still hot.

Transfer the mixture to a large bowl to cool, then beat in the sifted flour, egg yolks and sour cream. Season with salt and pepper.

Use an electric mixer to beat the egg whites until stiff peaks form, then carefully fold the beaten egg white into the potato mixture, using a metal spoon or spatula.

Heat 1 tablespoon of butter in a large, heavy-based frying pan over medium heat. Use two teaspoons to measure out heaped teaspoons of mixture, forming them into rounds.

In batches of four, fry the scones briefly on both sides, until golden, being careful not to flatten them too much. Repeat with the remaining mixture. Transfer the scones to a plate covered with a tea towel (dish towel).

To serve, offer sour cream for dolloping on the scones, salmon caviar for spooning over and snipped chives for sprinkling on top.

PIROSHKI

See story on page 18

MAKES About 24
PREPARATION 30 minutes,
plus 1 hour 15 minutes proving
COOKING 25 minutes

310 ml (10¾ fl oz/1¼ cups) milk
125 g (4½ oz) butter
2 tablespoons sugar
450 g (1 lb/3 cups) plain
    (all-purpose) flour, plus
    extra for dusting
2 teaspoons salt
1 x 7 g (¼ oz) sachet
    dried yeast
1 free-range egg yolk
1 free-range egg, lightly
    whisked, to glaze

Filling
50 g (1¾ oz) butter
1 tablespoon extra virgin
    olive oil
2 large brown onions,
    finely chopped
250 g (9 oz) speck,
    finely chopped
210 g (7½ oz/1 cup) sauerkraut
1 teaspoon freshly ground
    black pepper

Put the milk, butter and sugar in a medium saucepan and stir over low heat until the butter has melted.

Sift together the flour and salt in a large mixing bowl and stir in the yeast. Make a well in the flour and pour in the milk mixture. Add the egg yolk and stir from the centre, gradually incorporating a little more flour from the sides. Beat the dough with a wooden spoon for 3 minutes, until smooth and elastic – use your hands if you find it easier. Sprinkle the dough with a little flour and then cover with plastic wrap and a tea towel (dish towel).

Leave in a warm place for 1 hour or until the dough has doubled in size.

For the filling, heat the butter and oil in a large frying pan over medium heat and sauté the onions until tender and slightly golden, being careful not to brown them. Add the speck, sauerkraut and black pepper and cook for 5 minutes on medium–low heat. Remove from the heat and cool to room temperature.

Preheat the oven to 230°C (450°F). Line a baking tray with baking paper.

To assemble the piroshki, turn the dough out onto a floured work surface and knead lightly. Take a tablespoon-sized piece of dough in your hand, flatten it slightly into a thick disc in your palm and place 1 teaspoonful of the filling in the middle. Fold the edges over to enclose the filling, then mould into a small ball. Repeat for the remaining pastry and filling. Put the balls on the prepared tray. Cover with a clean tea towel and leave to prove (rise) in a warm place for about 15 minutes.

Brush the piroshki with egg and bake for 10–15 minutes, or until golden. Serve hot.

tip

These can be made ahead, baked for two-thirds of the time (8–10 minutes), and then frozen in plastic snap-lock bags. Bake from frozen until golden and heated through.

ROASTED TOMATOES *with* CHARRED CAPSICUM

See story on page 18

SERVES 4–6
PREPARATION 20 minutes
COOKING 50 minutes

2 garlic cloves, thinly sliced
2 tablespoons balsamic vinegar
2 tablespoons extra virgin
 olive oil
1 small handful basil leaves,
 coarsely torn
8 (about 600 g/1 lb 5 oz) ripe
 tomatoes, halved
sea salt flakes
2 tablespoons baby capers
crusty sourdough, to serve

Charred capsicum
2 large red capsicums
 (peppers)
1 garlic clove, thinly sliced
1 tablespoon Raspberry
 Vinegar (see page 113)
2 tablespoons extra virgin
 olive oil

For the charred capsicum, set a large chargrill pan over high heat until very hot. Put the capsicums on the pan and cook, using tongs to rotate, until they are blackened all over. Alternatively, hold one capsicum with tongs over a gas flame, rotating until it is black, then repeat. The skin should be blistered all over. Put the capsicums in a brown paper bag and close at the top, or place in a medium bowl and cover with plastic wrap. Set aside for 20 minutes to steam in their own heat.

Remove and discard the plastic wrap or paper bag, then pull the stalks from the capsicum with the seeds and discard, reserving any juice in a medium bowl. Put them on a board, cut them in half lengthways, and scrape the blackened side with a knife to remove the skins. Tear the capsicum into strips. Transfer to the bowl with the juices, add the garlic, vinegar and olive oil and toss to combine. Cover and set aside for the flavours to develop.

Preheat the oven to 180°C (350°F).

Combine the garlic, vinegar, olive oil and basil leaves in a large bowl, add the tomatoes and toss to coat. Marinate for 5–10 minutes, then season with salt to taste.

Arrange the tomatoes, cut-side up, with the basil, garlic and marinade in an ovenproof dish big enough to hold them in one layer. Roast for about 45 minutes, or until soft, then add the capers and stir gently to combine.

Toss the capsicum together with the tomatoes and juices on a serving platter and serve with sourdough.

tip

You can use sherry vinegar instead of raspberry, if you prefer.

PROFITEROLES

See story on page 19

MAKES 45
PREPARATION 40 minutes,
plus chilling
COOKING 1 hour 15 minutes

125 g (4½ oz) unsalted butter,
   coarsely chopped
1 teaspoon caster
   (superfine) sugar
½ teaspoon salt
150 g (5½ oz/1 cup) plain
   (all-purpose) flour, sifted
5 free-range eggs

Crème pâtissière
1 litre (35 fl oz/4 cups) milk
2 vanilla beans, halved
   lengthways, seeds scraped
8 free-range egg yolks
4 tablespoons plain
   (all-purpose) flour
4 tablespoons cornflour
   (cornstarch)
220 g (7¾ oz/1 cup) caster
   (superfine) sugar

Chocolate sauce
300 ml (10½ fl oz) thin (pouring)
   cream (35% milk fat)
250 g (9 oz) dark chocolate
   (at least 70% cocoa solids),
   finely chopped
50 g (1¾ oz) butter, softened

For the chocolate sauce, heat the cream in a medium saucepan and bring to the boil, then reduce the heat to low. Add the chocolate, stirring gently until melted.

Remove from the heat, stir in the butter and allow the sauce to cool to room temperature. Reheat when needed.

For the crème pâtissière, combine the milk, vanilla beans and seeds in a medium saucepan and bring to a simmer over medium heat. Remove from the heat, cover and set aside.

Beat the egg yolks, flour and cornflour together using an electric mixer. Add the sugar and beat until pale and thick.

Reheat the milk to a simmer, remove the vanilla, then slowly add to the egg yolks, whisking continuously. Return the mixture to a clean saucepan and cook over low heat for 8 minutes, stirring continuously, until thick.

Scrape the vanilla crème into a bowl and cover the surface closely with baking paper before cooling completely.

Preheat the oven to 200°C (400°F). Lightly grease two baking trays.

In a medium saucepan, combine the butter, sugar and salt with 250 ml (9 fl oz/1 cup) water. Bring to the boil, then stir in the flour. Cook, stirring constantly, over medium heat, until the mixture comes away from the sides of the pan.

Transfer to the bowl of an electric mixer and leave to cool slightly. Beat in the eggs, one at a time, on low speed, until the mixture is shiny and smooth.

Use a piping bag with a plain 1.5 cm (⅝ in) nozzle to pipe high mounds, about 2.5 cm (1 in) wide, onto the prepared trays, leaving space between for spreading. Bake in the oven for 20 minutes, then reduce the temperature to 190°C (375°F) and bake for a further 10 minutes, or until golden brown and crisp. Turn off the oven and leave the profiteroles to cool in the oven.

Pipe crème pâtissière in through the base of the profiteroles. Arrange on a platter, then drizzle over hot chocolate sauce.

tip

This makes 45 profiteroles. You can freeze half the batch of unfilled puffs in an airtight container for another time, and only make half the quantity of crème pâtissière.

NEW AUSTRALIANS

From the age of two, Margaret, her older siblings and her parents lived in Glen Innes, a town about 600 kilometres north of Sydney. Her father was a tailor and the children were dressed impeccably in sensible Scottish wool and sturdy leather. Margaret always wanted to wear something pink as a little girl and – pushing it – some patent leather shoes.

Other girls didn't wear tweed overcoats and lace-up brown shoes with buttons, they weren't nicknamed 'Scotch'. Other girls were not immigrants, whose father had packed up his entire family, overhauling life plans on the say-so of a letter from a fellow tailor who had moved from Scotland to Australia and found wealth (as a farmer, he neglected to note). Other girls didn't have little velour hats like the ones worn by the English Princesses Elizabeth and Margaret Rose: they were different. Margaret was different.

Two of her three brothers also longed to be like the local boys, who stumbled out of bed at dawn, year round, milked the cows and then rode their horses ten kilometres to where the bus picked them up for school. These eight- and ten-year-olds' heads fell into the crook of their elbows during class, their red and rough hands falling limp as they slept at their desks. John and Alex Fulton envied their hardship, coveted their position on the brink of manhood.

Meanwhile, Margaret joined the swathes of immigrants who were yet to be wholly accepted in small Australian country towns, but who were beginning to form part of the structure of things. Chinese migrants ran the local department store, Kwong Sing's; Greeks ran the Paragon Café; Lebanese ran the draper's shop – and the local tailor was a Scot.

'The Australian children called us Scotch, Chink, Dago, worse. But it didn't matter, everyone had their adversities, and that wasn't so bad,' she tells me.

When her father told her stories of Scottish heroes, she felt much less of an outsider.

'I went home to hear stories of William Wallace, or red-headed Scottish warriors withstanding the Romans, tales of Robert the Bruce, and I was proud of where I'd come from.'

'Queen Margaret was my namesake,' she says.

Her parents claimed it was this wife of Malcolm, King of the Scots – who spent her childhood in Hungary; introduced spiced meat and French wines to the court in 1066; brought ballads, singing and dancing to the stiff-collared aristocracy – whom she could thank for her name.

'But it's more likely I was named after Aunt Maggie, my mother's older sister,' she chuckles to herself.

As the Great Depression pushed more people out of work, men travelled into small towns looking for jobs, often arriving at Margaret's father's tailor shop to see if he could use them; a shilling or two was better than starving. He found odds and ends for them: re-rolling fabric and sharpening scissors, sweeping floors and tinkering with plumbing. When their token chores were done and he handed them something for their work, Alexander sent them on to his wife, giving them directions and suggesting they may be useful there. They pulled weeds from the garden and beat the dust from rugs, polished cutlery and pruned trees.

Families pulled together meals from the cheapest cuts, and tripe – the rippled insides of a cow's stomach – appeared on tables everywhere. Tripe and onions, boiled into a stew, became a popular staple during the Depression and while her friends hated the dish, Margaret loved how her mother made it. The flavours enveloped each other, rich and textured. Bread and dripping were served with mutton for bulking up meals and mopping up juices. Bread was often saved for dessert if treacle was on hand, a sweet, luxurious treat.

'Australian women became very adept,' says Margaret now. 'They had very little at this time, but they made the effort, especially when a guest was coming. It wasn't uncommon to travel three or four hours to have afternoon tea. So you had the feeling that you had to do something really proper and special. It's not as though you could run down to the shops to pick up a cake. Women took a lot of pride in their skills in the kitchen.'

Margaret's mother Isabella was no different. She took her recipe cues from the Country Women's Association and the Presbyterian Women's Association cookbooks, learning new ways to bake. She stumbled over the chocolate cakes and sponges her Australian peers had mastered – it didn't come naturally. Margaret envied her friends who arrived home to jam tarts and gingerbread cake; she was handed an apple when she walked in the door. There was usually shortbread, that crumbly and buttery Scottish biscuit, and Dundee cake, a dense fruitcake that Margaret adored, but both were for special occasions, for guests who travelled miles for afternoon tea.

Sitting with a bowl on her lap in the afternoon, Isabella used her hands to beat butter and sugar until it resembled whipped cream, to make one baked thing she did perfectly: shortbread. The warmth of her hands softened the butter as she pinched her fingers into a whisk shape – no utensils needed. Scots often add ground rice to their shortbread, giving the whole thing a coarse grittiness. But the texture also comes from using coarse flour, hand-ground where possible. Margaret and her sisters never agreed on how their mother made the recipe, what was 'proper'. So from this brood of children came a handful of different recipes for shortbread, and each continued to make her own version of their mother's recipe throughout their lives. Catherine, Margaret's oldest sister ('She makes a very good shortbread,' says Margaret diplomatically), doesn't knead the shortbread, but Margaret remembers her mother working away at it in a bowl, 'so I knead'. Jean, Margaret's closest sister in age, 'kneads a little bit'. But Margaret says it's important not to knead the dough too much nor overwork it.

'It needs lightness of hand and good judgment. If the ingredients are worked too much, shortbread becomes tough and chewy, instead of short and melting in the mouth.' (See recipe on page 35.)

Jam tart shortages aside, there was food. Baskets of lemons, beef heart tomatoes, bunches of basil and rosemary, green beans and yellow squash, baby zucchini and tamarillos, spinach, silverbeet and guavas arrived in great bounty at the door. In lieu of actually paying Alexander for his work as a tailor, customers often turned up to the house loaded with boxes of produce from their gardens. There were cabbages and turnips, carrots and even fish that people caught themselves, all offerings in place of money. When they grew nothing, customers found other ways to pay. Many baked. While the Fulton clan was not exactly rolling in money, there was always plenty to eat.

Margaret's mother had a way to use everything. She found something to love in every onion, stalk of celery and bunch of carrots, and giant pots of stock sat on the stove all afternoon, barely simmering, to create bases for soups and stews.

One day Margaret opened the door to a stranger, an apron wrapped tightly around his portly shape.

'Hello, dear, could you please open the door as wide as possible,' and he gestured to his right, out of Margaret's view. She slipped out the door and almost ran into a teenage boy with a whole creature slung over his shoulder.

'It's for your mother, love. Yer father said to just bring it on up here, said to put it in the kitchen. It's payment for the work he's been doin' for us.'

'Oh!' said Margaret. 'Yes, please follow me.'

And the young man traipsed after her through the house, a whole lamb, skinned and gutted, over his shoulder. He laid the carcass on the kitchen table in the middle of the room, nodded at Margaret, and walked back through the house.

All of this bartered food was hand-reared and homegrown, homemade. We tend to remember vividly our first taste of fresh-pickled pine mushrooms, fresh baby peas right out of the pod, homegrown sorrel folded into butter and slipped under the skin of a pasture-fed chicken. And having eaten Mrs Magoo from Glen Innes' chocolate cake – a most perfect combination of dense and rich – and the freshly picked produce arriving at the door, Margaret rebelled against anything that would put her in the way of eating ordinary. The more hand-reared baby milk-fed lamb and beetroots straight from Mr Bluster's garden she was given, the more heightened her senses, the stronger her appetite for good ingredients.

Isabella was an alchemist in the kitchen, and followed her countrymen's tradition of turning food that might seem to be lead into gold. What was a humble shoulder of lamb or mutton neck, an unlovely strip of stomach, became complex broths and wonderful brews. Margaret witnessed tough, veiny hunks of meat go into the oven and come out, hours later, the sauce reduced and the meat darkened, sweet, salty, transformed.

She didn't make haggis, though. In Scotland, butchers tackled the complex procedure themselves, and the family bought it for New Year's celebrations to have with 'neeps and tatties' – mashed turnip and potato, lots of butter. But in Australia, it was not so readily available.

What is haggis? It's the butt of culinary jokes about Scottish people, for one. It's the Thing Never To Be Eaten Under Any Circumstances for culinary cowards. And it does sound terrifying to the uninitiated: a hot sticky mix of sheep's 'pluck' (the whole oesophagus, lungs, heart and liver, yanked from the sheep in one go) finely ground and mixed with oatmeal, chopped onions, lots of black pepper. The gooey filling is stuffed inside a sheep's stomach, steamed slowly and then whisked into the oven. Then, the stomach peeled back and the innards revealed, it's served hot. A dram of single malt works well with it (more as a lick of courage than anything else). There's no romantic way to write about it. On paper it's barbaric, but the reality is quite the opposite.

Margaret's mother did turn to another Scottish classic for her brood, however: Scotch broth. It is indeed a broth, but with carrots and other root vegetables, lamb slowly cooked so the gnarly fatty bits, the shin or neck, fall from the bone and become so tender, so remarkably soft and flavoursome that the Scots have handed the dish their country's name in its honour (see recipe on page 36).

Isabella took a saw and sharp knives to the whole lamb and butchered it herself. Lamb shoulders and neck, trimmings, ribs, chops – the family ate lamb in various guises for weeks. Margaret watched her mother create the broth, as she had done many times before. She sautéed vegetables in butter until they turned aromatic and golden, added the lamb's 'lesser' cuts with stock and barley, and simmered the lot for three or four hours. It was this broth that was simmering gently when two strangers came for dinner.

The sound of whispering in the kitchen drew Margaret across the house. She recognised her parents' voices, but there were other voices too, hushed but emphatic. When she entered the kitchen, two men stood up from the kitchen table suddenly. They held their coats in front of them, their skinny frames draped in clothes a few sizes too big. Margaret smiled and, as she drew nearer, saw the deep lines in their faces, which were brown and worn. Their hands were rough and blackened and their slender necks too old, their eyes too sad for their years. It was not the first time men like this had stood in the kitchen. They dropped their eyes when they saw her.

Isabella, Alexander and the six siblings joined their guests at the table that evening. Isabella asked the children how their days had been, and the boys beamed about their neighbour's offer of one of their horses to ride one weekend. Isabella spoke of a recipe she'd heard about on the wireless. The communal chatter warmed the small room. Margaret's father asked the guests where they'd been looking for work, where they would head next. These men were going for days without anything to eat. They'd left their families behind in search of work, sending money back where they could. The Fultons scrimped to pay for electricity, and fabrics for clothes were not easy to come by – but they would eat, and they had each other at the table.

SCOTTISH SHORTBREAD

See story on page 30

MAKES 36 x 6 cm (2½ in)
round shortbreads
PREPARATION 30 minutes
COOKING 30 minutes

250 g (9 oz) butter, softened
110 g (3¾ oz/½ cup) caster
   (superfine) sugar, plus extra
   for dusting
300 g (10½ oz/2 cups) plain
   (all-purpose) flour
150 g (5½ oz/1¼ cups)
   cornflour (cornstarch)

Preheat the oven to 160°C (315°F). Lightly grease two baking trays and line with baking paper.

Use an electric mixer to cream the butter until pale, then gradually add the sugar, beating the mixture until it is pale and creamy.

Gradually work in the flour and cornflour, then knead for about 5 minutes, until it becomes a very smooth dough.

Roll out the dough on a lightly floured work surface until it is 5–6 mm (¼ in) thick and use a 6 cm (2½ in) fluted round cutter to cut out rounds. Put on the prepared trays and use a fork to prick shortbread in a decorative pattern. Dust lightly with extra caster sugar.

Bake the shortbread in the lower half of the oven for 25–30 minutes, or until very lightly coloured and crisp, swapping trays halfway through for even baking. Cool on the trays for 10 minutes, then transfer to a wire rack to cool completely. Store in an airtight container for up to 3 weeks.

SCOTCH BROTH

See story on page 32

SERVES 6–8
PREPARATION 20 minutes
COOKING 3 hours 50 minutes

2 tablespoons olive oil
25 g (1 oz) butter
1 onion, finely chopped
2 carrots, diced
3 celery stalks, sliced
1 swede (rutabaga), parsnip
   or small turnip, peeled
   and diced
3 lamb shanks
2–2.5 litres (70–85 fl oz/
   8–10 cups) homemade
   vegetable stock
100 g (3½ oz/½ cup) pearl
   barley, washed
½ savoy cabbage, tough
   stalks removed, chopped
   into 1 cm (½ in) pieces
sea salt and freshly ground
   black pepper
coarsely chopped flat-leaf
   (Italian) parsley, to serve
sliced crusty bread, to serve

Heat the olive oil and butter in a large saucepan or stockpot with a lid, then add the onion, carrot, celery and swede and sauté until the onions are softened. Add the lamb shanks and 1.5 litres (52 fl oz/6 cups) of the stock. Stir with a wooden spoon to combine, bring to the boil, then reduce the heat, cover, and simmer for 2½–3 hours, or until the lamb is starting to fall from the bone.

Add the pearl barley, stir to combine, and then cook for a further 30 minutes, adding some of the remaining stock if needed. (It shouldn't be stodgy – it should have the consistency of soup.)

Remove the shanks and meat from the pot – it should definitely be falling off the bone by now. Let the shanks cool a little while the broth bubbles away gently over medium–low heat. When the shanks are cool enough to handle, remove the bones and use two forks or your fingers to shred the meat coarsely into bite-sized pieces, discarding any surplus fat or gristle.

Add the cabbage to the pot with as much of the remaining stock as you like, depending on the consistency you want. Return the lamb to the pot and simmer for 10 minutes, then season to taste.

To serve, place the pot in the middle of the table to allow people to help themselves to the hot broth. Serve the parsley for sprinkling over the broth, and accompany with sliced bread.

IT'S NOT OUR ROOSTER

'Pig's feet and cauliflower,' Mum giggled to herself.

It was a running family joke: Mum refusing to risk the slumped shoulders and moans when she told us what we were really having for dinner. If she'd made roast chicken and we'd been hoping for lasagne: disappointment. Rissoles, when all day we'd been wishing for roast chicken: disaster. It was our spoilt daily tussle and Mum dodged the ramifications of our expectations simply by skipping over them altogether. The answer to the inevitable question of 'What are we having for dinner' was often, then, the worst possible imagining of what a person could ever eat, ever: 'Pig's feet and cauliflower.'

The result of her tricky mum-ness was that we were never actually disappointed when we sat down to a meal. It may not have been soy-marinated chicken wings, as we'd privately hoped, but it could have been much worse, too. Just once it was worse, but it wasn't her fault.

Something was up with this food. I knew it and my sister knew it, but the adults were not letting on. We were already suspicious because we were staying with Aunty Leslie and Uncle Graham in New Zealand, and perfectly extraordinary company as they were while we were netting for flounder, diving for scallops or steaming fresh-caught cockles on the beach in Auckland, they didn't know our dietary requirements, which included – my parents obviously forgot to mention when they packed us off in a plane to the New Zealand family for a holiday (their holiday) – nothing suspicious.

Being two years younger than me, Louise had the youth that brought with it the luxury of naïvety. Two years goes a long way when you're only eight; the age gap equated to a quarter of my life, but a third of hers. Those extra years gave me the power of culinary insight, and set me up with the role of grand-inquisitor-of-all-suspicious-things-on-plates.

Louise was less guarded and therefore less analytical, and began a meal simply by eating it. Not me. I'd spooned avocado flesh from its half shell, I'd ploughed into broccoli and anchovy spaghetti, hell, I'd polished off a can of smoked oysters at my parents' dinner parties when nobody was looking. All in all, I was adventurous. But this – odd, lumpy, meaty bits in white sauce, with some carrots – was not right. The adults were not letting on.

'What is this, Aunty Leslie?' I asked as I prodded a lump with my fork.

'Do you like it, dear?'

She was standing in the kitchen, and I did a 180-degree twist in my chair to face her. My sister and I were having an early dinner before the adults had theirs. For me, this was just another notch on the wall of things that were weird. I kept eye contact, so she went on.

'It's meat in white sauce, some lovely onions, herbs, parsley, I think,' and she rattled off another herb or two, trailing off while she poured herself a glass of wine.

When adults generalise about some parts of a story, but are specific about other parts – going into great detail, charming you with colour – it's the general bit you need to try to hang on to. This is a difficult trap to navigate because by the time you've heard all about the onions from the garden and the flat-leaf parsley, not the curly kind, and learned that the chicken in the back garden loves to eat the stalks of the carrots on your plate (let's go and see the chicken after dinner!), you forget what it was you had asked.

Rattled, I turned back to my plate. The meat, the meat.

'And the meat, Aunty Leslie?'

'I'll tell you what else; there's jelly and ice cream for dessert if you eat all your dinner.'

I knew I'd been had. I hadn't fallen for her detour, but I wasn't going to pass up jelly and ice cream either. The bribery worked. Plus, how bad could it be? The meat wasn't so horrible, a little spongy, veiny, the outside with tiny little bumps on it. I had barely swallowed one piece before I deciphered the remaining three-centimetre-long chunks on my plate.

I turned to watch my sister plough into one more piece of meat, waited for her to put it in her mouth before I released the hounds.

'I know what this is, Louise.'

Her sweet little face looked up at me, still chewing.

'It's tongues.'

She looked at me, waiting for the next bit of the joke. You can't *eat* tongues. We looked down at our plates. Louise's eyes widened.

'Tongues?' she repeated. She put her knife and fork down and stared at her plate.

'What tongues? Kate, what sort of tongues?'

We looked at each other, frozen, trying to work out what to do. Jelly and ice cream could go to hell.

The shape was disconcerting, reminding me that the tongues had been sliced off, as far back as possible in the mouth. Of course the lambs were probably dead by then, weren't they? We looked closer into our plates, inspecting. It's not as if they'd slice off the tongues and let the lambs go back into the paddocks, traumatised and bleatless but otherwise intact.

It took some steely determination to reveal to Aunty Leslie that we would not be eating our tongues, our mouths scrunched shut for effect.

'Our girls eat lamb's tongues all the time. They love them!' she said, which only made us quietly question the sanity of our cousins, and draw some dark conclusions about New Zealand. We blinked comprehension but, seeing us still frozen, our aunt resigned herself to the inevitable. We finished off our carrots on clean plates while our aunt spooned 'recovery jelly' into bowls.

It's not as though our own parents had never worked to evade our keen culinary tuning. They'd done the 'little trees' metaphor when trying to give us broccoli – hyperbole that wasn't actually needed when broccoli was cooked al dente, given a slab of butter and scattered with sliced toasted almonds anyway.

Playing one day in our garden in Sydney's inner west, my sister and I counted the chickens. They had their own little nook at the bottom of the property, a tree for sitting in and fresh sawdust for scratching. The ducks, Indian Runners, were there; they'd joined us in the paddling pool earlier that day, dipping under the water to wet their backs, quacking while we, naked, chased them around the garden. But the rooster was missing. Next thing, we were sitting at the dinner table with a great pot of coq au vin.

It's just a fancy name for a chicken stew, but made with a gamey, definitely free-range, strong-boned bird, some aromatic bacon, tender little mushrooms and half a bottle of half-decent wine. The other half of the bottle goes to the cook while she's waiting for the long, slow cooking. It's the sort of dish you can eat as well in Annandale as you can in Alsace or Burgundy. Coq au vin is better made with a slightly older bird. The older the bird, the richer the sauce. The long cooking transforms the otherwise tough meat and the whole thing starts falling off the bone in soft, tender pieces. Some butchers will order in an appropriate chook for you, but otherwise the best hunting grounds for an older bird are farmers' markets, by special request … or in your own back garden (see recipe on page 42).

'Missing rooster, chicken for dinner.' I put it straight to Mum and Dad.

'It's not our rooster, darling. We wouldn't eat our own pet for dinner.'

They caught each other's eye and then quickly got on with the matter of serving, spooning the chicken pieces out of the pot with the rich hot sauce, juicy mushrooms and soft baby onions turned translucent and soft. My sister and I exchanged glances, narrowing our eyes as we scanned our parents' faces. It wasn't our rooster, fine. Something was odd – but it wasn't our rooster, it wasn't our rooster.

There was still the matter of the missing bird. Days later, I brought it up with Mum and Dad again: if he wasn't in the coq au vin, where is he? Dad sat us down, like any father would who has to break the news of the birds and, if not the bees, the missing rooster.

'He was a terribly noisy little blighter and the neighbours complained. You can't have a noisy little trickster in your back garden, waking the whole of Sydney up every morning,' he began.

My sister and I froze. Had our parents *lied* to us?

'And the rules are that if you have a noisy bird keeping the city awake, then you can't keep him. It's not just us: Sue and Paul had to get rid of their rooster, too.'

So it was a case of the great rooster switcheroo. We'll take your cock, if you take ours.

'Next time, just give us pig's feet and cauliflower for dinner.'

Years later, I developed a recipe for that very dish that had secured itself in our family lexicon: pig's feet and cauliflower. As the nose-to-tail trend swept its way across the blogging, cookbook, dining scenes, I realised Mum might have been onto something all along.

I tested trotters in cauliflower hash, perused a little further up the leg and did hock in roasted cauliflower soup, a kind of tilt on the pea and ham classic. But pigs' lower leggy bits, at their very best, are smoked and slow-cooked, then pulled apart in shredded, sticky pieces. And so I did that, folded the meat into a rich béchamel and rolled crispy-shelled croquettes. Panko crumbs on the outside hold together the salty, soft, almost gooey centre. To tart the whole thing up, flavour-wise, a sharp, crunchy cauliflower pickle (see recipe on page 44).

I recently asked Mum and Dad for dinner.

'What are we having?' Mum asked.

COQ AU VIN BLANC

See story on page 40

SERVES 4
PREPARATION 30 minutes
COOKING 1 hour 15 minutes

1.6 kg (3 lb 8 oz) free-range or
   organic chicken, jointed into
   8 pieces on the bone, skin
   on, at room temperature
sea salt and freshly ground
   black pepper
1 tablespoon rice bran or
   grapeseed oil, plus extra
   for frying
250 g (9 oz) bulb spring
   onions (scallions), peeled and
   trimmed, leaving 1–2 cm
   (½–¾ in) green stalk
150 g (5½ oz) button
   mushrooms, halved
200 g (7 oz) oyster
   mushrooms, trimmed
1 brown onion, finely chopped
2 celery stalks, chopped
4 garlic cloves, sliced
150 g (5½ oz) pancetta, cut
   into 5 mm (¼ in) strips
2 tablespoons plain
   (all-purpose) flour
750 ml (26 fl oz/3 cups) dry
   white wine
2 tablespoons cognac
juice of ½ lemon
250–500 ml (9–17 fl oz/
   1–2 cups) homemade
   chicken stock
40 g (1½ oz) butter
6 tarragon leaves
boiled potatoes and salad
   leaves, to serve

Season the chicken pieces with salt and pepper. Heat the oil in a large heavy-based saucepan or casserole, with a lid, over medium–high heat. Add the chicken in batches, skin-side down first, and cook until golden, but not quite brown, on both sides. Transfer to a large plate and repeat with the remaining chicken pieces. Remove all the chicken pieces from the pan.

Add the bulb onions to the pan and toss in the oil until lightly browned on all sides, then transfer to another plate. Add the button mushrooms and cook until golden. Stir in the oyster mushrooms and cook until wilted. Transfer the mushrooms to the plate with the bulb onions.

Heat 1–2 teaspoons extra oil in the pan, if needed, reduce the heat to low, add the onion, celery and garlic and sauté until softened but not brown. Add the pancetta and cook for 2–3 minutes. Stir in the flour and cook for 1–2 minutes. Stir in the white wine, cognac, lemon juice and 250 ml (9 fl oz/1 cup) of the chicken stock and season to taste.

Return the chicken and any juices to the pan, pushing the chicken down a little to submerge it in the liquid – add another 250 ml (9 fl oz/1 cup) of chicken stock if needed. Add the mushrooms and bulb onions to the pan. Cover with the lid, bring to a simmer, then reduce the heat to medium–low so the sauce bubbles gently, and simmer, partially covered, for 40 minutes. Remove from the heat and transfer the chicken to a bowl.

Bring the sauce back to a simmer, allowing it to reduce and thicken a little. Stir in the butter, return the chicken to the pan and cook over low heat for 2–5 minutes, or until the chicken is heated through. Scatter with tarragon and serve with boiled potatoes and salad leaves.

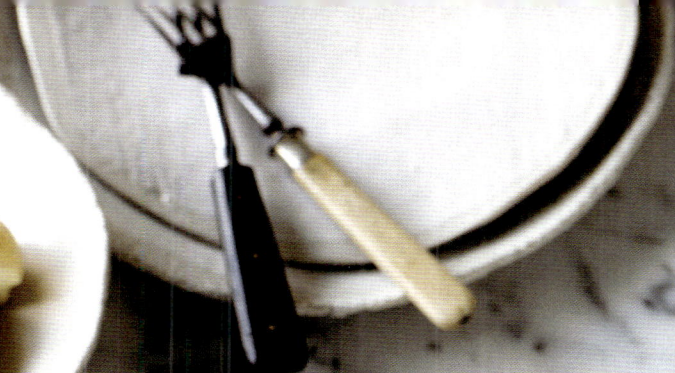

PORK CROQUETTES *with* CAULIFLOWER PICKLE

See story on page 41

MAKES 12
PREPARATION 30 minutes,
plus 2 hours chilling
COOKING 4 hours 55 minutes
Start this recipe 1 day ahead

450 g (1 lb) free-range smoked
   ham hocks
½ brown onion, halved
1 celery stalk
½ carrot, coarsely chopped
1 fresh bay leaf
½ teaspoon black peppercorns
2 tablespoons olive oil
60 g (2¼ oz) unsalted butter
½ leek, diced
100 g (3½ oz) plain
   (all-purpose) flour
500 ml (17 fl oz/2 cups) hot milk
freshly ground black pepper
whole nutmeg, for grating
100 g (3½ oz) panko
   breadcrumbs
25 g (1 oz) manchego cheese,
   finely grated
2 free-range eggs,
   lightly whisked
1 litre (35 fl oz/4 cups)
   rice bran oil

Cauliflower pickle
500 g (1 lb 2 oz) cauliflower,
   cut into florets
375 ml (13 fl oz/1½ cups)
   white wine vinegar
1½ tablespoons coarse sea salt
2 teaspoons sugar
2 garlic cloves, crushed
1 teaspoon black peppercorns
1 teaspoon black mustard seeds
1 fresh bay leaf

For the cauliflower pickle, pack the cauliflower florets tightly into four 250 ml (9 fl oz/1 cup) sterilised glass jars. Put the remaining ingredients in a saucepan with 500 ml (17 fl oz/2 cups) of water. Bring to the boil, reduce the heat and simmer for 5 minutes. Turn off the heat and cool to lukewarm. Pour the liquid over the cauliflower to cover, place the lids on the jars and leave to cool. Chill overnight in the fridge. (The pickle will keep for 1 week in the fridge.)

Put the hocks, vegetables, bay leaf and peppercorns in a saucepan with 1 litre (35 fl oz/4 cups) of water and bring to the boil. Reduce the heat to low, cover, and simmer for 2½–3 hours, or until the meat is falling off the bone.

Leave the hocks in the stock until cool enough to handle, then remove. Strain the liquid into an airtight container for another use. Pull the meat off the bones, discarding the bones and skin, and shred into 1 cm (½ in) pieces. You'll need about 140 g (5 oz) meat – refrigerate the leftovers for another use.

Heat the olive oil and butter in a medium saucepan over medium heat. Add the leek and sauté for 5 minutes, or until softened. Turn the heat to low, gradually stir in the flour and cook, stirring constantly, for 8–10 minutes. Slowly add hot milk, stirring constantly. Cook for 10–15 minutes, or until thickened. Season with pepper and a little grated nutmeg. Transfer the mixture to a bowl, press plastic wrap closely on the surface to stop a skin forming and then refrigerate for at least 2 hours, or until firm.

Combine the breadcrumbs and cheese in a shallow bowl and put the beaten egg in another. Divide the firm béchamel mixture into 12 even portions. Flatten one portion into a disc and fill with one-twelfth of the shredded pork. Close up the edges to enclose the filling and roll into a short cylinder shape, about 3 x 4 cm (1¼ x 1½ in). Roll in the beaten egg, then the breadcrumb mixture to coat completely, then place on a plate or board. Repeat with the remaining mixture.

Line a plate with paper towel. Heat the oil in a wok or small saucepan to 180°C (350°F), or until a cube of bread turns golden in 15 seconds. Fry croquettes in batches of two or three for about 2–3 minutes, turning with tongs until golden all over. Transfer to the plate and repeat with the remaining croquettes. Serve hot with cauliflower pickle.

NO ORDINARY GIRL

A sign at the Glen Innes railway station read: 'Is your journey really necessary?' During the Second World War rail travel in Australia was discouraged, even locally.

'Yes,' Margaret remembers saying under her breath. 'It is absolutely necessary.'

And she boarded the train to Sydney.

Armed with a small suitcase stuffed with clothes, Margaret moved through the carriage looking for a seat. She examined the faces of other passengers as she passed them, all off on their own journeys: travelling salesmen and soldiers arriving home, some returning to work after visiting family in the country. How many, like her, had never left home before? How many were embarking on the greatest adventure of their lives? She found a seat as the train pulled away from the station. She was off to become a dress designer in the Big Smoke.

'It wasn't particularly practical,' she tells me now.

Margaret knew her way around a piece of fabric with sharp scissors, thanks to her father's trade. But clothes rationing in Australia, in 1942, brought with it austerity measures such as clothing coupons and 'Victory suits'. Excesses such as pleats, cuffs, pockets and linings were trimmed down in designs, and lapels narrowed to save fabric – saving means Victory! Some of Margaret's friends fashioned clothes out of old tablecloths.

'Household linen hadn't been rationed yet.'

But Isabella kept a trunk of remnants, offcuts of fabric too small or misshapen to use and, with the help of some Vogue patterns, Margaret made her own clothes. She went for the slinky and flamboyant looks of Hollywood stars: Ginger Rogers and Rita Hayworth, Betty Grable.

The 'frock shop' chain Coral Lea and French couturière Madame Pellier both declined the country girl's sartorial innovations; they had no room for new talent when people were reducing the size of their wardrobes. The surest way into the highly competitive clothing workrooms then was via war work in the essential industries. And so, in a bid to prove her skills as a seamstress, her proficiencies with fabric, Margaret took a job at Turner's parachute factory. She imagined working on giant parachute masterpieces that would show her talent, give her some practice with a sewing machine and, hopefully, assist young Australian troops jumping out of planes carefully in the process. But something else was falling out of the sky, too: aeroplanes. Margaret was shifted to the 'nuts and bolts' department and specifically the X-ray machine, to assess why planes were literally breaking apart mid-air. She became a service girl, X-raying millions of aircraft nuts and bolts and naval radar equipment at the Munitions Supply Laboratories in Lidcombe. It wasn't the job she had fantasised about when she left home.

'I dreamed of nuts and bolts every night.'

Margaret was an eighteen-year-old country girl in the big city. She was dazzled, if not by the lights – traffic lights were replaced by policemen to save electricity, department store windows were boarded up in case of invasion, 'brown-outs' were imposed at night so the city was not so visible from the air – then by the theatres and the seven or eight nightclubs in Sydney in 1943. At the Trocadero in George Street, as many as two thousand people danced six nights a week, and they could stay up until the early hours of the morning. They had to order their drinks before six o'clock – country-wide pub closing hour – but if you ordered before then, the club could get a bottle or two in (usually at black-market prices). A concrete air-raid shelter was set up in the middle of Taylor Square in Darlinghurst, and covered trenches were cut into Hyde Park. Barbed-wire entanglements ran the length of most beaches. The Manly ferry had to pause mid-passage in every commute it made to allow an anti-submarine boom net across the harbour – running from Watson's Bay to George's Head – to be opened and closed for it.

There were men, boys, everywhere. Sydney was teeming with servicemen on leave, Americans looking for girls to entice with silk stockings. They came armed with Lucky Strike and Camel cigarettes to pacify worried fathers while they borrowed their daughters for a dance. But Margaret missed out on all this.

'There was no strolling in the arms of a Yank for me.'

She was teaching people how to cook.

Food. As a career, it was not what all the girls wanted to do. It was while she was X-raying nuts and bolts for two years that Margaret met a woman through mutual friends who changed her life, spun her in a new direction. Olwen Francis, the cookery editor of *The Australian Women's Weekly*, offered Margaret some advice.

'After the war, food, energy and cosmetics will grow, and these will be the areas for the new progressive woman.'

Liking the sound of 'new progressive woman', Margaret chose food. Her friends were off liaising with American soldiers, wearing silk stockings. But Margaret sponged coffee essence on her legs and drew a line down the back for a seam instead; she made do without the finer things and the attention of a uniform, for the sake of a burgeoning career.

Sneaky manoeuvrings or desperate lies, she wasn't sure what to call it: probably both. Helping to save lives at the munitions supply lab was well and good, but believing she was onto something more worthwhile, Margaret approached her boss in his office with a resignation letter.

'You're pregnant, Margaret?' he said, scanning her figure for signs of proof. She lifted her chin and her eyebrows, put her hand on her stomach and confirmed that indeed she was.

He looked at her, down the end of his nose and into her eyes, squinting. She looked back at him, refusing to falter. The words not being said out loud popped in the air around them. Not married and pregnant or lying to get out of work; either way Margaret was no ordinary girl. She was released from her job as a nuts and bolts X-rayer.

In a new position at the Australian Gas Light Company, first as a clerk but then in the Home Service Department, Margaret taught Australian women how to save gas, and how to use the company's appliances: turn this dial, press this button, the pilot light flicks and 'Aha! Now we're cooking!'. It wasn't much of a show if there was nothing to put in the ovens, so Margaret made little scones and patty cakes, shortcrust pastry and sponge cakes, pretty edible things that showed how gas achieved the best results. She taught women how to bake dainty biscuits, and how to repeat the recipe at home with their new gas appliance – how pleased your husband will be!

Her boss approached her one day with a challenge to teach groups of blind people how to cook using the new gas ovens, literally to feel their way since they couldn't read the thermostats. This is when Margaret Fulton rather famously taught the blind how to cook scones (see recipe on page 50). Her students moved gingerly into the classroom and stood at the benches allocated to them. Margaret told them how to measure the flour, feeling the ridges on their measuring cups as though they were braille, portion the milk, and rub the butter into the flour with the tips of their fingers. They turned the mixture out onto a floured board, cut out the scones and placed them on trays. She taught them how to put their hands into the oven to check it was hot enough and, when the 15-minute timer beeped, she tapped the underside of the scones, a hollow sound revealing they were done. The smell told them as much as the golden tops would have told those who could see.

'Then they made their own batch of scones without my help,' Margaret says. 'It was bedlam.'

Layered sponge cakes four times a day, batches and batches of scones, neat finger sandwiches every day of the week: Margaret was a one-woman production line of baked things. She tweaked recipes, refining and perfecting for best results. For her scones she replaced milk with buttermilk to make them lighter. She showed women how to know when cream was perfectly whipped and enthralled them by rescuing the cream if they'd taken the peaks too far, adding a splash of cream before the lot was spoiled. Learning from her mistakes, repeating the recipes every day and making up her own – it was a far cry from her first brains in black butter sauce.

Cooking most of the day, she found a new interest in food. Suddenly, Sydney wasn't just taped-up fashion stores and bung traffic lights; it was Victor's Sydney rock oysters and the Hotel Australia's American club sandwich, it was Cahills Restaurants' butterscotch fudge sauce, their lamb cutlets – it was all about the food.

SCONES

See story on page 48

MAKES 25 x 4 cm
(1½ in) scones
PREPARATION 20 minutes
COOKING 15 minutes

450 g (1 lb/3 cups) self-raising
   (self-rising) flour
1 teaspoon sea salt
60 g (2¼ oz) butter, chopped
375 ml (13 fl oz/1½ cups
   buttermilk, plus extra
   for brushing
whipped cream, to serve
jam, to serve

Preheat the oven to 230°C (450°F). Lightly grease a baking tray and line with baking paper.

Sift the flour and salt together in a bowl, then rub in the butter, using your fingers. Make a well in the centre and mix in the buttermilk, using a wooden spoon. Add a little more buttermilk, if needed, to make a soft dough.

Knead the dough, being careful not to overwork – too much handling can make the scones hard and heavy.

Roll out the dough on a well-floured work surface until about 2.5 cm (1 in) thick. Use a 4 cm (1½ in) cutter to cut rounds in the dough. Pull together the scraps of dough, knead a little, just until it comes together, then cut out another couple of rounds.

Put the rounds on the prepared tray and brush tops with a little buttermilk.

Bake for 12–15 minutes, or until the tops are golden, then transfer to a wire rack. Cover with a clean tea towel (dish towel) to keep warm.

Serve warm with cream and jam.

DOWN TO CHINATOWN

For me growing up in Sydney, Chinese food was short soup, mermaid's tresses and pink lemonade. It was recurring pots of green tea and dipping my finger into the froth of Dad's beer. Chinese food was a family outing treat that catered to my sister and me, Grandma, Mum and Dad; the tables were ridiculously big and therefore *amazing*, nobody cared if you spilled food on the starched white tablecloth, and the lazy Susan kept my sister and me entertained through the entire meal.

'Louise, would you like some sticky rice? Be quick...Too late!'

The dish speeds past her on the wheel. She stretches out her arm, spins the wheel full circle again to get to the rice. The joke replays.

'Ginger chicken, Kate?' she says, hand poised.

She spins the wheel so fast that Mum has to slam down her hand to stop the entire meal landing in our laps. Grandma steadies her tiny cup of tea.

At home we'd have braised Chinese pork, master stock beef, steamed chicken with ginger and shallot dressing, homemade noodles and extraordinarily textured hot pots filled with tofu and lotus root, mapo dofu, eggplant and black bean stir-fries. But that was just Mum's cooking – to us it had no nationality. A Chinese–Australian family friend John also made great banquets of steamed fish and hand-spun noodles with chilli and black vinegar, sticky rice with one surprise bean stuffed at the end of its lotus leaf wrapping, quail eggs dipped in sichuan pepper and five-spice salt.

But as far as my sister and I were concerned, Chinese food was what we had when we ate out: crunchy spring rolls with fluorescent dipping sauce, tiny little bowls of crab and sweet corn soup, chilli mud crab, bowls of golden sticky chicken with lumps of pineapple. And we were allowed soda, which never happened at any other time. Specifically, we were allowed one, maybe two, lemonades with pink cordial, loads of ice and a little umbrella. Three, if my parents lost count.

In the mid-1980s, Chinatown was like Disneyland – all bright lights and foreign smells, but with better catering. My sister and I would climb the two bronze dragons that guarded the entrance to this exotic wonderland, claiming one each and pretending to be Kings of the World until our parents threatened to disappear from view in the largely Asian crowd. Those red neon signs twinkled and steam pumped from air-conditioning units above giant doorways.

We oscillated between one or other of the fine establishments in that fair quarter, some gilded, red carpets leading the way up to a space as big as a ballroom, standard-issue Chinese restaurant chairs with vinyl seats, velvet backing. Or we'd tuck into a tiny porthole of a space, where barbecued ducks hung in windows and scrawny chefs whacked cleavers down on red roast pork, cutting straight through bone at super speed.

Sydney's Chinatown thrummed with colour and sound, but mainly smells. Fresh herbs and dumpling steam, braised meats and tripe hot pots, it all melded together on Sussex and Dixon streets. My sister and I walked through it, holding onto the corners of Dad's jacket, taking giant breaths, wary of hitting something too fishy, too meaty. But that added to the thrill. We held our noses down back alleys, where garbage rotted sourly by the roadside; these were strange, wet, dank alleyways with sewage wafts.

For my sister and me – dressed in our corduroy overalls with tight-neck skivvies or, in summer, little corduroy overall dresses with t-shirts underneath – the drive from Annandale to the city in our ageing navy-blue Renault was like being beamed into outer space, to a world where they play haunting instruments, speak other languages, eat chicken feet. We'd be jolted from our dreamy browsing by belting drums that forced your heart to change beat, and turn to see tiny men do backflips in costume, leap into the air under the batting eyelids and head of a *dragon*. You could buy firecrackers in Chinatown. (I can still feel the anticipation as Dad pushes one cracker into a bucket of sand, lights the wick, and hear the hiss as it flies into the air, ending in a perfect ball of golden sparkles.)

Live fish gurgled in plastic buckets, there were great stacks of misshapen turnips, fresh turmeric and dried galangal, piles of coriander with their roots still attached. I looked up and down as a child here, I saw scrunched-up tissues and glitter in the road, arching tree branches holding red paper lanterns above my head, a man flick his stunted cigarette by my feet. It was beauty and horror and fantasy and muck.

We'd wander into grocery stores, open later than our bedtime, and I'd trace my fingers along rows of dusty sweets: chewy ginger things individually wrapped, little discs of dried reconstituted pawpaw wrapped up liked coins in paper (slightly grainy but pleasingly saccharine), fluorescent jellies laid out on styrofoam plates, squished multi-coloured cubes tightly covered in plastic wrap. Mum and Grandma bundled jars of fermented pastes, dried shrimp, packets of fresh, flat noodles into plastic baskets, holding up pastes and chilli sauce, mooting recipe concoctions, a dish they'd eaten in Hong Kong and how to recreate it.

And then, the food. Sitting next to Grandma in a brand-new seafood restaurant, my neck craning to see the front window display – ten, maybe twenty tanks of water holding fish, crabs, lobsters – she put her hand on mine on the table.

'I'll come over with you, darling,' she said, and pushed her chair away from the table.

Together we weaved through the large tables, where other voracious eaters and bargain hunters came together to feast and mess up the tablecloths, share food and break, if not bread, then great mounds of rice. My head was just above table height and, from here, plates of braised abalone, dark vegetables licked with soy and sesame oil, bowls filled with dark, wobbly things enchanted me. We peered into the fish tanks, where snapper and perch pecked at the glass or sat motionless, levitating in the crowded water, some gasping for oxygen by a mechanical bubble shaft.

Grandma leaned in and introduced me to the lobsters.

'They have had happy lives under rocks, exploring the sea, darling. They haven't spent their lives in here. But now the bigger, older ones have to move on. It's okay, they're not in any pain, and they won't be here for long.'

The Peking duck arrived and we fell on it. Mum shook out her swan-folded serviette and Louise and I wore ours as hats.

'I'm the King of Peking,' I sang.

I smeared hoisin sauce on my pancakes, carefully layering one piece of meat, a piece of skin on top, then handed the plate to Dad, so he could remove the fat. A stick of cucumber and a stick of shallot, and then I rolled the pancake so tightly that most of the duck fell out the end. I picked up the remnants, shoved them into my mouth, and reached for another pancake, looking up to Mum for permission as I did. She nodded, smiling.

FISH, PLEASE

Margaret ordered the fish at the bar at Victor's, in King Street. The tail was lightly poached in fish stock, a creamy sauce holding six plump fresh oysters poured over; a slab of white bread, chewy and fresh, came with butter on the side. The twenty-two-year-old leaned her elbow on the white marble bar, watching the cooks, a cloud of steam billowing from the pots of stock and soup in front of her.

She ordered oysters too, sometimes, served natural in their shells with brown bread, shucked to order and tasting of the sea. Margaret watched the chefs prepare oyster soup, rich with fish stock made from snapper heads and water, white wine, a carrot and an onion cut into quarters, a few peppercorns and a couple of handfuls of fresh oysters. Eating out became a means to discover, learn, taste – it was more than a practical answer to sating routine hunger. She repeated the recipe at home, pouring the hot soup over the oysters in the bowl so they weren't cooked through but turned plump in the heat.

Margaret followed the Gas Light Company's rule of 'discreet makeup', no nail polish, as she turned up to give cookery classes every day. She wore a hat and gloves travelling on the tram. After work, she'd walk down George Street, Pitt Street, down Elizabeth, looking in windows and sometimes stepping with friends into the Hotel Australia – which has since been knocked down 'in the name of progress'. She loved the marble staircase, the sophistication, how the clientele dressed in fine fabrics and hats. The Hotel Australia served American food: hamburgers and club sandwiches, layered with crispy bacon and chicken. There was American-style coffee, poured through a filter and served black, with milk on the side.

Sydney's food scene in the 1940s was buoyed by Americana. Creamy mayonnaise, bacon and chicken together, corn and chunky salads appeared on menus everywhere. A waiter brought Margaret a cob salad at the tiny restaurant known as the Martha Washington, in Martin Place. She pulled her chair in a little bit tighter, leaning in to examine her meal, and picked up the single utensil she was supposed to eat it with, a Splayd.

'It was an all-purpose eating instrument, a spoon and a fork together, with a knife on one of its edges, a sharp cutting side,' Margaret says now. 'It reflected the American way of eating food, which seemed completely foreign to me. They cut up the food with a knife and fork, and then transferred the fork into their right hand to eat the meal, moving the cut-up food into the mouth. Very strange. But the Splayd became a hot craze,' she says. 'Anyone getting married would receive a set of these Splayds.'

Margaret loved one particular outlet of the restaurant chain Cahills, the one by the Hotel Australia. Crumbed lamb cutlets and other breadcrumb-coated food – also croquettes – were in high demand. It was a fancy rendition of the food she knew: crisp and golden-coated things, some with creamy melting centres of minced chicken, beef or lamb, a different sauce for each item. For dessert she would have a banana split – sometimes an ice cream sundae – served in a pressed glass dish and topped with crunchy toasted nuts, fresh fruit and chocolate fudge, butterscotch or caramel sauce. Nowhere else could you find anything so elaborately delicious.

When Isabella visited her youngest daughter from Glen Innes, taking the train by herself and staying with Margaret, the pair included a trip to David Jones department store's main restaurant. It spread across the ground level of the building, great arched windows allowing light to stream in across the tables. The room was divided in half by a strip of carpet; at the entrance, a couple of birdcages on pedestals, and at the other end, a little band played jazz and gentle classical music. Parents from country towns took their career-minded daughters and sons to lunch, a special treat. Waitresses wore little folded white scarves over their heads and pinafores that ran to mid-calf. Margaret and Isabella looked up at the art deco chandeliers, the decorative garlands; they caught up over the starched white tablecloth and, being so close to the sea now, they ordered the fish.

SHOOT DAYS

A cast of thousands took over our house twice a month in Sydney for magazine and newspaper photo shoots. It was the world I came home to growing up. Black bags filled with lenses, the dining room table moved outside for better lighting, media people writing in notebooks and crossing the names of dishes off lists, ironing linen and scattering parsley. A photographer would set up outside, his assistant holding a massive reflector over some scene: a champagne jelly stuffed with summer berries, a jug of water sparkling with lemon slices, bright striped linen evoking a pretty afternoon tea, the Christofle polished and smelling of Silvo. Rodney Weidland, or another great Sydney food photographer of the 1980s and 90s, pressed a Polaroid between his hands, tore off that protective coating and checked his image. He lined up rolls of film, waved a light meter over the jelly – then, click, click, click, click.

In the kitchen, my mother and her assistant Amber Keller cut potatoes into fondant shapes, blunt at the ends with seven equal sides. They sautéed and reduced stocks, pulled whole roasted pork loins, crackling and blistered, from the oven. One of them ground cardamom seeds in a mortar and pestle, while the other picked through baby cos leaves in the sink. One checked the pots de crème, while the other melted chocolate and butter in a bain-marie. The house was noisy with the clatter of sauté pans and the hum of whisking, the smell of pungent vinegar over heat before butter mellows it suddenly – then, click, click, click, click.

Grandma and Mum breezed from the kitchen to the set outside. Mum held a small tongful of pappardelle high above a plate, turning them slowly so the pasta fell into a pretty twist. She cut into layered galettes, starting the point of the wedge a little out from the centre of the cake to achieve a better-looking slice for the camera. Balancing peas on sprigs of watercress, lifting a stew with chopped herbs, spooning the perfect mouthful from a crème caramel, Mum created pages of inspiration for *New Idea* and *Home Beautiful* magazines. Grandma checked and ticked everything that went in front of the camera, commenting that you never use a spoon to eat pasta or that the chicken needed brushing with its own jus.

'It's growing weary as it waits for the camera.'

An assistant would jump in and fuss over the food again. When the fresh Vietnamese rolls were lined up on their turquoise plate, Grandma commented that they looked too big, 'too phallic'. Mum rolled her eyes, then sliced them in half diagonally.

'Better, Mum?'

'Much.'

My sister and I would run down the street after school on photography days, our oversized navy backpacks shifting up and down as we raced each other home. We loved descending the stairs to the door from the gate, hearing the bustle of people, smelling perfume, curries, laundry, rice pudding rich with cardamom. We'd wave to familiar faces and enter the kitchen, peek into the fridge and into saucepans, gliding along the benches to examine every possible contender for afterschool snacks.

I had friends whose parents were great believers in takeaway; they had their reasons. One mother claimed we lived in cosmopolitan Sydney, where any variety of 'ethnic cuisine' was available at the end of the phone. Food in a plastic container? Call it dinner. Some kids I knew survived on a steady diet of cheese and crackers, apples and pad-thai-from-up-the-shops. It's true that cooking does account for only one part of parenting. Foodists and zeitgeist nutritionists may like to look away now, but there can, indeed, be love, humour, responsibility, support and dedication, without the homemade vats of lemony hummus and carrot sticks, the steamed broccoli, the elaborate homemade birthday cakes.

My friend Grace endured versions of a family dinner that involved her mother tearing up an iceberg lettuce and pouring over bottled caesar dressing, with 'bacon bits' from a shaker as the final flourish, to go with the containers of spaghetti bolognese and fettuccini carbonara from the Italian takeaway down the road. I asked her about these meals recently and we cringed, remembering the thick Spanish onion rings her mother decorated the pasta with to make it 'genuine Italian'. Maybe feeling ungrateful or disloyal, Grace changed tack, as though she had to sing and dance her mother back into my good graces.

'She worked long hours at the library, she took us kids to netball every weekend, she ironed the bed sheets, for God's sake. I really can't complain about her mothering,' she said. 'Love is possible with takeaway, too.'

'You must eat very well at home, lucky thing,' friends' parents often said to me, after school.

'Yes,' I'd reply.

'What's your favourite food?'

'We have roast chicken sometimes, and I love macaroni and cheese too.'

They'd look at me, nodding and smiling but clearly puzzled. I was puzzled too. I used to wonder, do they think because Margaret Fulton is my grandmother that means we are having partridge for dinner? Sometimes, I didn't particularly feel like a stir-fry and I wasn't a fan of steak and kidney pudding (although I liked the pudding part with the gravy from the meat spooned over). But otherwise, yes, we ate pretty well. Just normal dinners: spaghetti bolognese sometimes, roast pork with crackling and apple sauce at other times.

It has taken me years to realise what they meant. It wasn't what we ate that they imagined was remarkable, but how we cooked it – and the priority we gave to food and cooking.

THE MAKING OF A FOODIST

I'm sitting on a wooden stool in a restaurant deep in China's Wuyi mountains in my pyjamas. Eight other Australian twenty-year-old girls, also in their silky, gingham, slightly see-through outfits, join me at the round table. And there's Colin, a forty-something. We order ten bottles of Tsingtao beer and when it arrives we wipe the bottle mouths with paper serviettes before we drink, a suspicious habit in a foreign world. It's dark outside, and wind and rain beat against the walls. We drink our beers, icy, clean and soothing. We're about to eat the best meal in the world.

As teachers in training, we went to China because we were travellers yearning, kids dying to be somewhere other than on campus, facing another lecture on Ethics in Education. We signed up to take our 'prac' session – the compulsory in-class training for our degrees – for five weeks in a city called Fuzhou, in the Fujian Province. While others were being vetted at Glebe High School and Scots College, we packed our bags, elated.

Our local contact and fixer, Colin, was a well-connected guy employed by the University of Sydney. Patient, an experienced teacher himself, and wise to the strange politics and bureaucratic dealings in China, he organised accommodation, teaching posts, translators, money exchanges. He found roles for each of us in small schools during the week, and in the local university on weekends. He sourced matching navy polo shirts with the university logo with a little 'China teaching excursion 1998' sewn in.

It was summer in China – dusty, humid, frazzled. We were on the outskirts of Fuzhou. A worse-for-wear concrete block was our digs for the month, grass mats for beds. A small barred window, with no glass, brought hot air into the room and open green pipes dripped rusty water into buckets. We used the same buckets to wash our hair. Three to a room at night, we wrapped up in sleeping bags from home. Every day we were woken at sunrise by a tannoy call for local men to road-building work. Bulldozers were tearing up roads as part of China's rising industrial overhaul, and the workers of the world seemed to be uniting on the job outside our bedrooms.

After school we folded up on flimsy, stiff chairs in each other's rooms and broke open drinks and snacks: beer, chewy fluorescent sweets, tangy crisps made from radioactive salts and fats, everything tasting like Asia. Loaves of bread were fluffy, sweet, pink. Someone bought a packet of cryovacked meatballs, insipid pale-pink mystery meat in plastic wrap. Rolling around on a plastic plate, the balls were the culinary unknown, and we dared each other to take one into our mouths. I pinched one between my fingers and sniffed it, the girls urging me on. Someone waved their hand over the plate, presenting it like a celebrity on a food show.

'These Chinese balls really are the dog's bollocks!'

We were on a permanent sugar rush, dehydrated and laughing at each other, the food, the foreign world around us. Later, in the cooler early evenings, when the beers turned warm and the snacks ran out in our rooms, we'd go looking for a decent meal in the town. I had become a food canary on the trip, tasting noodles first to test for chilli, the hot pot first to decipher ingredients. My best mate on the trip, Sonya, would hold up an item between her chopsticks, a kind of holey potato.

'Lotus root,' I'd nod her on.

Karen, another friend, would peer into her bowl and then look up to make eye contact, checking.

'It's fine, eggplant and tofu, like a vegie mapo dofu.'

Fresh razor clams sat like twigs in shimmering black sauce. Soups arrived full of indecipherable produce, the language barrier impossible to penetrate so we'd use chopsticks to dig in for prawns and tofu, taro, eggplant, chunks of tender bamboo shoots, fermented beans and pork. The girls would send me into the coalmine, and I'd chirp that it was good down there, in the delicious depths.

Halfway up the main road one evening, I smelled something wonderful and stopped. I stepped into an open kitchen where a long bar stretched past two giant woks and flames. Concrete floors and a few lino-topped tables, metal chairs and handwritten menus stuck on the otherwise bare walls. A gappy-mouthed man at the woks smiled as we entered. He held a wad of pork fat between long wooden chopsticks, wiped it around a black wok being licked by flames, then threw in chunks of garlic and bitter melon, cucumber, tomato and eggplant, chilli and vinegar. Cucumber, let alone tomato, in what was essentially a stir-fry, was new to me. Walnut-sized uneven chunks, slightly crushed, were barely warmed through, giving the stir-fry a pleasing crunch. The eggplant was rich and creamy, coated in just-cooked garlic, still with a sharp bite. I loved this food.

A second course arrived and it was something we all recognised: ribs. The dark meaty splinters were piled onto an enamel plate, spiced with star anise and soy, and caramelised until they had turned sticky in their own juices, then carved up into individual bones. The owner stood next to our table and nodded for us to begin, standing and grinning. Only half realising he was still there, we each put down our polished bones and licked our thumbs clean, then looked up at him.

'Ah!' he said. 'Now have '

He presented a bowl he'd been hiding behind his back.

'Please,' he said, and placed it on the table, attempting an energetic thumbs-up and signalling that we should dip the bones in. We dipped. The sweet and sour caramelised pork ribs were, one by one, dunked into the bowl, and we gnawed on the bones.

'Oh, my God!' said Sonya.

The sichuan-spiced salt, with chilli, fragrant with lemon rind and, maybe, cinnamon, turned the humble ribs into a magic trick. We each dipped our fingers into the bowl, tasting again.

'What is that?' someone said.

Years later, when ribs took over as a culinary cult back home, I could shrug them away, take or leave them, knowing that without the sweet and salty, sharp and sour, aromatic dipping bowl to go with them, they would never match up. But at home, when the grill is blasting over the marinated bones, I'll be grinding spice and salt in the mortar and pestle (see recipe on page 65).

When the teaching was done for the month, we packed into a white van, two more to the vehicle than there were seats, and drove about half a day to Wuyi Mountain, north-west of Fuzhou. With so little room in the van, we packed just clothes for the night. Outside the window, mile after mile of rural fields, farmland dotted with men ploughing and beating into the earth with large wooden tools, a string of stalls selling water spinach and dried mushrooms, bitter melon and chilli, all swept past, glimpsed for a second and then gone.

It became clear on this journey why the workers outside our bedrooms in Fuzhou were overhauling the roads; they just hadn't reached this stretch yet. They had hit one section of it, and we delayed forty minutes while cars bottlenecked and veered off-road to avoid the bulldozers, detouring as best they could into ditches and fields, then back on the road again. At one interminable hold-up, we crawled past a stall owner selling live ducks. A purveyor picked up a white-feathered fellow, its eyes wide and terrified as his wings were forcibly outstretched so the punter could see his plump breast. The customer nodded and the stall owner pinned the duck down on a scarred wooden block. I screamed. I may have been a determined foodist, but I was still a fledgling. Right there, I turned vegetarian, and remained no-meat for the next five years.

It was mid-afternoon when we arrived in the mountains. It was June, about as out of season as off-season can be: hot, humid, with a constant downpour of penetrating, unforgiving rain. The van pulled up at the beginning of a long forest walking trail that we'd follow to our hotel. We tumbled out of the van like eggs from a turtle: plop, plop, stumble.

It was one of the most beautiful places I'd ever been, a UNESCO-listed site for biodiversity conservation, the best example of a largely intact Chinese forest, with ancient, relict plants, amphibians and insects. We squinted in the downpour, unwrapped blue plastic bags with holes cut out for head and arms, and attached attractive little plastic bonnets to our heads. We pointed at each other and bent over laughing.

'Let's go!'

We ran the first bit, pleased to be out of the van and in the fresh air. Maybe it would be raining less a bit further along. Every metre proved us wrong. An hour in, and our shoes were slopping with every step. Even Colin's moustache looked sad and bedraggled.

It *was* beautiful though, in the mountains. Giant rocks forced their way out of the landscape, reaching into the clouds and mist. Trees grew where they could on these grey shards. It was the China of my dreams: ancient, moody, romantic and misty. A wide, dark-green river snaked its way through the steep landscape.

In a small village, water fell in sheets from unguttered corrugated iron, which protected, barely, makeshift houses. The street was banging with bartering and the sound of rain, loud swooshes and efforts to sweep away leaves with broomsticks fashioned from branches. The streets were mud, and we strode over little rivers that carried with them odd clumps of leaves, branches, a Coke can. Women squatted beside upturned wooden boxes, improvised stalls from which they sold whole bamboo shoots and liquid washing detergent.

In the hotel, we found real beds. Mattresses. Side tables. Sheets. There may have been carpet. Best of all, there were showers. We hung our clothes up outside on little standing-room-only balconies that looked out in to the rain, mist and forest. Sonya, my roommate, and I took turns to shower, our first in more than a month. I recovered under the heat of the water, let it run over me as I breathed and remembered the dust, the rain, the duck, the snakes, the cucumber stir-fries, the children I'd taught. Water brought it all back, but I knew we were nearing the end and I'd miss it here.

I was throbbing from the hot shower, the long bus trip, the eternal rainy walk. Sonya and I stretched out on top of our beds. A knock at the door.

'Dinner upstairs when you're ready, girls,' sang Colin. 'Oh, and the others are wearing their pyjamas because their clothes aren't dry.'

We felt our clothes.

'Same.'

And so I ventured to dinner in a white singlet, baggy grey marle bottoms; Sonya wore her tartan ensemble, no shoes but socks. Cold beers came and we took large first gulps. Chilled bubbles ran down our throats; clean, bitter and gentle. Colin ordered our food in his best Mandarin. My companions had also adopted the no-meat policy, still suffering from the post-traumatic duck situation. Three large oval plates of dumplings turned up. Handmade, pleated, steamed purses, little flour-and-water dough casings, each with pan-fried bottoms.

I take a dumpling in my little white bowl and drizzle over vinegar and soy, a dot of chilli oil. Holding it in chopsticks, I bite into the doughy morsel and the hot, soft insides spill into my mouth and down my throat like lava – melting tofu and steamed eggplant. The pure, hot, silken insides, comforting and gentle, bring tears to my eyes. The fresh dumpling has been made only moments earlier, and the sticky bottom gives them a toasted aroma, with the crust and chew of a hot pretzel. The creamy centre, set against the vinegar and soy, is flawless. The food warms and reassures us, exhausted kids in a foreign place. The dumplings take each of us home – to Sunday mornings with the family in Chinatown, to soothing soups made by Mum or Dad when we weren't well, and steaming home-cooked dinners – those hot, enveloping, perfect meals.

PORK RIBS *with* SICHUAN SALT

See story on page 61

SERVES 2 as a main,
or 4 as a snack
PREPARATION 10 minutes,
plus overnight marinating
COOKING 15–20 minutes
Start this recipe 1 day ahead

125 ml (4 fl oz/½ cup) light
   soy sauce
3 tablespoons brown sugar
1 tablespoon malt vinegar
½ teaspoon roasted and finely
   ground sichuan peppercorns
160 ml (5¼ fl oz) shaoxing wine
2 teaspoons sesame oil
50 g (1¾ oz) fresh ginger,
   peeled and finely grated
6 garlic cloves, finely chopped
1 fresh small red chilli, sliced,
   with seeds
2 x 600 g (1 lb 6 oz) racks of
   free-range pork, separated
   into ribs
2 tablespoons vegetable oil
coriander (cilantro) sprigs,
   to serve
toasted sesame seeds,
   to serve
lemon cheeks, to serve

Sichuan salt
3 tablespoons sea salt flakes
1 tablespoon roasted and
   ground sichuan peppercorns

Combine the soy sauce, sugar, vinegar, sichuan pepper, wine, sesame oil, ginger, garlic and chilli in a bowl, add the ribs and turn until well coated, then cover with plastic wrap and refrigerate overnight.

For the sichuan salt, combine the ingredients in a bowl and set aside.

Heat a barbecue or chargrill pan to medium heat and lightly brush with the vegetable oil. Cook the ribs, turning them regularly and basting them now and then with the marinade, for 8–10 minutes, or until slightly charred and cooked through.

Meanwhile, in a small pan, bring the remaining marinade to the boil, reduce the heat and simmer for 5 minutes.

To serve, put the ribs on a board, pour over the remaining marinade, sprinkle with coriander and sesame seeds. Offer sichuan salt for dipping and lemon cheeks for squeezing.

BREAK
the
MOULD

WEDDING BELLE

'Don't worry, Mummy, Aunty Margaret can always get a divorce.'

Nine-year-old Billy Hatfield, Margaret's nephew, was sweetly attempting to reassure his mother, Margaret's big sister Jean. These words, which have become part of our family lore, set the tone for the wedding of Margaret Fulton and her beau Trevor.

'He had a big smile, a lairy hat, the shortest shorts and cute legs,' Grandma says now.

But her main reason for marrying the army lad was revealed when the bride wore the palest possible shell blue, 'like a duck egg'. She felt dishonest wearing traditional white now she was no longer a virgin and believed nobody else would have her. Marriage was her only path to security.

'In those days, good girls kept themselves for their husbands. I don't know how many really good girls were around.'

Isabella and Alexander took a small plane from Glen Innes a few days before the wedding. As I've been told the story, Isabella wondered why none of her daughters, almost all now married, had planned a trousseau, organised a kitchen tea, or involved their mother in choosing a gown for their respective weddings. These traditions, which Isabella herself had grown up with, were ignored as a new generation, her own daughters, cast them aside. As the aircraft made its way through the light clouds, she had a sinking feeling. Margaret – that young, bright girl, who had almost risen above this, who had better sense, who might have done brilliant things, who aspired to more – was now marrying a man she didn't love. She knew her daughter well enough to know she wasn't being happily hitched.

The groom's family was not faring much better.

'Don't look so worried, Irene,' said a family friend to Trevor's mother at the wedding, which took place in Manly, on Sydney's northern beaches, on 7 August, 1948. 'Look at it this way: you haven't lost a son, you've gained a daughter.'

'I haven't lost a son,' came her reply. 'And I didn't need a daughter.'

'It wasn't a proper Scottish wedding,' Margaret tells me. 'It wasn't really a proper Australian wedding. It was real enough, however. I was now Mrs Trevor Wilfred Price.'

Margaret catered the wedding herself and planned a spread of things she'd mastered at the Gas Light Company. Asparagus rolls, involving canned asparagus rolled in fresh white, crustless buttered bread; little homemade sausage rolls; red salmon brown bread sandwiches cut into fingers; plump oysters in a creamy sauce set in crisp vol-au-vent pastry – all appeared on the lace tablecloth. She rolled prunes in bacon, fixing them with a toothpick, for devils on horseback, and created a batch of their celestial altar ego, angels on horseback: fat oysters rolled in bacon, speared with a toothpick and grilled. She made shortbread and the wedding cake, which she iced and decorated.

Isabella advised her daughter to call for gastronomic backup. In 1948 Sydney, nowhere did wedding reinforcement better than the department store David Jones. The food department delivered sandwiches, 'savouries' and hors d'oeuvres, as well as petits fours. Meanwhile, Alexander took care of the alcohol.

'Whisky for him, gin for them,' Margaret says now.

Trevor brought out his guitar and sang to his new wife. With his large flashing smile, he played some of the latest jazz, the song 'Lover' and Benny Goodman's 'How High the Moon'.

Margaret watched her new husband, with his one leg crossed over the other, strumming quaintly, winning over the group with his cheery voice. She felt some relief with the music and his fun happy song. She skimmed her eyes over the faces of her new family, who were rocking gently to the music and applauding in all the right places. She found her mother's face in the crowd. Her mother was trembling, filled with apprehension, seeing it all as so foreign and so elaborately forced, a sort of performance to gloss over the truth that this wouldn't make Margaret happy.

'At that moment,' Margaret remembers now, 'I knew I was getting married for all the wrong reasons.'

Life with Trevor was 'suburban, rather dreary in many ways', says Margaret. He spent all his spare time polishing his car, which he loved. On Sundays, Margaret and her new husband drove to the beach, usually Cronulla, with his mother Irene in the back seat. The trio picked up prawns or fish and chips from Tom Uglys Point on the way. Margaret was bored. But on weekends, when her husband parked himself beside his car with spit and polish, she went to the Art Gallery of New South Wales. She gazed at the new Archibald Prize–winning portrait of Margaret Olley by William Dobell, as well as the same artist's *Storm Approaching Wangi*. She returns to these two paintings, still, many years later.

So she was married, and that was that: done. Her parents rarely visited and her new life was with her husband, a man she lived with but barely shared her life with. On her birthday that year, in October, Margaret would receive a chicken in the post from her mother. It was to be sent as a lone voyager, trussed and plucked, on the train. Isabella wrote to her daughter to pick it up from Sydney's Central Station.

The chicken wrapped on her kitchen bench, ready to send to Margaret, Isabella put another log in the fuel stove, to keep it from burning out while she went to the station. She opened the roaring door and slipped in the piece of wood, catching her finger on a splinter as she tossed it in. Weeks later, Isabella told Margaret that she had a wound on her finger that wouldn't heal. As the days passed and the infection grew, Isabella bandaged it up, covered it over. But it worsened, and she could no longer do household chores. The puzzled doctor sent her in for further tests, and later revealed to her that she had cancer of the uterus.

Isabella had neglected telltale signs; she had pushed aside the regular bleeding and pain as minor bothers. Had she been in Scotland, she might have told one of her sisters, but it was nothing to bother her children or husband with. By the time she was diagnosed, cancer had spread through her body. Margaret rushed to Glen Innes to care for her mother, who was sixty years old, and was by her side when she died on Boxing Day.

Heartbroken, Margaret was lost in pain. Completely grief-stricken, she spent the weeks following her mother's death with her father and family in Glen Innes. It was there, in her old home amongst the Scottish wools and beside the wood-fired stove, that Margaret and her father hatched a plan. Isabella had wanted to return to Scotland to visit the family, explore the Highlands, breathe the air. They would still go.

A year later, in July 1949, the duo threw streamers from the upper deck of the P&O liner, *Strathaird*. Passengers tossed bright ribbons into the sprawl of hats and faces below, crying, waving farewell. As the ship bellowed, Margaret cheered and turned to sing along with the brass band: 'Wish me luck as you wave me goodbye.'

'Travelling P&O was *posh*,' Margaret tells me.

The boat itself was pristine white with a navy trim, but the 'Port Out, Starboard Home' acronym for the word *posh* stuck with Margaret; she liked the word's literary origins and so was pleased with the whole P&O thing. On the *Strathaird*, her nightdress was laid out on her bed every evening, the soft silk folded and draped, nipped in at the waist, ribbons prettily arranged. A laundered white linen mat was refreshed beside her bunk every day, her slippers propped on top.

On the sea journey to Southampton, Margaret and her father joined in the captain's cocktail parties at night, and regularly ate at his table. Four or five courses included crème Constance, a soup involving butter, onion, curry powder, chicken stock and coconut milk, garnished with cream and lemon. A consommé royale was also served on board, a clear soup served with pieces of firm, savoury custard floating in it. Fish came next, either filet de sole meunière, a fillet of sole, dredged with flour and milk, fried in butter and served in a brown butter sauce with lemon; or sole Colbert, for which the fish is dipped in milk and breadcrumbs and served with a melting nugget of parsley butter. A roast duckling often followed, with a classic bigarade sauce, basically duck à l'orange, but with a bright and fresh orange salad on the side. A fillet of beef with pommes rissolées, or French-browned potatoes, and watercress salad, a roast pheasant served with grapes – the dishes kept coming. The food was rich and constant and as the days passed, Margaret and her father traipsed up and down the smooth wooden deck, reading in the shade, pulling up for another long meal at the white cloth-covered tables with their immaculate silverware, Alexander pouring whisky for him, red wine for her.

'Following dessert, in deference to an English gentleman's preference to end the meal on a savoury note, we'd have a hot cheese soufflé, cheese croquettes, roquefort toast or Buck's rarebit. Then we'd retire to one of the lounges for petits fours and drinks such as Drambuie, crème de menthe or cognac. Then I'd go outside and watch the moon,' Margaret remembers.

The rocking seas, the rich food, the interminable onslaught of butter, cream and cheese, took their toll on Margaret only a day or so into the trip. Moonlight gazing could do nothing to divert her from the seasickness that distracted at first, and soon overwhelmed.

'Going across the Australian Bight, I was seasick. In Colombo, I was seasick. Going through the Suez Canal, the Mediterranean, the English Channel, still seasick.'

Margaret tried to walk it off, sleep it off, starve it off, eat it off, but nothing could shake the swooning, rocking ruptures of seasickness, which stayed with her for more than eight weeks. On the train to Scotland, she was still seasick. In Glasgow, Dr Finlay confirmed his diagnosis: Margaret was with child.

'I decided to put it out of my mind for the time being and enjoy myself instead.' The elated mother-to-be she was not.

LEAVING

There's something to be said for dropping everything and leaving.

I went to London because a friend bothered to read the 'Jobs Vacant' section of *The Sydney Morning Herald* on the same weekend that my head was buried in a pillow in my new Woollahra apartment, tears soaking through to my mattress.

It was 2002, and I'd moved in with my high school sweetheart, Abe. I had been working as an English teacher in a Sydney high school for more than a year, making the best of an Education degree from the University of Sydney. Every morning, I dreaded the fifty-minute drive west, the prospect of doing this job for the rest of my life. I felt trapped in the wrong career.

In the classroom itself, with the students, I found strength and brilliant distraction through the books and studying them. We laughed and invented. They dreamed of greatness and I was there to witness it, nurture it, and put better grammar around it. Some days, I wondered if I'd exaggerated my tears, when this – teaching – was the most important possible job in the world. I was privileged; the sadness would surely pass.

And so it went, until I found myself in a staff meeting one afternoon. The boardroom table spun around me, my head was noisy and numb. I felt sick. I excused myself for some fresh air, made it to my car and burst into tears. There was terrible sadness and panic. I called my sister from the car.

While I curled in a ball on the front seat, she spoke to me gently, reassuring and promising me that none of it had to continue as it had, that I could change whatever I wanted. I listened to Louise's words, and everything became clear. I quit my job the next day.

I enrolled in a Master of Arts in Journalism at the University of Technology in the new year. I wrote to some local newspapers with a pitch or two. I bought a double-shot latte from across the road, and then another. I waited for class. I vacuumed, both literally and personally. It wasn't enough; nothing was enough.

Abe left in the morning to work in a Surry Hills restaurant as a chef. At night I pulled myself together, just to prove that while I couldn't stop the tears or change my dismal interior dialogue, I was not totally out of control. I was glad to see him. He brought light and life back into the house and I lived off it. I knew things were getting bad when I stopped cooking. Not doing enough, and debilitated by it, I couldn't see the point.

Then one day in class, my friend Fleur reached her pen over and wrote on my notebook.

'I found the perfect thing for you.' Smiley face.

She placed a torn square of newspaper in front of me, an advertisement: 'Teacher/Journalist, wanted for position in London. Starts immediately.'

I applied; I got the job. The *Evening Standard* newspaper would fly me to London to go undercover as a teacher in one of the city's worst schools, and write about it. For the first time in a year, I was awake. I was a journalist.

I could feel an inch of daylight opening in my mind. Suddenly, I could sleep, and I dreamed of climbing out of a ditch and forward.

The day after I got the job I walked outside, squinting like someone who has just been released from confinement. As I walked to my local shops in Woollahra, the day was like a holiday, as though Paris had fallen just here and made everything smell like sun and laundry and green leaves. I filled my tote with fennel and a tub of ricotta, herbs, a loaf of sourdough. I stalled, taking some joy in the company of strangers, the dialogue of their daily routines. In a bookstore, I bought Nigella Lawson's *How to Eat* and *Paris Out of Hand: A Wayward Guide* to a place I would soon visit. I picked up a bunch of poppies and three baby squid from the fishmonger on Queen Street – and went home to cook.

I tore the bread into bite-sized pieces and dried it out in the oven. I whipped together grated lemon zest and ricotta in a bowl with extra virgin olive oil and drizzled red wine vinegar over the slightly crunchy bread pieces. I tossed the roughly cut squid into a hot chargrill pan and watched it curl, dancing and crackling and browning. Food recovery.

Abe walked into the kitchen and, for the first time in months, we were together again. He sidled up to me with a wink, facing the bench next to me, then sliced the fennel with a mandolin and tossed it into a bowl. I added mint leaves and parsley. I finished the squid with lemon ricotta and placed the pretty platter on the kitchen table (see recipe on page 74). He pulled me towards him, arms around my shoulders and smiled.

'Sorry,' I said. 'I've been unbearable.'

'You haven't,' he answered. 'It has. And now you're back.'

We set our tiny kitchen table and I filled a jug with water for the poppies.

'You should get a job in England and leave me forever more often,' he said, smiling, and placed his hand on mine. 'At least I get dinner made.'

A week later, I landed at Heathrow by myself.

CHARGRILLED SQUID *and* FENNEL WITH LEMON RICOTTA PANZANELLA

See story on page 73

SERVES 4
PREPARATION 40 minutes
COOKING 10 minutes

½ x ciabatta loaf, oven-
toasted, coarsely torn into
2–3 cm (¾–1¼ in) pieces
60 ml (2 fl oz/¼ cup) red wine
vinegar or Raspberry Vinegar
(see page 113)
80 ml (2½ fl oz/⅓ cup) extra
virgin olive oil, plus extra,
to serve
4 (about 450 g/1 lb) small–
medium squid
½ teaspoon each of sea salt
and freshly ground black
pepper, plus extra, to taste
½ teaspoon chilli flakes
½ teaspoon ground sumac,
plus extra, to serve
1 small fennel bulb, thinly
sliced, using a mandolin
1 small handful (¼ cup) torn
mint leaves
1 handful (⅓ cup) flat-leaf
(Italian) parsley leaves
juice of ½ lemon

Lemon ricotta
200 g (7 oz) fresh
ricotta cheese
zest of 1 lemon
1 tablespoon extra virgin
olive oil
1 large pinch of sea salt

For the lemon ricotta, put the ricotta, lemon zest, olive oil and salt in a bowl and mix until well combined. Set aside.

Put the torn bread in a bowl. In a separate bowl, whisk together the vinegar, 2 tablespoons of the oil and a pinch of salt and pepper. Pour over the bread, toss together well and let sit for 10 minutes for the flavours to develop.

To clean the squid, carefully pull the tentacles away from the tube over a bowl or the sink (the intestines should come away at the same time). Pull the clear cartilage from within the tube (discard), and scrape and discard the insides. Place the tentacles on a board and carefully slice them just under the eye to remove the squid intestines and eye (discard) and keep the tentacles in one piece. Slice off the wings from the body with a sharp knife and halve. If the skin is thick, remove it from the body by running your finger underneath the skin, then peeling it off in one piece and discarding. If the skin is very thin, leave it on.

Cut the squid tubes open and score the inside flesh in a cross-hatch pattern, taking care not to cut all the way through. Cut each squid into 3 x 5 cm (1¼ x 2 in) pieces and put in a bowl with the remaining olive oil, sea salt, pepper, chilli and the sumac. Add the tentacles and wings to the bowl and toss to combine. Cover with plastic wrap and set aside.

Heat a barbecue or chargrill pan over high heat until smoking. Cook the squid in batches for about 30 seconds, or until it curls at the edges, then turn and cook for a further 30 seconds–1 minute. Do not overcook or it will become tough.

Scatter the fennel, mint, parsley, squid and torn bread in a shallow bowl. Season with salt and pepper to taste. Dollop over spoonfuls of the lemon ricotta, sprinkle over some more sumac, then drizzle with the lemon juice and extra olive oil before serving.

SCOTLAND

Those who say it's all about the journey could not have persuaded Margaret Fulton of that sentiment in 1949. After a punishing sea voyage and the discovery that she was pregnant, all she could think about was the destination. Travel has a way of either making or breaking us, and until she walked into her family's home in Glasgow, Margaret worried that, this time, it might be the latter.

'The Scots are not very huggy-kissy,' Margaret says now.

But her cousins, Catherine, Hugh and Tom, her Aunt Maggie, and her father's sister, Jean, took turns embracing Margaret and her father, roaring with jokes and laughter when they met at the railway station, the boys in their kilts. They brought the beleaguered travellers back to the grand house where they lived. Inside the large rooms with their high ceilings, surrounded by Scottish furniture, Margaret felt as though she had come home. She watched her Aunt Maggie, the spitting image of her own mother, and her eyes filled with tears. She missed her.

'The Scots are not very demonstrative, but you know from the tilt of the head, the glint of eye, the unspoken word, what their feelings are. I was one of them,' says Margaret now.

The world of her husband, the tedious car trips down to the beaches, the muffled feelings of a sedentary marriage, seemed further away than ever.

'They were my ain folk.'

'The thing about the Scots is their sense of humour,' says Margaret. 'I find people are always shocked when you say things, but the Scots just take it with the flow of conversation. People get so sensitive and worried, they get very serious over a naughty joke.'

She loved their intelligence, banter and quibbles.

Glasgow had a working-class vibe. It was as if they'd sorted all the gruff, no-nonsense and often very funny citizens with beautiful, but impenetrable, accents into one corner of the world.

'We were an opinionated lot and sparked off each other. I voiced many ill-formed judgments. It didn't seem to matter.'

Everything dull was turned into something funny, or witty, she says. And they could eat.

Aunt Jean laid a large table out, flicked over a large damask tablecloth. Margaret watched the fabric billow in the air, perfectly laundered, and remembers thinking to herself, 'I know how to iron that.' Places were set with silverware and china, a pretty silver and crystal condiment set. High tea drew everyone in from their chores, the laundry, or a lingering chat with the neighbour out the front. It came after the large dinner in the middle of the day, at about that time when you can't possibly fit in another thing, except maybe some tea – and some jellied tripe.

Margaret walked around the large table laying thick soft white napkins, trying to get the look right or risk being labelled as not-one-of-us. Aunt Jean sat at the head of the table as everyone pulled in their chairs, surrounded by jugs of hot water and a few pots of tea. Attending to each member of the family, one at a time, Jean pointed around the table, asking each how they liked their tea, and then serving them directly. When it was Margaret's turn, the novice suggested she could just pour her own, trying to make it easier on her host. Everyone turned to face Margaret, silenced, and then looked back at Jean, eyes wide and holding back smiles.

'Just this once,' her aunt replied, a gentle reprimand for Margaret having clearly forgotten the traditions of Scottish life while in Australia.

Margaret leaned over the table for the jellied tripe; at least she could help herself to that. Jean made the various savoury concoctions for high tea, and Margaret joined her in the kitchen to help stuff a cow heel into an earthenware pot with the knuckle bone and cutlet-sized pieces of tripe. They covered the jar with the lid, placed it in a cauldron of hot water over the fire and left it there, simmering, for a day. The tripe turned tender and the knuckle and cow heel turned the whole thing to liquid jelly. They removed the bone and let the tripe set in jelly as it cooled. It could be kept in the cold larder for weeks. They served the jelly in slices, with sea salt, hot English mustard and roasted onions (see recipe on page 81).

Margaret's uncle, a Scottish butcher, came to the door with a paper-wrapped parcel. A few nights later, cold-pressed tongue appeared on the high tea table. Food rationing restricted various cuts of meat, but offal had no limitations, and so trotters and tripe, tongue and blood were turned into whatever mysterious Scottish concoction that could be found in some century-old scribble of a family recipe. All the various meaty, jellied dishes, if not so attractive in appearance, were 'lifted' by vinegar or mustard, a sharp pickle or spiced condiment.

When Margaret's father, Alexander, didn't get up for hot supper one evening, the group began to worry.

'Ah, no. It's just a wee upset stomach.' He patted his belly.

But they were worried, nonetheless, and called in the doctor the following day. The doctor propped his bag by the bedside and walked into the kitchen to tell the family his prognosis.

'Now, he says he's been eating Scotch woodcock for his hot supper,' referring to a meal served late in the evening, just before bed. 'And mushrooms on toast, followed by a rather generous wedge of cheddar, or a scoop of blue Stilton.'

The family nodded.

'Yes, yes,' said Aunt Jean. 'But what is wrong with him, doctor?'

'I'm afraid to say that sir is going to have to change his diet. He can't be eating this rich food so close to bed. He's having digestive problems,' the doctor said, patting his own stomach now.

Scotch woodcock involves beating anchovies, cream, chopped hard-boiled egg yolks and butter into a cream, heating it and serving it on toast. And Alexander's stomach had rebelled. The family shook their heads in wonderment – fancy the food he was eating doing all that to his health!

The Fulton clan all got into a car and climbed, twisted and wound their way from Glasgow up to the Scottish Highlands, to the heather-clad mountains and Margaret's birthplace in Nairn. The winding roads had the same effect on Margaret as the sea journey did, and she turned green at every twist and turn. But she eventually settled in time for her first wild salmon and wild trout, caught in the local streams and served with asparagus and followed with fresh raspberries. That night, she rested.

Morning broke with the sound of a call from the pavement.

'Hot baps! Get your hot butteries!'

The local baker had arrived outside, stopping briefly on his morning rounds to sell those Scottish breakfast rolls, also know as flouries. The flaky kind of bap, the Aberdeen rowie, is a hybrid of the croissant and a breadroll, and slightly less rich, but still laden with butter.

The famous cook Elizabeth David once said: 'They don't look as showy as the croissants, but for all their homely appearance, I prefer them in some ways.'

And Margaret did, too. She bought a small bag of them and noted the recipe for future bap making (see recipe on page 82).

The Fultons donned kilts and tweeds, smart leather boots and appropriate hats, and took walks into the heathered hills, shaded with purple like a child's colouring book. Stags and deer stood in the misty distance. They took 'twilight picnics' to the Fairy Dell and sat quietly together, eating sandwiches and little cakes, drinking sparkling cider. But then December rolled on, the pipers played their farewells, and Margaret's uncle and cousins accompanied the Australian contingent to Glasgow station.

'I left my heart in Scotland,' Margaret tells me now. 'But my little bun in the oven knew the serene contentment of her mother, who had taken her to her spiritual home.'

POTTED HOUGH

See story on page 77

SERVES 10
PREPARATION 30 minutes
COOKING 3 hours 30 minutes

1.5 kg (3 lb 5 oz) beef shanks
   on the bone, cut into 3 cm
   (1¼ in) thick slices
2 fresh pig's trotters
1 bouquet garni
1 onion, quartered
4 whole cloves
8 whole black peppercorns
6 whole allspice
4 tinned anchovies, mashed
1 small pinch of ground cloves
sea salt and freshly ground
   black pepper
malt vinegar, to serve
hot English mustard, to serve
toasted baguette slices,
   to serve

Put the beef shanks, pig's trotters, bouquet garni, onion cloves, peppercorns and allspice in a large, heavy-based saucepan with a lid and cover with cold water. Bring to the boil and skim any foam from the top. Cover and simmer for 3 hours, then leave until cool enough to handle.

Strain the broth into a clean saucepan. Transfer the meat to a board, discarding the spices and herbs. Trim away the fat, gristle and skin and remove the bones. Using two forks or your fingers, shred the meat. Put the shredded meat into the saucepan with the broth and simmer, uncovered, for 20 minutes, to reduce. Add the anchovies and ground cloves, then season with pepper and a little sea salt, if needed. Simmer over low heat for a further 5–8 minutes, to allow the flavours to develop.

Transfer the mixture to a 1 litre (35 fl oz/4 cup) terrine or loaf tin and cover with plastic wrap or a lid. You can determine the amount of jelly in the finished hough by adjusting how much liquid you add at this stage (for a meatier result, don't add all the liquid). Chill in the fridge overnight, or until firm.

To serve, turn the potted hough out onto a plate and cut slices for sharing, or simply spoon directly from the terrine. Offer malt vinegar for drizzling and dipping, hot English mustard and toasted baguette for spreading. Cover any leftover potted hough with plastic wrap and store in the fridge for up to 10 days.

HOT BUTTERIES

See story on page 78

MAKES 12 generous butteries
PREPARATION 1 hour, plus
2 hours proving
COOKING 20 minutes

500 g (1 lb 2 oz) strong '00'
    plain (all-purpose) flour, plus
    extra for dusting
1 x 7 g (¼ oz) sachet
    dried yeast
1 tablespoon sea salt flakes
1 tablespoon soft brown sugar
350 ml (12 fl oz) warm water,
    plus extra, if needed
250 g (9 oz) unsalted butter,
    plus extra, to serve

In a large bowl, mix together the flour, yeast, salt and sugar until combined. Make a well in the centre and gradually add the warm water in a thin stream, stirring with a wooden spoon and incorporating more flour from the sides as you mix – you may need a little more water. The mixture should come together as a dough.

Turn the dough out onto a lightly floured work surface and knead gently for 8–10 minutes, or until smooth and elastic.

Transfer the dough to a clean, greased bowl and cover the surface loosely with plastic wrap that has been dusted with flour. Put the bowl in a warm place to prove (rise) for about 1 hour, or until the dough has doubled in size.

Meanwhile, cream the butter in an electric mixer until pale, then use a spatula to divide it into four equal amounts.

Roll out the dough into a 20 x 40 cm (8 x 16 in) rectangle, about 1 cm (½ in) thick. If it 'seizes up' while you're trying to roll it, set it aside for 2 minutes, then come back to it.

With the shortest edge of the dough facing you, spread one portion of the butter over the bottom two-thirds of dough. Fold the top third over the centre third of the rectangle, then fold the bottom third over the folded dough. You will end up with a rectangle three times its original thickness.

Roll out the dough to the same size as before. Spread another portion of the butter over the bottom two-thirds of the rectangle, and repeat the folding process. Roll out the dough and repeat twice more to use the remaining butter portions, then roll the dough out again to its original size.

Lightly grease two baking trays and line with baking paper.

Use a knife to cut the dough into twelve even pieces – in half vertically, then in six pieces horizontally. Shape each piece into a slightly flat bun – like a chocolate croissant with rounded edges (tuck the edges under so the tops are smooth). Transfer the butteries to the prepared trays, cover with plastic wrap dusted with flour and set aside in a warm place until they have doubled in size.

Preheat the oven to 200°C (400°F).

Bake for 18–20 minutes, or until they have risen and are golden-brown. Cool on a wire rack, or serve hot with butter.

RECIPE OVERHAULS

The concept of 'potted hough' held my sister and me in the same kind of wary disbelief through our childhood, as did pig's feet and cauliflower. Except one was real. We'd beg Mum to tell us again, again, the story of the potted hough.

'Well, it's not really a story, girls, it's a dish,' she'd try.

'Oh, go on, Mum! What's in it again?'

Pronounced 'hoff', the dish seemed about as appealing to us as lamb's tongues lapping around in white sauce, something to be squeamish about but secretly amazed by. Boiled and shredded hough, or beef shin, is set in thick jelly. It would be cut in wedges, if it had been made in a bowl, or slices, if from a loaf pan. It came with little dishes of English mustard and malt vinegar.

Mum would finish the story with this little nugget: 'And they put anchovies, mashed, in there too, and pig's trotters.'

My sister and I would hold our bellies over the table, dramatically groaning and blerking.

'Pig's trotters and anchovies! In jelly!'

In a bid to dig deeper into my Scottish heritage, I made potted hough. I didn't do it right and Aunt Jean would no doubt have pointed out the errors as Margaret Fulton and my own mother did. The hough our Scottish ancestors ate was a thick-set moulded jelly, with pieces of meat mottled through it. The meat is shredded, placed in the bowl or terrine, and covered with the hot jelly stock. I increased the cloves, and ground them up, tweaked the allspice, but otherwise followed the recipe. My version had a very thin layer of fat on top, something like a rillette. Next time I might carefully spoon the fat from the top before it sets, or I might not. The jelly becomes a kind of binding agent, rather than a feature in itself, a characteristic that appealed to me because the idea of meat jelly still sends me into quiet conniptions. It wasn't exactly what Aunt Jean made, but it was potted hough. And when we laid thin slivers of the stuff on crusty baguette, with a tiny lick of hot mustard and a decent drizzle of malt vinegar, I felt some smug Scottish know-how, even if it was recipe rebellion against years of steadfast tradition.

We're constantly dreaming up new ways to do old things. The drive to discover food and then overhaul it is natural. Just as every generation thinks they invent sex, especially interesting sex, every year brings a host of new ideas around food.

When I tested Margaret's baps recipe at home, my father and grandmother pulled the pastries apart. We ate them straight, still hot from the oven, and my dad and I decided no extra butter was needed.

'What are you talking about, Robert?' my grandmother said. 'Why would you go and say something like that?'

Taking butter from that Scot, we learned long ago, was not to be done.

'They are supposed to have butter on them, and so we shall put butter on them.'

Recipe overhauls, then, not permitted.

For me growing up, food was already done.

People would ask: 'Are you going to do what your grandmother and mother do? Are you going to write cookbooks?'

No, I wasn't. I don't need to do what they did, I thought, I am going to do something different and extraordinary, something new, something mine. I didn't know then what I know now: there are ways to reinvent anything. You can break any old mould and put it together again as your own, be it a sacred family recipe, or a career.

WE'LL BE GONE TOMORROW

Soon after my mother was born, my grandmother was faced with the battle of raising a child on her own.

'It was heaven,' she reflects now.

But it started out as hell.

Twenty-six years old and heavily pregnant, Margaret went along to mothercraft classes run by the state nursing association. She learned how to change nappies on a hard rubber doll, slipping her hand between the terry towelling and the puffy-eyed model, so as not to prick it. She did pelvic floor exercises and learned how to manage her expectations versus what was realistic, how to budget for baby. She tried to prepare her house for the new arrival.

But her husband refused to give her money to do it. He argued that frivolities, like baby clothes and nappies, were not his responsibility. When she asked him for cash to buy pins and bottles, he'd baulk.

'How do I know she's mine?'

'He often suggested I had other men. It was emotional cruelty, I believe,' she says now, with the wisdom of hindsight.

A lot happened behind closed doors in the late 1940s. A husband depriving his wife, humiliating her as she shuffled around the house, heavily pregnant, was not something particularly noteworthy, Margaret thought. That didn't mean she was going to take it. She got to work making baby clothes for my mother, but also for a wholesaler, who would sell the little dresses and bonnets on, giving Margaret enough cash to prepare for the imminent birth. She stayed up late into the night with a treadle sewing machine, her pregnant belly heavy on her thigh as she pedalled and stitched.

Inside their Victorian terrace, one night in early December 1950 – the year my mother Suzanne was born – a thunderous row mirrored the awful weather outside.

'I want to you leave this house, and take the baby.' Margaret's husband Trevor turned to her, pointing his finger at the door. 'Leave tonight, just leave now.'

Trevor had told her to leave before. But for my grandmother, a baby made it personal. Precious Suzanne deserved better. She looked out into the night, demurring about taking the baby into the storm. Where would she go? She had no money, no way of getting anywhere.

Their personalities wrestled through the evening, angry silhouettes fell on the wall and the thunder clapped around them. Oblivious to the magnitude of their words as they focused on absurd logistics, they settled on a compromise.

'Well, you can stay until the morning,' conceded Trevor. 'But then, out.'

The next morning, a bright new day streamed around Margaret in the garden, glorious and soothing. She reached on tiptoes to hang baby clothes on the line, allowing the warmth of the sun to soak into her body. The copper had been lit and nappies boiled in a pot. Trevor walked out into the garden to find his wife bending down to shake out another load of washing. The baby lay on her back on a rug on the grass, clacking a few pegs together and chirping happily.

He questioned Margaret on the multiple loads of newborn outfits hanging around them, apparently forgetting the previous night's battle.

'What are you up to?'

'We'll be gone tomorrow.'

She put a full stop on their life together.

Margaret packed her things into a small leather suitcase and waited by the front door in a floral short-sleeved summer dress she'd made herself. The baby's cot and the sewing machine that Trevor had given her years before sat on the footpath by her side. She held the baby to her chest and squinted up the road, waiting for the arrival of her sister Jean in a taxi, and her new beginning. As the sisters shifted Margaret's possessions into the car, grappling with the heavy cot, Trevor rushed out into the road. Faced with the imminent departure of his wife and child forever, he was suddenly able to focus on what really mattered – the sewing machine being hauled by the driver and Jean into the boot.

'You're not taking *that*,' he bellowed.

Margaret pleaded. He had given her the machine for her birthday.

'No way. Do you know how much those things cost? No, you're not taking that for free.'

And so, using all the money she'd saved making baby clothes through the night, she paid him for the machine, the one thing he'd ever given to her. But she had in her possession a much more precious gift: a gurgling baby girl who would be forever by her side. It was heaven.

THOSE WHO CAN, TEACH

England was burning. I turned on the television, opened up the newspaper – everywhere there were smouldering piles of livestock, a constant terrible butchery, and the body count was rising, as the country worked to eliminate a bovine infection that was costing it dearly. Beef was off the menu.

Seated at my desk, with a view from the side of the building on Derry Street all the way down Kensington High Street, I opened the paper every day, looking for inspiration. My boss Guy Eaton would stand in front of my desk, blowing cigarette smoke from the side of his mouth out the window, fanning it with his hand.

'This isn't bothering you, is it?' he asked.

It never was – I was in London, baby.

By nine thirty every morning, I had a list of feature ideas ready for him to take into the ten o'clock meeting with Veronica Wadley, the newspaper's editor. Guy scanned the news every morning.

'What else, Kate? What else is happening?'

He got me on the phone to celebrities, getting quotes on how fast they intended to run the London Marathon, or what they thought of Ken Livingstone's congestion charge. I called up John Cleese, Sophie Dahl, some busty newsreader, and even got through to some of them. Still, to this day, I have Mr Cleese's mobile number in my phone, a nostalgic nod to those first few months at the *Evening Standard* newspaper. I've not checked to see if it's still live, in case it's not. Guy remains one of the best editors I've ever known. His faith in me as a writer aside, it was his constant challenges to the story, his striving for impeccable, engaging and accurate copy, that have most influenced what I do now. If issues were left unanswered in a story I wrote, he made me chase them down, knocking bravery into me as I went back to the source again to clarify, chase a difficult lead, ask the awkward, challenging questions.

'One cannot write if one does not read,' he said. And so I do, constantly.

When I wasn't researching for a raft of veteran feature- and leader-writers, including Keith Dovkants and Christopher Hudson, or writing pieces on health, science, education and celebrity, I was working to be vetted for placement into one of London's schools as a teacher. I was going undercover, the journalist's equivalent of the deep end, where all the muck-raking, dirt-toiling happens. I was completely unknown as a journalist, with barely a by-line behind me. So, when a local recruitment agency did their background checks, they could see my university results, my history in a less advantaged school in Sydney, and were impressed. When I said I wanted to go somewhere rough, it was easy to slot me right into a secondary school, based in North London's Haringey, the dodgy part. The recruiter found me a job as an English and Drama teacher. To cover our legal bases, I officially terminated my employment at the *Evening Standard*.

In November, I knocked on Guy's door, peered in, and sat on the chair by his desk to run through a story. I mustered all the diplomacy I could.

'I have enough copy,' I said. 'I have enough for three features.'

I'd had enough.

The next week, my article appeared on the front page of the newspaper, with a picture of my best impression of a serious teacher. 'My London teaching nightmare' ran the headline. It opened to a double-page spread inside, and a full-length photograph of me, arms folded, with my story. The words traced the predictable saga of testosterone-fuelled insubordination, insults, rape threats and consequent non-education. I described how firecrackers were set off in my classroom; how I was accused of racism when I told one student he had to stay back during lunch; how one senior student pushed me across a desk so he could storm out of the class. The school had been disadvantaged when Tony Blair's government took it under its wing and invested in new all-weather sports pitches and paintwork, but the teachers bore the brunt of a kind of Sovietisation of British state education, and the idiotic paperwork that all state teachers had to endure. At the end of every day, teachers had to deliver detailed lesson plans and respective lesson outcomes to their head teachers, instead of being able to actually teach. In the month that I was at the school, five full-time teachers resigned. It was my first by-line.

The editor congratulated me on the story. I appeared on radio to talk about my experiences, and I saw little *Evening Standard* posters advertising the piece all over London. I'd unravelled my teaching career by completely sabotaging any possible future in education, at least in England. I was immediately officially re-employed at the *Evening Standard*, where I continued to tap up pieces for editors, Liz Jones and Guy. I did feel – and continue to feel – guilty. Not for betraying my fellow teachers and never revealing to them what I was really doing, because I knew the story would change things for them. The story meant that the need for so much paperwork was overhauled, so teachers could spend less time justifying their movements, their lessons, and more time actually educating and nurturing the children, who were starved of stability and continuity. But I did feel bad for the students. I felt guilty that I'd exposed their school, especially in a country where the reputation of your school might impact your future prospects for university and jobs in some of the more judgmental and prejudiced sectors.

After work, I knocked on the door of my journalist friend Meg who was working at *The Times*, handed her a bottle of red as I pushed through the door.

'Welcome to our tiny wine party,' she sang, wrapping her arms around my head and roughing up my hair.

Her husband Andrew walked in with a brown paper bag, put out cartons of chicken jalfrezi and palak paneer he'd picked up from the local Korma Sutra on Charleville Road. It was our petit family of three.

I'd sat behind Meg in first year at university and decided I wanted to be her friend. Less than a year later, it was Meg who was holding back my hair when we decided to share a bottle of vodka, Meg with whom I skipped the odd lecture and drove to Rozelle instead, to share one slice of rhubarb crumble cake, and then share another slice. It was Meg who sent me a box in the post from England when I broke up with Abe. Inside were a glass jar of Aveda tea, chocolate licorice bullets, paperclips from Paperchase, and a card saying 'Come home to where you've never lived, to play with me'. So I followed her to London, to come home to where she was.

It was one of those very rare moments, when everything clicks together and you thank every celestial thing you want to access, every momentous and tiny decision you made, however horrible, because now you are exactly where you want to be. Soon after the teaching article came out, Meg and I were shivering through Kensington Gardens, wrapped up in beanies and coats. She stopped to pick some duck feathers off her bag, disgusted.

'From now on,' she said, 'if it's terrifying and amazing, I know you're definitely going to pursue it.'

PADDOCK TO PLATE

In the tiny fishing village of Mooney Mooney, in the Hawkesbury River estuary, about forty-eight kilometres from Sydney, sat a little house at the bottom of a large terraced garden. It had originally been constructed as a guest room for the larger house at the top of the garden. But in this little space lived Jean and her husband Bill and their two children, Billy and Lois. When Margaret arrived with baby Suzanne, they took Lois' room and squeezed a cot between two single beds.

'How absolutely perfect,' Margaret said aloud as she opened her suitcase, then picked up the baby with a gleeful whoop to take her into the garden.

Margaret bathed Suzanne in the laundry outhouse, where a deep basin filled with warm water made a perfect soapy bath. Behind the basin, rows of shelves stocked jars of preserves, fruit, pickled cauliflower and eggplant. Tomatoes pressed up against the sides of canning jars, a metallic lid securing summer's glut for out-of-season recipes. Jean and Bill had lived in Italy and France years before and, still swooning with the love of Mediterranean vegetables, Jean had planted a garden that the entire brood could live from. And from a stint in Dorset, England, they'd learned to dig the asparagus beds deep, grow the whitest cauliflowers and snap-fresh beans and peas.

White China peaches grew beside a large plum tree, an experimental pawpaw and a fig tree inside a cage, to foil the birds. They grew a hybrid almond tree to eliminate cross-pollination. Margaret often found Suzanne

Above, l-r: Denis, Maureen Simpson, Alexander, Suzanne and Margaret on the Hawkesbury River; below: Suzanne, Margaret and Alexander.

as a toddler in the strawberry patch, mouth stained with red juice. When they wed, Bill had given Jean a bay tree as a gift and over the years it became enormous, taking pride of place in the middle of the garden.

Suzanne grew too and soon she was chasing the Muscovy ducks around the garden. The ducks thrived under the fig tree, feasting on the tree's fruit all summer. They'd be let out to explore the mangroves and Suzanne squealed and ran with them as they crackled through the sand, sifting for tiny crabs and worms.

'It gave the ducks a lovely gamey taste,' Margaret remembers.

Pens around the garden kept White Orpingtons and Rhode Island Reds, and their meat and eggs became table fare. Margaret collected the eggs from the Khaki Campbell ducks, playing with recipes and noting which eggs worked best in which dishes.

Margaret was put in charge of fish and she'd grab Suzanne early in the morning and head for Peats Ferry, where they'd throw a line in from a boatshed. When Suzanne was older, Margaret would slip a tiny yellow buoyancy vest over her head and together they'd row out to the deep. They'd always come back with snapper, bream or flathead. I've always liked to think of the crack fishing duo, my grandmother and Mum, rocking on the water as they sat in silence, each in her own thoughts.

Margaret reeled in a flathead that jumped and flipped in the bottom of the boat. Mum held onto her seat as her mother, in rolled-up jeans and open-toed sandals, a red scarf around her dark hair, smacked the fish over the head. Then she hooked another worm to her line and waited for the next sign of a bite. Mum, meanwhile, at just three or four years old, picked up the fish from the bottom of the boat and held it up to her face.

'Hello, fish! How are you today?'

As a child, Suzanne became completely unfazed by the concept of animal-into-meat, handling a plucked chicken in the kitchen and learning to stuff the insides with halved lemons and handfuls of herbs. She would hold up the filleted skin and bones of a fish, running her tiny fingers along the bones like a piano keyboard, before tossing it into the bin.

Margaret dusted the fillets lightly with seasoned flour and fried them in a hot pan with butter and sage or marjoram leaves from the garden, which turned crispy as they cooked. I still do it the same way, thinking of my fishing grandmother as I do. Broken apart slightly and scattered over a pillow of soft polenta, garlic, chilli and lemon zest too, with crispy speck adding a salty complement to the fish, it's about the best easy meal in the world (see recipe on page 95).

When their haul was too large, they exchanged the excess with neighbours, for milk and cheese. A surplus of peaches or tomatoes was a worthy barter for local oysters, prawns, crabs and sea mullet, when they were running. Cow's milk was an important trade because the children needed it, but when Suzanne's cousin Bill came out in allergic boils, Jean took matters into her own hands and threw herself into goat breeding. She raised russet-toned Toggenburgs and white Saanens for milking, and was soon churning butter and turning out discs of goat's cheese and bottles of cream.

If Margaret ever wondered about the life she was giving Suzanne, she was grateful for the step she had taken and the harrowing leap that had led her to take it. This was better – living on the waterways with a family who loved her, with cousins to play with. She looked across the room at her daughter whose chair was pulled into the kitchen table, her tiny fingers deciphering the mystery of shelling a couple of prawns. The little girl picked up the prawn and nibbled it out of its shell, rubbed her hands together, then moved on to the next.

'We're going to be just fine,' Margaret remembers cooing to her daughter. 'Aren't we, my beautiful little Suzie? Yes we are.'

SOFT POLENTA WITH FLATHEAD *and* PANCETTA

See story on page 93

SERVES 4
PREPARATION 10 minutes
COOKING 25 minutes

2 tablespoons extra virgin
  olive oil
50 g (1¾ oz) pancetta or
  speck, cut into 1 cm
  (½ in) lengths
2 garlic cloves, chopped
2 fresh small red chillies, finely
  sliced diagonally
600 g (1 lb 5 oz) small flathead
  fillets (or other firm, white
  fish fillets), skinned
sea salt and freshly ground
  black pepper
50 g (1¾ oz) butter, diced
1 small handful sage leaves
juice and finely grated zest
  of 1 lemon

Soft polenta
1 litre (35 fl oz/4 cups)
  homemade chicken stock
250 g (9 oz) instant
  polenta (cornmeal)
60 g (2¼ oz) Parmigiano
  Reggiano cheese,
  finely grated
50 g (1¾ oz) butter, diced
sea salt and freshly ground
  black pepper

For the soft polenta, heat 750 ml (26 fl oz/3 cups) of the chicken stock in a saucepan over medium–high heat. Whisk in the polenta and stir over medium heat for 5–6 minutes, or until cooked. Stir in the cheese and butter, and season with salt and pepper to taste. Cover and keep warm. Pour the remaining stock into another small saucepan, bring to a simmer, cover and keep hot.

Heat 1 teaspoon of the oil in a large frying pan over medium heat, then add the pancetta and cook until crispy. Add the garlic and chilli and cook until the garlic is golden. Transfer to a plate and keep warm.

Increase the heat to high, add the remaining oil, season the flathead fillets and cook for 2–3 minutes on each side, or until golden and cooked through. Carefully transfer to the plate with the pancetta and garlic. Add the butter to the pan, fry the sage until crispy, then transfer to the plate. Add the lemon juice and zest to the pan, scraping up any lovely crispy bits from the pan with a wooden spoon.

To serve, add the remaining hot stock to the polenta and stir well. Spoon the hot polenta onto a serving platter or board. Gently break the fish into 5–8 cm (2–3¼ in) pieces. Using tongs, carefully put the fish and pancetta on top of the polenta. Spoon over the lemony juices and scatter with the sage leaves. Serve immediately.

FOR THE LOVE OF BOOKS

I got carried away at a bookstore and what I realised when I got home with the *Momofuku Cookbook* by David Chang, *Cumulus Inc* by Australian chef Andrew McConnell and *The Fat Duck Cookbook* by Heston – and three birthday cards – was that I probably didn't need the third card.

When people proudly tell me that they never buy cookbooks and instead find their recipes online, I feel like shoving *Larousse Gastronomique* down their throats. A recipe online is a technical thing, catering to a get-it-over-with attitude to food and cooking that leaves me cold. Good cookbooks are highly personal, immaculately edited works of inspiration.

A cookbook is visual and physical: you hold it, browse it, touch it, come back to it. Cooks and chefs are physical people. We like the touch, the smell, we look for beauty, we want to feel things in our hands. There's an argument I like, that chefs and cooks make better lovers, and this might explain it. We don't want to get it over with. We crave the *process*.

At Christmas in 1952, Margaret made an extravagant purchase for her sister Jean: the cookbook *The Garrulous Gourmet* by William Wallace Irwin. Jean unwrapped the brown-paper package tied with red ribbon and the two of them spent the rest of the day reading the book, transported from the Hawkesbury River to Paris and the French countryside, to the regional towns and cities of France. They pictured themselves in Les Halles, the Paris food markets, where produce was scrutinised, inspected, weighed, smelled and bargained for, before being packed off to the great restaurants of Paris.

Margaret turned on the oil lamp next to the kitchen sofa she called a bed when other friends came to stay in Jean and Bill's house in the Hawkesbury, and examined the soupe à l'oignon or French onion soup. She practised the recipe time and time again, sometimes with a slice of baguette laden with gruyère cheese set neatly in the bowl (see recipe on page 100).

One day Jean came home to find Margaret finely slicing nearly a kilogram of onions, tears running down her face. She announced that she was making a variation of their French onion soup, enriched with eggs and Swiss cheese. Jean joined her at the kitchen bench, and together they heated butter and oil – 'a compromise between the olive oil used in the South of France and the butter used in the North' – and cooked the onions gently.

They held their breath for that sacred moment when, eggs in a bowl, one turned the egg beater steadily while the other poured boiling onion stock into the bowl and the soup became pale and creamy. With the addition of a tablespoon or two of brandy, it was lifted from 'the merely good to the semi-divine', just as *The Garrulous Gourmet* promised.

The pair sat down at the kitchen table, surrounded by a clatter of saucepans and whisks, and drank their velvet soup. With fresh goat's cheese from Jean's goats and garden chives they had grown themselves, the sisters made a simple dish as served in a Parisian artist's studio in *The Garrulous Gourmet*, which not only prescribed the recipe but set the scene as well.

'We put the cheese in a bowl and added some snipped chives,' Margaret remembers now. 'The artist in the book would go to his window box. We went to our herb patch, but the effect was the same. Then, a careful sprinkle of cayenne pepper and a little salt. This we beat, adding, from time to time, some cream. We served it, as instructed, on brown bread. And so we found ourselves in Montmartre, or the Latin Quarter of Paris — artists entertaining each other until there was no more left to enjoy.'

The chickens kept laying and laying and every day Margaret walked into the garden to find another half dozen dispatches, often more, from the prolific birds. She unravelled her apron of eggs onto the table.

'What do you say we do a 'slobbery omelette'?'

The 'slobbery omelette', or l'omelette baveuse, is not just any omelette. *The Garrulous Gourmet* describes the 'square gobs' of egg he had eaten in Germany and Russia, but 'this is one of the great national dishes of the French'. 'Slobbery' conjures a quivering and wobbly thing. Except when it comes to omelettes. They absolutely must be slobbery on the inside, Margaret still argues, as evidence of perfectly cooked eggs.

They practised with the chickens' surplus, breaking eggs into the bowl with their swift wrists, shaking the pan to stop it sticking, turning it out onto a plate with a rounded flip.

Cookbooks tell you where you've been, says Margaret. When she was a little girl at home in Glen Innes, her mother went to hospital for a procedure while the children were minded by their grandmother, who was visiting from Scotland. Isabella arrived home to her happy brood, who grabbed her around her legs or politely kissed her on the cheek, depending on their age.

'Oh, Mother, Grandmother cooked all our favourite meals,' they cried.

Later that night, Isabella asked her mother how she knew what to cook for the children.

'It was simple,' she replied. 'I just looked for the splattered pages.'

'The best recipes are always on the splattered pages,' Margaret tells me.

My friend Meg asked me recently why her boeuf provençal didn't taste like mine. I love her boeuf provençal, but it is definitely hers.

'Did you follow the recipe?'

'Yes!'

'Did you soften the onions until translucent and completely tender? Did you brown the meat and not overcrowd the pan? How long did you cook it for? A couple of hours?'

I was teasing, but I sounded like a stern mistress. Well, she did ask.

She dropped her head back: 'Ugh. Nooo.'

For such a pioneer – something she was yet to prove – Margaret was resolutely stubborn when it came to following the recipe. And she still is.

When Australian talk-show host Andrew Denton asked Margaret for the secret of good cooking, she put it down to the recipe. That may just be a veteran cook justifying her career, but she's determined.

'Well, I'll tell you what the secret is. It's so easy. It's like when people make a casserole and they fiddle around with it until it tastes like the casserole they always made. Whereas, if you actually stick with a new recipe, you've got a new flavour and you're keeping your mind open and you're keeping your mind expanding,' she said.

'See, I…you're talking to…I'm a very limited cook and I find recipes quite scary, to be perfectly honest,' Denton attempted.

'I find gardening quite scary. [Laughter] I snip off next year's growth.'

'No, but you see with cooking, you see, the thing about recipes is…What infuriates me is they'll say 'cook until brown'. Now what does that mean? Are we talking dark brown or are we talking light brown? [Laughter] So I usually err on the on the side of cooking till dead.' [Laughter]

'No, that's silly.'

'Well, no, but it's…[Laughter] But you're not being supportive here, Margaret…What you're saying is with a recipe you've got to stick to the recipe. But what I've heard is that you should take the recipe but you should play around a little bit and have the confidence.'

'Well, I don't say play around a bit. I say follow the recipe.'

Margaret and Kate at Margaret's home.

FRENCH ONION SOUP GRATINÉE

See story on page 96

SERVES 4–6
PREPARATION 25 minutes
COOKING 1 hour

45 g (1¾ oz) unsalted butter
1 tablespoon olive oil
1 kg (2 lb 4 oz) brown onions,
    thinly sliced
2 litres (70 fl oz/8 cups)
    homemade beef stock
2 teaspoons plain
    (all-purpose) flour
125 ml (4 fl oz/½ cup) dry
    white wine
sea salt and freshly ground
    black pepper
1–2 tablespoons brandy
10 thick slices sourdough
    baguette, toasted
100 g (3½ oz/1 cup) finely
    grated gruyère cheese
fresh thyme sprigs, to garnish

Melt the butter in a large, heavy-based saucepan, add the oil and onion and sauté gently for 30–40 minutes, stirring occasionally, or until softened and deeply golden.

Meanwhile, heat the stock in another saucepan until it is very hot.

Add the flour to the onion and stir over moderate heat for 3–5 minutes, to cook the flour. Add the hot stock and wine, season to taste and simmer for 20 minutes, then remove from the heat and stir in the brandy.

Turn the grill (broiler) to medium–high. Spoon the soup into 4 large or 6 small individual ovenproof bowls and place them on a baking tray. Divide the toasts between the bowls, overlapping a couple of slices to fit. Push the toasts down a little so they soak up the soup. Scatter over the cheese and place the tray under the grill until the cheese melts and turns golden.

Alternatively, if the bowls will not fit under the grill, divide the cheese between the bread slices, grill until melted and golden, then slip a slice or two into each bowl of hot soup.

Garnish each bowl with a thyme sprig and serve.

FOOD IN THE BLOOD

'How the hell do you truss a chicken?'

I slammed a packet of butter on the bench, untangling it from the curling, bloody (literally) string I'd been working at for ten minutes on the raw birds.

'Damn it.'

I had vast polished stainless-steel benches. I had access to a Kitchen Aid stand mixer in my beautiful Barons Court rental in London. The oven was preheated; I had even found a jar of preserved lemons at Tesco's. Roast chicken? Easy. I'd seen it cooked a million times. I'd slipped butter under the skin as an eight-year-old, picked rosemary from the garden and shredded the sharp little needles from their woody stems. But what was I supposed to do with the timing of the bird and the potatoes, the green beans with slivered almonds and capers and the bread and butter pudding I did not know. Where was *The Margaret Fulton Cookbook* when you needed it? On the end of the bloody phone. What time is it in Australia?

'Kate! How are you, darling?'

'Mum, sorry to wake you up. I have two chickens at room temperature but when do I put them in? Is 200°C good? Everyone is coming in, like, forty minutes. Do you have to par-boil potatoes? I think they're overcooked.'

'Oh! Now. Ahh…'

I'd literally woken her up.

'Sorry, Mum.'

'What time is it there?'

It was nearly three o'clock on a Sunday afternoon in London, and I'd taken the idea of a Sunday lunch and run with it. There's something about London that just calls for it. Every Saturday night, while my friends danced in some club in Clapham, or jumped around to the Pixies or the Smiths at one of our houses, glasses raised, singing in drunken harmony, we'd plan for Sunday pub lunch. Next day we'd drag ourselves out of bed at midday, crawling from sofas in each other's houses, downing bottles of energy drink, and go to the Gold in Notting Hill, the Ladbroke Arms, or just for a pint at the Hillgate. While I knew I couldn't reproduce the whole-beast carveries of London's finest, I could do home-cooked as well as anyone.

Except, at the precise moment that the potatoes were turning to crumbs and the raw chickens had surpassed room temperature and were reaching blood-temperature, I realised that, maybe, I hadn't actually done this before, by myself, from start to finish. It was all well and good to say 'read the recipe', except I didn't have one, and my 2003 Nokia didn't do anything useful internet-wise. But it could call for help. It was just before 6 am in Sydney.

'The chickens need to cook for an hour, darling.'

'And when do I put the potatoes in? They're…*very* par-boiled.'

'Do you have any more potatoes? Uncooked?'

'No.'

'Okay. Well, cook them ten minutes before the chicken has finished, and more while it's resting. And turn the temperature up to 220°C. They will be a bit crumbly but should form a nice crust. Just dry them out well first. They will be delicious.'

When Tamar, Foordy, Kitty, Cara, Yiannis and Dimbleby walked through the door, I asked, 'Where's Roby?'

'Hung-over,' said Tamar.

I pulled the glistening golden chickens from the oven and placed them on the stovetop. They were the most beautiful chickens I had ever seen. Their feet were bound with a string bow as a last-minute alternative to trussing, but the whole birds stayed together and rich lemon-butter oozed through their thin and crispy skin, keeping the flesh moist. The potatoes were done, to say the least. I bundled them into a bowl and scattered over some mint leaves, a splash of white balsamic. The bread and butter pudding came out after cheese and more wine, crunchy on top with velvety custard inside. We lay back on the navy-blue sofa and spent the rest of the day laughing and teasing, family for now. And cooking made it more so.

Early on a Saturday morning I hit the Borough Market for the first time. I stood in the middle of a great hall, London's oldest fruit and vegetables market, and watched the whirlwind of activity around me. Two heavy men wrestled an enormous wheel of cheese onto a foot-thick wooden bench. Another ladled hot mulled wine, fragrant with orange and cloves, into cups. A couple selling eggs had their cartons piled up in front of them, more than a metre high, hundreds and hundreds of free-range eggs. A man scraped the halved edge of a melting ogleshield – a large salted, pungently flavoured cheese, not unlike Switzerland's raclette – which blistered under an open grill. He slid the bubbling cheese onto plates of boiled baby potatoes – an oozing concoction of molten, rich, crispy, gooey lunch.

Duck confit sandwiches, pork rolls with layers of meat and cabbage, sauerkraut on a great two-hands-needed bun, pork pies, Spanish stews – each stallholder had their specialty. In England's supermarkets, everything was pre-packed and plastic-wrapped, but here, food came alive with great piles of stunning produce and pastry. The air smelled of roasting meat and fish, fried onions, melting cheese and great wedges of stilton and cheddar.

I pushed up to a stall to buy what I'd come for. An entire carcass of venison hung from a rafter behind the counter, whole fluffy rabbits and pig's ears were on full display. Placing two large and meaty smoked hocks into a bag for me, the butcher winked.

'Pea and ham soup?'

I felt predictable. He wiped his hands on his apron, already pawed with blood, and gave me a huge ruddy smile.

'Yes, but with green peas. I'm trying a twist. And I'm making my own stock...' I trailed off, running out of wow-worthy things to add.

'Of course.'

He handed the parcel over and lifted his chin with a nod.

'Thinly slice the skin too, it adds a good bite.'

'Of course.'

As I walked back to London Bridge Station, my mobile rang: Roby. 'Hey ho, Gibbs.'

'Hi, how are you?'

'What are you doing tonight? Want me to come over and bring some wine and you can make up for me not turning up to your place the other day, even though it was unforgivable of you.'

He walked in an hour later, carrying a bottle of pinot noir and a bunch of tulips. We played Scrabble on the kitchen table while the stock bubbled, rich with onion, wine and smoky ham (see recipe on page 106). Two hours later, when the soup was finally ready, we were starving. I semi-puréed the fresh peas, so the soup was a little chunky and a little velvety, returned it to the pot with the slow-cooked ham, and spooned crème fraîche from the markets over the top. I carried over another small bowl and Roby peered inside.

'You don't have to, but the guy at the markets said it adds *bite*.'

We both scattered the sliced skin into our bowls and gave it all a half stir. He held up his glass to me.

'Oh to be fed by the Gibbs.'

GREEN PEA *and* SMOKED HAM SOUP

See story on page 104

SERVES 4
PREPARATION 20 minutes
COOKING 3 hours

800 g (1 lb 12 oz) smoked
   ham hocks
1 leek, halved lengthways and
   coarsely chopped
1.5 litres (52 fl oz/6 cups)
   homemade vegetable stock
½ garlic bulb, halved
   horizontally
1 fresh bay leaf
2 tablespoons extra virgin olive
   oil, plus extra for drizzling
½ brown onion, finely chopped
125 ml (4 fl oz/½ cup)
   white wine
600 g (1 lb 5 oz) fresh or
   frozen peas
sea salt and freshly ground
   black pepper
6 rashers free-range streaky
   bacon, very thinly sliced
3 tablespoons crème fraîche
mint leaves, to serve

Put the hocks, leek, stock, garlic and bay leaf into a large saucepan with a lid, bring to the boil, then reduce the heat to low. Cover and simmer gently for 2½–3 hours, or until the meat is almost falling off the bone.

Using tongs, remove the hocks carefully from the stock and put them in a large bowl. Strain the broth into the bowl, discarding the leek, garlic and bay leaf. Leave until the hocks are cool enough to handle, then remove them from the broth and pull the meat from the bones in bite-sized shards, discarding the excess fat, gristle and bones. Either discard the skin, or finely slice half or all of it and reserve it with the meat.

Heat the oil in a medium saucepan over medium–low heat. Add the onion and cook until translucent and soft, but not browned. Stir in the wine and bring to a simmer, then cook for about 5 minutes, or until almost completely reduced. Add the reserved broth and bring to the boil, then add the peas and simmer for 10 minutes if the peas are fresh, or 5 minutes if frozen.

Use a hand blender to lightly blend the soup, so some peas remain whole but the soup is thick and creamy. Add the ham meat and cook gently for 5–10 minutes with the lid off, or until the desired consistency is achieved. Test for seasoning and add a little salt if needed (the ham hocks and bacon are salty), and freshly ground black pepper.

Heat a frying pan over medium–high heat and cook the bacon for 8–10 minutes, or until very crispy. It will curl as it cooks – let it. Transfer to a plate lined with paper towel.

Serve the soup in individual bowls. Put a small dollop of crème fraîche in each bowl and swirl it through a little. Scatter over the bacon and mint leaves and drizzle with extra olive oil.

THE KINDNESS OF SWARTHY STRANGERS

A Sydney girlfriend Samantha lived in London too. We met up three or so mornings a week before work to drink (but not savour) horrible London coffee. Being kindred spirits, we'd invest in a meal out about one evening a week. To say that our meagre London incomes got us down would be an overstatement, but it definitely hindered our consuming the kind of food we were used to. We economised by sharing everything. We found a cool Italian spot on the King's Road and shared the platter of beef carpaccio topped with shaved parmesan and baby rocket leaves, then a soft porcini risotto, poured into the shallow bowl like a thick perfect puddle. And when the glass of zabaglione – a creamy boozy foam – arrived at the table, we both dug our spoons in. Being cash-strapped wasn't going to hold us back culinarily. But one time we had to rely on the kindness of swarthy strangers.

It's hard to say whether he had an account at the gilded department store, was some kind of British billionaire who owned the building, or both. Sam still swears it was Mohamed Al-Fayed who paid for our groceries that particular day. We'd been inside Harrod's food department for an hour: two blondes with wide eyes and empty baskets.

'Eccles cakes! Oh, Sam, my parents bought eccles cakes from Fortnum & Mason in 1969. I'm getting them.' (See recipe on page 110.)

I dropped them into her shopping basket, which otherwise contained a tin of tea shaped like a double-decker bus that Sam was sending home as a gift. We traced our fingers over packets of French chèvre, great wheels of cheddar, and fogged up the glass cabinet containing smelly blues and rinded squares.

'Better not,' said Sam. 'Let's just get dinner at Sainsbury's. This is getting depressing.'

I rested my forehead on the glass and sighed.

Sam was already halfway through a sentence in a conversation with a gentleman behind us by the time I turned around, and I just picked up the ending: '...absolutely glorious, isn't it.'

I raised one eyebrow at her, half nodding, to say, 'Yep, yep, let's go.' She didn't budge. Was she being charmed by this olive-skinned gentleman, his smart, light cashmere coat dropping nearly to the floor and well polished shoes? By a man in his sixties, or older? I squeezed her elbow and listened in, waiting. She nudged me off. He was charming her. This was weird. Sam laughed loudly.

'No, no, no,' she said. 'We're heading home to get dinner now, but we wanted to just be here for a little while, have a look. It's complete heaven.'

Their conversation trailed off. But as we stepped away, he turned back to us. I'm not making the next bit up.

'You ladies should continue shopping. Please, just catch my eye before you leave and I'll escort you out.'

'Ah, pardon? Sorry?' I definitely unwittingly pulled a face at this point.

He rephrased: 'I'd like you to continue enjoying your experience here. Please fill up your baskets with whatever you like, and signal to me when you're leaving. Just give me a nod, it's fine. Please enjoy.'

'Oh, no. No. Thank you,' Sam said, more politely than I would have.

'Please,' he said. 'It's really nothing for me.'

At this point, Sam seemed to register something that I did not, and she nodded to me.

And so we did. We filled up a basket, all the while debating her who-it-was theory. We added perfectly wrapped parcels of cheese, another box of tea, more eccles cakes. Sam ordered free-range, rare-breed ham, sliced from the bone, and prosciutto: thin, long flags striped with gorgeous fat. We added about ten punnets of raspberries. They were on sale (as if that were relevant), but still, ten! Olives, a trussed chicken decorated with lemon and rosemary, all went into the basket. And, as we approached the exit to the food hall, our man nodded to a uniformed chap who escorted us to the checkout. Our parcels were packed into a few Harrod's branded bags and we were thanked for visiting. Pleasure, Harrod's, it was a pleasure. Over the next two weeks we kept referring to the various produce as Mohamed's prosciutto, Mohamed's ham.

'Thank you, Mohamed!' we'd cheer as we popped another olive into our mouths or a martini.

We'd gone nuts on the raspberries. I made raspberry vinegar (see recipe on page 113). Mum used to keep the homemade version at home, a kind of balsamic substitute that was as perfect drizzled on raw sliced fennel as it was on barbecued chicken, and I'd missed it. For months we used the slightly sweet, intensely raspberry-flavoured vinegar to dress salads, or had it as a kind of tart cordial, topped up with ice and soda, sometimes vodka. We called it 'Mohamed's Cheers'.

ECCLES CAKES

See story on page 108

MAKES about 30 cakes
PREPARATION 1 hour
30 minutes, plus 2½ hours
chilling pastry, plus
macerating overnight
COOKING 25 minutes
Start the filling 1 day ahead

450 g (1 lb/3 cups) plain
   (all-purpose) flour
½ teaspoon salt
185 g (6½ oz) unsalted butter,
   chilled, diced
80 ml (2½ fl oz/⅓ cup) chilled
   water (approximately)
55 g (2 oz/¼ cup) raw sugar
2 free-range egg whites,
   lightly whisked

Filling
320 g (11¼ oz/2¼ cups)
   currants
2 teaspoons ground allspice
1 teaspoon freshly
   ground nutmeg
finely grated zest of 2 oranges
60 g (2¼ oz) unsalted butter
60 g (2¼ oz/¼ cup) dark
   brown sugar
60 ml (2 fl oz/¼ cup)
   orange juice
2 tablespoons brandy

For the filling, put the currants, spices and orange zest in a bowl. Heat the butter and sugar together in a medium saucepan until the butter is melted, then add to the currant mixture with the orange juice and brandy. Mix well, cover and leave in the fridge overnight, to allow the flavours to develop.

Sift the flour and salt into a bowl. Rub in the butter until the mixture resembles breadcrumbs. Make a well in the centre and add enough of the chilled water to make a firm dough. Do not knead. Form into a ball, roll in plastic wrap and chill for 1 hour.

Preheat the oven to 190°C (375°F) and line a baking tray with baking paper.

Roll the pastry out to 5 mm (¼ in) thickness and cut out circles with a 9 cm (3½ in) round cutter. Gather the scraps and re-roll. Place a heaped teaspoonful of filling in the middle of each pastry round, fold in half and tuck the pointy edges under, shaping the cake into a flattish round. (To work faster, spoon out 5–10 dollops of filling at a time, then wrap and shape.)

Make three slashes in the top of each cake (tradition says this number is important). Put the sugar in a shallow bowl. Use a pastry brush to paint the top of each cake with egg white, then dip the tops in the sugar. Place each cake on the prepared tray.

Bake for 15–20 minutes, or until golden, being careful not to let them burn. They can be eaten hot or cold.

RASPBERRY VINEGAR

See story on page 109

MAKES 800 ml (28 fl oz)
PREPARATION 10 minutes,
plus 3 days macerating
COOKING 30 minutes

500 g (1 lb 2 oz) fresh or
    frozen raspberries
500 ml (17 fl oz/2 cups) good-
    quality red wine vinegar
75 g (2¾ oz/⅓ cup) caster
    (superfine) sugar

Put the raspberries in a glass or ceramic bowl, pour over the vinegar, cover and allow to macerate for 3 days.

Mash the raspberries in the bowl, using very clean hands or a fork, then strain the liquid through a fine-mesh sieve lined with muslin (cheesecloth). Squeeze the fruit firmly in your hands to extract every last drop of flavour from the raspberries.

Combine the raspberry vinegar and sugar in a saucepan, add 80 ml (2½ fl oz/⅓ cup) water and bring to a gentle simmer (not a boil!) for 30 minutes. Let cool completely, then transfer to sterilised bottles.

Use immediately or allow the flavours to develop as the months go by. It will keep for up to 12 months.

ALMOST
PERFECT

THE ROCKS

By the time Margaret returned from Mooney Mooney to the world of Sydney circa 1953, the Korean War had ended and Britain had exploded its first atomic bomb in the Monte Bello Islands off Western Australia. King George VI had died and the lovely Queen Elizabeth celebrated her coronation with a poached chicken dish involving curry powder, crème fraîche, flaked almonds and raisins.

Everyone wanted the recipe, developed by the inimitable British cook of the Cordon Bleu cooking school Rosemary Hume. A few years later Hume teamed up with her friend Constance Spry, the royal family's flower arranger, to publish the best-selling *Constance Spry Cookery Book*.

Also newsworthy, a royal commission was looking into whether television should be established in Australia. (Just three years later the whole country collectively sat down on the sofa, and has barely got up since.) A writer named Ian Fleming had high hopes for his first novel involving a chap called James Bond, in a book called *Casino Royale* – a touch of glamour to alleviate the post-war gloom. Others were recommending another new book, *The Catcher in the Rye*. In Sydney, Waverley Council maintained its ban on the bikini from its beaches including Bronte, Tamarama, Coogee and Bondi.

In Britain, many women in the 1950s had to surrender the hard-won freedoms of being able to work throughout the Second World War in order to become perfect housewives. And that was also the case for many women in Australia. In the post-war boom, Australia was manufacturing washing machines, ovens, refrigerators, freezers, food mixers and saucepans. David Jones, the Sydney department store, was building up its homewares section. Men dropped by on their way home from work, picking up little gifts – such as the latest garlic crusher – for their lucky wives, so they could cook dinner for their husbands even better than before.

Margaret wanted a piece of it – not by staying at home, leaning on her washing machine and dreaming up ways to use her new food mixer before she scrubbed the floors, but by selling the new contraptions to the domestic-bound females herself. While it was expected women with wartime jobs would abandon their careers so returning soldiers could have them, there was one place only a woman would do – teaching other women how to spiff up their home skills. Women at home were scrubbing and cleaning from dawn to dusk, and someone had to be there to show them how to do that.

Margaret took a part-time job at David Jones in 1952, leaving baby Suzanne at home in Mooney Mooney with Jean – two days one week and three the next – and hitching a ride to Sydney. Bikini-clad girls might not have been allowed on the beaches of Sydney, but Margaret's bare leg, peeking underneath her calf-length skirt, lifted slightly, reliably stopped passing traffic. She jumped into purring saloon cars and rumbling utes on the main road and rattled into the city to her new job.

Margaret practised her sales pitch at night, describing the qualities of the front-loading Bendix washing machine, Sunbeam cake mixers, Kelvinator freezers, various pots and pans, and other dazzling labour-saving devices. When one of the department store's buyers enthusiastically bought thousands of vegetable peelers – a new contraption for the Australian consumer – it was Margaret's job to sell them. She was escorted with a couple of young female colleagues, each in her white starched uniform with a bright handkerchief tucked into a breast pocket, to the ground floor of the building. They were propped by the front entrance, beside a table piled high with raw carrots, cucumbers and potatoes. They were not impressed.

The top level of the department store was a kind of educated saleswomen's domain, where knowledge of a product was more important than the pitch. But here, on the floor, they felt like regular spruikers. Margaret struggled with the peelers, the cucumbers, the carrots, fumbling over their elongated shapes and trying to demonstrate the peeling process at the same time. One customer returned moments after a sale, handing his paper bag back to Margaret with a head tilt. She peered inside. There sat a lonely carrot, partially peeled.

'My apologies, sir.'

And she swapped a peeler for his vegetable.

A roar of laughter came from a salesman at the adjoining Dunhill cigarette counter and Margaret threw him her iciest look. At lunchtime the salesman asked her to join him for a cup of coffee. The handsome, moustachioed Douglas Fairbank lookalike was not Margaret's type, she told herself. She saw his brand-new Fuji silk shirt, his perfectly pressed pinstriped tailored suit, his silk tie with matching kerchief in his breast pocket and well-manicured hands and thought 'no thanks'. She was after a craggy artist or writer, with baggy corduroy velvet trousers, Viyella shirt, some loose hand-knitted sweater or tweed jacket, instead. She is often specific about these things – planning out the fantasy.

But Denis managed to weave his way into her life, accompanying her on the train back to Mooney Mooney, only to U-turn all the way back to Sydney again without stopping in. It was his way of wooing her. But having to catch the bus and train, instead of hitching a ride as she would had she been alone, was an expense for Margaret. Her usual route was to catch the train to Asquith, where there was usually no one to punch the tickets, and hitch a ride from there. She worked short shifts, so had no time to hang around after work and she didn't have money to be throwing around for cups of coffee. She has never been a coffee drinker, either.

Nonetheless, these Denis-accompanied trips went on for months and not once did Margaret invite him into the house at Mooney Mooney, thinking he'd never fit in. Until she did. Then he dropped in on weekends and stayed for supper in the evenings. He joined Bill, Jean, Suzanne, Margaret and a new friend of Margaret's, Maureen Simpson, on fishing days on the Hawkesbury, where they'd row out to Snake Island or under the bridge.

'Down hooks!' Bill would call out, and they'd pull back in jewfish or flathead. Then, 'Show hooks, they've gone', and they'd return home to a fish dinner. Some summer evenings, they swung into a riverbank to light a fire and cook the fish, restoring themselves when it turned chilly with a mug of hot Bovril. The thick, salty meat extract from the United Kingdom, swilled with hot water and a good dash of Bundaberg rum was loved by all fishermen in these parts.

Denis became part of the furniture. He loved fishing and the local fisherman loved his Irish humour. He helped clean the fish and told fishy tales – plus he could drink, so he blended in well at the local Brooklyn pub. They'd cook fish and chips, a luxury meal in the 1950s except to those who could catch their own. Margaret would bring out a bottle of Penfold's golden dry sherry while Denis threw an old army blanket over the table, and the adults played cards, five hundred specifically, into the night. Someone would bring out the Penguin edition of *Hoyle's* to sober many late night arguments.

My mother has often spoken of these nights – which went on in various guises for years, in different locations, on stolen weekends away, during school holidays – and confesses she used to lie awake listening to their laughter and conversation, game concentration broken by roars and cheers as the adults played hour after hour and into the morning.

'It was reassuring,' she tells me now. 'I loved it, hearing them next door erupting with joy through the evening. I wasn't allowed to go in, but it was comforting having them near.'

She feels the same about the party boats, or 'disco boats' as she calls them, that now travel back and forth past my parents' house on the harbour into the small hours on weekends. They're way too noisy and disruptive, arguably rude in their dismissal of people trying to sleep, but she loves to hear their innocent fun, their laughter, and she sleeps more soundly when they're there.

By the end of 1953, Margaret grew tired of hitching and the ongoing commute from the Hawkesbury into the city and back home again. She packed up her bags and her inquisitive three-year-old to face the brave new world of Sydney. She moved into a flat with a single woman before moving into her own place in Essex Street in Sydney's centre, in a quaint sandstone-clad location called The Rocks. Now a little plaque pinned to the wall inside her old house commemorates her time there. But instead of being a two-storeyed terrace house on a steep road, it's now the public bar called Harts Pub. The spot was once called Hangman's Hill, because there on its muddy slopes, unfortunate convicts got their come-uppance on the public gallows. It was already paved by the time Margaret lived there and the road was blocked off to traffic. Around the corner were the offices of *The Bulletin* and *The Sydney Morning Herald*, but the area's meagre rents drew in a community of struggling artists, poets, writers, models, actors, students, ladies of the night – and Margaret Fulton.

Margaret's life revolved around her work and a flourishing career, but she soon realised she must take on more hours to support herself and her little girl. Margaret's father, Alexander, found himself on a rotating homestay with his various children. He lived with Jean and Bill for months on end and then packed up his meagre belongings to move in with Margaret, and less frequently with their older sister Cath. Suzanne and Alexander bonded.

'Somebody gave me a canary,' Grandma tells me. 'I don't know why, what a mad idea.'

But every day she fed the bird, refreshed its water, and put its cage by the window so it could look out.

One day when Margaret was out at work, little Suzanne and Alexander spent the morning learning to play cards. Looking for more things to do, they peeked in at the canary, tapping at the cage to say hello.

'Let's feed her,' Alexander said.

He opened the cage door to scatter some crumbled bread crust inside, imagining the canary would warily drop down, once they were well gone, to peck nervously at the bounty. But when he opened the tiny palm-sized door the bird flew out into the room, banging into teapots and a pile of papers, scattering them all over the floor. Alexander grabbed a rolling pin and Suzanne a tea towel, neither completely sure what their choice of tool would accomplish, but waving them helped shift the bird around the room – to nowhere in particular. The bird perched on the doorframe for a moment, looked down at them, their weapons raised to the ceiling. The yellow chap tilted his head to both sides and did a swift dip out the window, disappearing into the sky.

'Let's get out of here!' Alexander charged, rolling pin now acting as knight's sword, leading his men (girl) to safety and out the front door.

They walked down Essex Street and into The Rocks, meandered around the water, bought ice creams and lay in the park under the Harbour Bridge.

Suzanne turned pavement tiles into a game of hopscotch. The pair was buying time until my grandmother returned home, avoiding the scene of the crime.

Margaret arrived home with a paper bag of groceries and seeing the window open and the papers scattered on the floor, nobody home, she assumed the worst. She tidied up, sat at the kitchen table and fretted. When Alexander and Suzanne returned, Margaret swung the door open wide, relieved.

'Oh! I've been so worried, it's such a mess in here. Where on earth have you two been?'

'We've been gone for hours and hours,' said Alexander. 'Oh, the mischief we've got up to outside the house.'

No valuables seemed to be missing and the trio inspected the room; everything was in order.

'Right!' said Alexander. 'A wee dram, Margaret?'

Later that evening, when she went to cover the canary's cage and noted its absence, Margaret figured out their hatched plan and burst into laughter.

'The two of them had this marvellous escape,' she tells me, laughing. 'See, these are things grandpas and grandmas do,' she says, nudging me with her elbow.

TINS OF SPAGHETTI

It was a long drive to far north Queensland from Annandale and our blue Renault couldn't handle it. So here we were, pulling into the Tenterfield Golf Club in a loan car, so ours could be fixed overnight.

'It's not so bad,' said Dad, negotiating a parking space. 'Do you know who was born here? Peter Allen.'

Louise and I kicked off with Dad in chorus.

'*Wooah, wooah, when my baby...When my baby smiles at me, I go to Rio. De Janeiro. Myo, Meo.*'

It was our dance marathon song, which basically involved my sister and me doing run-ups to Dad in the living room so he could lift us in the air and then swing us either side, like dancing superstars. The song, played on his record player, was our cue. We'd start by jumping around the room and then when the long and boringly protracted instrumental bit started in the middle, we'd do our high lifts in the air. It was pretty amazing. But stuffed into a car for five hours and with no jumping room to let our dance out, giggles were the only outlet for two girls under nine.

We weren't dressed for a golf club, even one in Tenterfield. Mum searched through her bags in the boot of the car, hoping to find something to up the aesthetic average of our ruffled crew. She pulled out a large cashmere scarf, with intricate patterning in gorgeous deep reds, and wrapped it around her neck and shoulders.

'Mum bought this at Liberty's in London,' she told us. 'This will do.'

'Right. Let's go, girls,' said Dad. 'Follow the scarf.'

We all burst out laughing. Our wrinkled couture would be outshone by Mum's single display of elegance.

'Let it out,' said Mum, as we walked towards the restaurant. 'Because when we get inside, we have to behave properly. No more giggles.'

'Now would you like the filet mignon or the penne, which I'm sure we can get with tomato sauce and without the marinara,' said Mum. 'How far inland are we, Rob? Yes, too far for seafood, I think.'

It was too late. We were delirious. Tiredness, puffy legs, excitement that we weren't back at school for another six weeks; it was too much. I leaned under the table to try and get the giggles out, but every time I looked over at Louise she was smiling and it would set me off. I'd close my eyes, focus, focus, but the harder we concentrated the more the laughs had to escape. Then we'd swap; just as I was getting it under control she'd smash the peace with a sideways, eyes-wide, pursed-lip face.

'Girls!'

'Yes, come on, girls,' Dad backed Mum up. 'You really have to get it under control…'

'Yes,' says Mum, putting the menu down, 'or you will never be invited to the Tenterfield Golf Club again.'

That did it. Louise and I exploded, and even Dad started laughing, looking at Mum and shaking his head. Dad grabbed us by our hands and led us outside into the carpark, while Mum begged the waiter for takeaway. When she walked out of the restaurant and into the chilly night with her containers of penne pomodoro, the three of us sang in unison:

'Never be invited to the Tenterfield Golf Club again!' and we all burst out laughing.

'I know, I know,' Mum shook her head, laughing too. 'The moment I said it, I regretted it.'

The best thing about arriving at a motel in Australia is that little sheet of paper where you get to tick what you want for breakfast, delivered to the room, the following day. For Louise and me, this was about the best part of the trip. You start with what juice you want. Always apple for me, always orange for Louise. English breakfast tea for Mum and Dad. Fruit salad or half a grapefruit, tick. Yoghurt, tick. Then, your choice of what to have on white-brown-multigrain toast: Vegemite, honey, marmalade, strawberry jam, tinned baked beans or tinned spaghetti. The spaghetti, always heated to either lukewarm or blisteringly hot, came slopped on toast. I ordered it every possible road trip. It wasn't good, but it was fascinating. I'd rarely eat it, instead kind of forking it and picking the odd strand from the fluorescent puddle of sugary, salty sauce. But as far as we were concerned, that kind of food – meals in cans – didn't exist outside the road trip. So we took advantage of it when we could.

The appeal died out by the time we reached our teens, and we grew wearily fussy as the years rolled by. Now when I feel frustration rising at some last-resort supermarket chain that's still neglecting to stock grass-fed beef instead of grain-fed, I try to remember those mini tins of spaghetti and realise that I've come this far, that somehow I will survive, that compromise is not necessarily death. I won't actually buy the feed-lot beef that's been shovelling down mouldy grain for a good part of its life, only to be sent to slaughter without the free-grazing on green pastures it was owed, but I'll calm down a bit.

Oh, the fussiness. It's impossible not to sound like a complete tosser when you have an opinion on quality. I've tried for years not to sound like an impassioned and unrelenting bore when I plead with a boyfriend not to pull in at McDonald's. I'm determined to take on Ronald, the Colonel and the King on the streets, because that's the only power we have left, you and me. And in the name of thoughtful, seasonal, whole and real food, I'll spurn their sugary buns and their spongy cage-bred chicken-fat extracts, formed into bite-sized pieces and deep-fried, because I know better. I know that eating that stuff will make me sick. No matter how many lean chicken wraps ensnared in nutrient-void lettuce they throw at us in the name of health, I will still source my own free-range chicken, a purple cabbage, some avocado, a sprig of rocket from a pot on the window sill, a squeeze of lemon juice and a drizzle of extra virgin olive oil and do it better and cheaper than they can. I choose flavour and nutrition, sustenance

Above: Kate aged six, with her sister, Louise, aged four; below: Five-year-old Kate.

and a respect for the planet over the salt-and-sugar-churned junk they're peddling. Tins of spaghetti: calm.

My great-grandmother, Isabella, once used a phrase I like to replay. Someone had baulked at a pile of fresh vegetables, fruit and meat she had bought, staggered at what it must have cost her.

Isabella replied: 'My grocery bills may be great, but my medical bills are nil.'

That just about hits the nail on the head for me.

RESPECT THE INGREDIENT

When summer rolls around and that perfect fruit – the peach – turns from bud into perfection, it's time to take them on in their glorious glut. I drive out to the produce markets and pick up trays like a crazed peach monopolist, turning the fruit into various guises meant for keeping or straight eating. It starts with that first glorious bite, the juicy flesh giving way to a fragrant sweet elixir, which runs down your throat and your chin. Then, as the week rolls by, we start concocting recipes to use up the excess. It's then that they're thinly sliced and delivered on pastry, scattered with crunchy sugar, cut up and frozen in smoothie-worthy pieces, puréed for a week's worth of yoghurt dolloping, roughly chopped and macerated, spooned over whipped cream for that other summer ritual, the pavlova. A tumble of fresh fruit, cut into wedges and encased in pastry, is the most perfect of the season's desserts: the peach crostata. A simple sheet of homemade shortcrust folds around the pretty pile, which is then baked and brought out in a display of the best possible homemade thing (see recipe on page 126).

Suddenly, a molten and cloying 'apple' (choko) pie from the drive-through just doesn't compare.

Respecting the ingredient is no longer an economic necessity in much of the emerging world. Many of us don't technically need to eat all the grisly bits from the animal, or tomatoes only plucked from the vine in the height of summer. But here it is: if you eat peaches and tomatoes in summer, and Jerusalem artichokes, kiwifruit and mandarins in autumn and winter, you're going to eat better, and cheaper, and hook yourself into a growing culinary global coterie that cares about the environment as well as what it eats.

Almost perfect

My chef friend Aaron Teece is completely obsessed with this idea, to the point where if he can't pick it, fish it, hunt it or gather it himself at a certain time of year, he's not going to bother. The guy pulls on a wetsuit when he wakes on wintry mornings and dives around the Sydney beaches armed with a stick and a pair of gloves, knocking sea urchin from the rocks like an underwater nomad, gathering the spiky creatures for their precious roe.

He picked me up on the side of the road near Kangaroo Valley in autumn after rain. I jumped in the front seat and turned around to the back to give Luisa Brimble, a photographer, a high five. We were joining Aaron, the foraging professional, happy to be along for the ride, for the intrepid road-trip excursion into a pine forest in search of new-season mushrooms.

Luisa snapped in the name of blogging and I picked mushrooms in the name of eating. Aaron walked ahead, tapping the ground with his feet to get our attention. We brushed the pine needles aside, lightly pinched either side of the hand-sized mushroom, gave it a twist and checked its underbelly for quality. Then, layering the saffron-coloured fungi upside down in a bucket between scatterings of pine needles, we moved deeper into the forest. I ran my finger over each dense piece I picked, over its dark orange gills, and breathed in that musty raw earthy aroma. An hour or so later we had a bucketful, enough to serve in Aaron's Redfern-based restaurant for a couple of days, enough for me to experiment with at home.

That night, I sliced three of the smaller mushrooms into thick slices, discarding the thick end of the stalks. A large frying pan sat over the gas flame, while I took out a large knob of hand-churned local butter, brought a large flank steak to room temperature. The grass-fed steak smelled sweet and charred as a crust formed on its seasoned exterior. The steak rested on a board while I wiped down and reheated the same pan until it was hot, threatening to smoke. Doused in extra virgin olive oil and salt, the mushrooms fried, enough space around each piece to prevent it sweating. A golden sear turned the saffron a darker shade, and I added the knob of butter at the end. The steak, thickly sliced, rested and rare, was transferred to a large plate. I spooned over the browned butter and the mushrooms and joined my Dad at the dining table.

When we took a few mouthfuls of the buttery sauce, the firm earthy mushrooms and the clean perfect meat, we both giggled a little, amazed (see recipe on page 128).

PEACH *and* ALMOND CROSTATA

See story on page 124

SERVES 6–8
PREPARATION 30 minutes, plus 45 minutes resting
COOKING 45 minutes

900 g (2 lb) ripe peaches, cut into sixths and pitted
75 g (2¾ oz/⅓ cup firmly packed) soft brown sugar
25 g (1 oz/¼ cup) almond meal
1 egg, lightly whisked
demerara sugar, to sprinkle
35 g (1¼ oz/¼ cup) sliced almonds, toasted
whipped cream, to serve

Pastry
225 g (8 oz/1½ cups) plain (all-purpose) flour, plus extra for dusting
2 tablespoons caster sugar
¼ teaspoon salt
125 g (4½ oz) unsalted butter, chilled, diced
60 ml (2 fl oz/¼ cup) chilled water

For the pastry, combine the flour, sugar and salt in a food processor. Add the butter and pulse to form large crumbs. Add the water, a little at a time, and pulse to a dough. Pull the dough together on a lightly floured work surface and shape into a disc. Cover with plastic wrap and refrigerate for at least 45 minutes.

Preheat the oven to 200°C (400°F). Line a baking tray with baking paper.

In a medium bowl, toss the peaches and brown sugar together, and set aside.

Roll out the pastry on a lightly floured work surface to a 30 cm (12 in) round and transfer to the prepared tray. Sprinkle over the almond meal, leaving a 5 cm (2 in) border around the edge. Mound the peaches and their juices over the top of the almond meal, leaving the edges untouched. Fold the edge of the pastry up and over the peaches, leaving an open circle in the middle. Gently press the pastry where it folds on itself to help support it. Brush the edges of the pastry with a little beaten egg and sprinkle with demerara sugar.

Bake for 40–45 minutes, or until the pastry is golden and the peaches tender. Remove from the oven and cool for 15 minutes on the baking tray.

Scatter over the sliced almonds and dollop cream in the middle of the tart. Serve immediately, cut into wedges.

tip

Peaches will only be tender if ripe, so buy them a few days in advance and allow them to ripen at room temperature. They will also soften a little during cooking.

FLANK STEAK WITH MUSHROOMS *and* SWEET POTATO CHIPS

See story on page 125

SERVES 2
PREPARATION 25 minutes
COOKING 20 minutes

450 g (1 lb) flank steak, at
    room temperature
sea salt and freshly ground
    black pepper
2 tablespoons extra virgin
    olive oil
20 g (¾ oz) butter
2 French shallots,
    finely chopped
350 g (12 oz) pine mushrooms
    (or Swiss brown and flat
    mushrooms), thickly sliced
a few thyme sprigs
micro herbs, such as red
    cabbage cress or sorrel,
    to serve

Sweet potato crisps
2–3 small orange sweet
    potatoes, peeled
1 tablespoon rice bran oil
¼ teaspoon fine sea salt
1½ teaspoons ground sumac
1 teaspoon flaked sea salt

For the sweet potato crisps, preheat the oven to 200°C (400°F). Lightly grease two large baking trays with oil.

Use a mandolin to slice the sweet potato into very thin, almost transparent rounds.

Put the sweet potato in a bowl with the oil, fine sea salt and sumac, and toss to coat completely. Arrange the slices on the baking trays in a single layer, being careful not to overlap them. Sprinkle over the flaked sea salt and bake for 5–6 minutes, or until they are slightly golden brown with a little give in the centre (they will firm up). Check them regularly as they cook to make sure they don't burn, and turn them with tongs halfway through cooking. Depending on the size of your oven, you may need to bake them in a few batches.

The crisps will keep for up to 15 hours, stored in an airtight container (the fresher they are, the crisper they will be).

Heat a large frying pan over high heat until smoking. Season the steak with salt and pepper and rub over half the olive oil. Add the steak to the hot pan and sear for 4 minutes on each side, or until a crust forms. Transfer to a plate to rest for 5–10 minutes.

Reduce the heat to medium–low, add the remaining oil and the butter to the pan and fry the shallots for 5 minutes, or until softened. Add the mushrooms and cook until golden brown, being careful not to overcrowd the pan. Add the thyme sprigs and cook for a further 1–2 minutes.

To serve, put steak on a serving board and cut across the grain into 2 cm (¾ in) thick slices. Spoon the mushrooms over the top with any remaining pan juices. Scatter over micro herbs and serve with sweet potato crisps.

THE NEW YORK CHEESECAKE

Cheese. In a cake. The idea was foreign to Australians in the 1960s. But they did understand cream cheese. The height of dinner party know-how was French onion dip, my mother tells me. The recipe: pour one packet of dried French onion soup powder into a bowl, spoon in Philadelphia Cream Cheese, mix to combine, serve with crackers. On toast, in sandwiches, churned into dips, stuffed into filo pastry triangles and baked – cream cheese took Australia by storm. People began to see it as a healthier alternative to butter. And then Margaret Fulton went ahead and introduced everyone to the New York cheesecake (see recipe on page 133).

Restaurateur Johnnie Walker, not the whisky one, got Margaret on the phone. The owner of various Sydney establishments, including the Rhine Castle Cellars in Pitt Street and later the Bistro in Angel Place, begged for her assistance to deal with a rogue teacher in one of his new cooking schools. Evie, a cook and tutor, was so nervous before each class that she worked to fix herself with a large glass of brandy.

'One evening, during a lesson on cooking a large snapper fish, Evie simply gave it a good slap and put it in the oven,' Grandma tells me. 'Somebody piped up: "Don't you scale it or clean it first?" '

Margaret giggles as she retells the story. 'She said: "Only if you're really fussy." '

Evie would disappear behind the scenes mid-class and pupils would hear the squeak of a cork coming out of a bottle, and the plonk of it being pushed back in. A moment's silence, then another squeak, and so on.

'Johnnie was growing concerned,' Grandma tells me. 'All these well-heeled Eastern Suburbs and North Shore matrons and young business executives had paid good money to learn how to enrich their lives and buy Johnnie's wines.'

He had a nervous drunk on his hands. Margaret arrived as reinforcement. She stood at the stove facing a large oak semi-circular table, a mirror overhead reflecting her various searing, sautéing undertakings. The class started with a glass of wine 'to get us in the mood', Margaret says. She would demonstrate a first course, a main and a dessert, and did lunches and cocktail party variations.

In one of her earlier classes, Margaret was demonstrating some intricate step, piping whipped seasoned egg yolk into a halved boiled egg white

– a mouthful for sophisticated dinner parties – when she looked up to ask if everyone was following. One woman's hat caught Margaret's eye, distracting her. As the woman nodded with her classmates, acknowledging the various steps of the piping bag, a large flower on her hat bobbed up and down. Directly above the wobbling bloom, perched on a whole tortoise shell hanging on the wall behind her was, to Margaret's horror, a large brown rat. Margaret turned to her assistant, Mary.

'Would you please ask the kitchen, Mary, to do something about the rat.'

The class tittered, assuming it was one of Margaret's jokes. Mary just stood there, puzzled. When the class was done, Margaret ushered her students into another room for champagne and a chance to sample the food. When they left, Margaret turned dead white, relieved they'd got away with it, and called for a stiff brandy just as her predecessor had done.

The 'sinfully rich' cheesecake was introduced to a Sydney clientele, already enamoured of cream cheese because of its versatility. They loved it on sandwiches especially, and used it to replace butter, which was gaining a bad reputation as a saturated fat. People had heard rumours, and travellers had witnessed it – the New York cheesecake was a dense biscuit base, topped with a whipped cream cheese filling spiked with lemon, glazed with sour cream and dusted with freshly grated nutmeg. Margaret taught the hordes of aspiring domestic pundits how to cook it. The recipe came from Lindy's restaurant in New York, and the fervour with which Australians adopted the cake surprised everyone.

'They were mad for it,' Margaret tells me.

What the cheesecake did, actually, was transform the way Australians baked. It was the first time people at home had heard of the spring-form pan. All the fluffy sponge cakes and denser loaves had called for plain tins, but this idea of a clip on the side for the easy removal of the tin base, transfixed Margaret's audiences. The sales of spring-form pans went up everywhere. Margaret had launched her career in food on the back of selling the new potato peeler, and now a new contraption would overtake it as the must-have item for the discerning home cook.

NEW YORK CHEESECAKE

See story on page 130

SERVES 10–12
PREPARATION 45 minutes,
plus 8 hours chilling
COOKING 25 minutes

80 g (2¾ oz) ginger nut
  biscuits (ginger snaps)
80 g (2¾ oz) plain,
  digestive-style biscuits
60 g (2¼ oz/½ cup)
  almond meal
60 ml (2 fl oz/¼ cup) thin
  (pouring) cream
75 g (2¾ oz) butter, melted
1 pinch of sea salt
whole nutmeg, for grating,
  to serve

Filling
500 g (1 lb 2 oz) cream
  cheese, softened
110 g (3¾ oz/½ cup) caster
  (superfine) sugar
2 free-range eggs,
  at room temperature
grated zest of 1 lemon
2 teaspoons lemon juice

Sour-cream glaze
370 g (13 oz/1½ cups)
  sour cream
1½ tablespoons maple syrup
1 vanilla bean, halved
  lengthways, seeds scraped

Line the base and side of a 23 cm (9 in) round spring-form cake tin with baking paper.

In a food processor, process the ginger nut biscuits and plain biscuits into fine crumbs. Add the almond meal, cream, butter and salt and pulse until a coarse mixture forms. Press the crumb mixture into the base and 5 cm (2 in) up the sides of the prepared tin. Chill in the fridge for 2 hours.

Preheat the oven to 190°C (375°F).

For the filling, in an electric mixer, beat together the cream cheese and sugar until well combined. Beat in the eggs, one at a time, then mix in the lemon zest and juice. Pour the mixture into the chilled tin and bake for 20 minutes.

Remove the cake from the oven, finely grate over some nutmeg and leave the cake to sit in the tin to cool to room temperature.

Increase the oven temperature to 220°C (425°F).

For the sour-cream glaze, put the sour cream, maple syrup and vanilla seeds in a bowl and mix with a wooden spoon until very smooth. Spread evenly over the cooled cake, using a spatula to smooth the top.

Bake for 5 minutes, or just until the surface forms a glaze. Remove from the oven and leave to cool in the tin, then refrigerate for 6 hours before serving.

To serve, finely grate over a little more nutmeg.

tip

This cheesecake will keep in the fridge for up to 3 days in an airtight container, but the base will soften slightly.

WRETCHED RULES

Families can be such beautiful things. It's a precious, lifelong relationship with people you pretty much got stuck with at birth. But, all going well, these people are your security and comfort, unwitting recipients of your love, and you theirs.

Of course, there is also a trade-off: being in each other's pockets for so many years means you can forget how to behave with decorum. There's something about a house full of people related to each other that induces complacency. Despite the best intentions to raise their children as future prime ministers, great thinkers, the next in line to run the family restaurant, parents end up with two kids trying to out-belch each other after dinner. Talking openly about bowel movements, or balancing one foot on the edge of the table to carve dead skin from their feet with a butter knife, is all framed by the over-used non sequitur: 'What? It's just *family*.'

Like other parents, mine planned well. My mother, I see now, was ridiculously helpful on the matter of chores. She did all our washing, made our lunches every morning and constantly untangled the hair of two girls with abnormally thick, unfashionably bobbish, fringed dos. My dad tutored us through our homework into our teens and then enlisted some other poor soul to come and do it. He dropped us at parties and then stayed up half the night so he could collect us from under-18 nightclubs across the other side of Sydney. In recompense, I was expected to employ basic hygiene, clean up after myself, and maintain a scent that didn't offend passers-by. Seemed simple enough, but I was pulled up constantly. Toilet seat down, wring out the flannel, put your dirty sheets in the laundry basket. There was a lot of instruction around wet towels. No wet towels left on the bed, no sandy (wet) towels left in the car, no chlorine-dank towels left in your schoolbag, no wet towel wrapping up your wet hair during dinner, no wet towel fashioned into a cooling blanket for the cat.

Mostly, it paid off. We'd greet school friends at the door on the weekend and promptly offer them a refreshing beverage. After our birthdays, we'd sit at our desks to write thank-you notes for presents. There was even one for the great aunt who gave me the assortment of floral mini soaps wrapped in a plastic bag that had previously held fish fillets, so the syrupy clear blood had soaked into the bar of 'lavender fields'. We were forced to be grateful for the thought and we drew big thank-yous on paper with coloured pencils, glue and glitter. I resented having to put so much effort (and good stationery) into it.

'Can't I just give back the soap?' I'd beg my mother.

'Such lovely girls,' my Mum's friends cooed.

Things amped up when it came to table manners. My mother got so tired of constantly telling us to remember the rules – no elbows on the table, no hands in your mouth, no picking your hairline, no plucking your eyebrows, no feeding the cat, chew your food enough, enunciate your words, offer food to others before you help yourself – that she developed verbal shorthand for each.

'ELBOWS!'

We'd jolt upright in our chairs.

'MOUTH!' was an abbreviation of 'close your mouth when you're chewing'. Sometimes, the instructions were general.

'BACKS!' was a gentle reminder to sit up straight. And we all would, to attention. Sometimes the instructions were targeted.

'Kate, HANDS!' was shorthand for me to not touch my mouth, put my fingers in my mouth, scratch my lip. I'd hear it all the time, and this one lasted for months, possibly years. Whether I was sitting at the table or trying on some new jeans, posing in the mirror, I'd be sharply pulled into line from the other side of the house: 'HANDS!'

I've heard horror stories of the current state of raising teenagers. Parents nowadays are apparently stumbling over hurdles that my parents never even had to jump, for the simple reason that technology wasn't really an issue back then. We didn't have earphones, we didn't have mobile phones. But even if we did, there is *no way* I would have been allowed to use these contraptions at the table. But for the sake of imaginings, let's conceive that I had tried to bring, say, a Walkman to the table. I imagine my mother and father would have desperately referred to lessons from their own youth. And so will I.

IN DEFENCE OF A HAPPY TABLE

Margaret's boyfriend Denis squirmed when peas fell onto the table as my mother, a child of seven or eight, worked logistics around her plate with a knife and fork. He'd baulk if she dropped crumbs on the floor, or spilled water from the jug onto the table. He got so worked up, watching her during mealtimes, telling her to use the serviette on her lap and placing a coaster under her drink, correcting how she held her knife, that he'd let his own meal go cold. The atmosphere was chilly, too.

Margaret told him to focus on his own meal. Suzanne was just a child and was doing the best she could.

'I can't bear sitting here watching this,' he countered. 'Suzanne, put your knife and fork down between each mouthful. Suzanne, knife and fork down. That's it.'

One day he cracked. He stood up in the middle of a meal and picked up a newspaper, announcing he'd had enough. And then he took the broadsheet and flicked out a double page. He planned to layer the floor around Mum with newspaper, as though he were dealing with a naughty guinea pig, whose cage needed cleaning.

Margaret was furious and ordered him to stop. They looked at each other for a moment, a red-eyed bull threatening a mother's calf, the mother standing firm between them. He pulled out his chair and harrumphed back down, his face purple. But he'd retreated, and he sat in gorgeous silence for the rest of the meal.

The fighting continued and crescendoed years later, when Mum was nineteen and finally took a stand against this moustachioed bully. But, meanwhile, she had an ally in her mum.

It may not have been happy families, but Mum would be given the chance to sit down at the table and eat in comfort. Defence of this basic right came from a woman who had already struggled for peace, and she was going to guard it for her child. But I believe now there was also something else at play. This was also my grandmother emphasising the moral imperative of keeping things up to scratch. And that included not bullying a child at the table, or ruining the look with newspaper.

LONDON GRIME

Irish blood, English heart and essentially a handsome version of that Morrissey guy from the Smiths. I met this London boy in a Notting Hill pub called the Gold at lunchtime on a Sunday. He was tall and dark, with doughy brown eyes. He had this whole Hugh Grant thing going on, plus his pale-blue rolled-up-sleeves shirt worked for me.

A smooth six months of friendship later, Roby and I confessed love and, after a few stolen lunch hours at his place and evenings spent kissing in Kensington's private gardens, he popped the question: Would I like to move in with him, and the guys?

'And the guys' was Shihab and Foordy. Three boys in one apartment, with a sign at the door – Campden Mansions – and now me too. I was so happy, I mistook the squinty haziness of the apartment as my rose-tinted love rather than what it actually was: a literal film of grime over everything. Empty pizza boxes waited by the door for three days, but I didn't mind. I was so joyous about every damned thing.

I recently found a postcard to my parents dated March 2003, soon after my sister's wedding: 'It must feel a bit quiet now with me out the door and the blonde one off and married. But the neighbours have called and will you keep the Bob Dylan and Mahler down a notch please. I am liking Roby more and more. The other day we made a deal that I would cook dinner and he would tidy his room. When I went in to say it's ready I found an immaculate Roby in an immaculate room, playing air guitar to Led Zeppelin. Work is good and things are just swell. Love you both.'

Things were swell, but so was I – literally swelling. Gloriously content with a couple of beers and hot Thai green chicken curry from the local pub, the Churchill on Kensington Church Street, we'd eat around a coffee table that Roby had fashioned using a sheet of glass placed over a turned-sideways wine rack. As the weeks rolled by, we all began to get slightly rounder too, physically speaking.

Breakfast and lunch I had under control, turning out my must-have porridge every morning using the one clean saucepan we owned. At lunch I ducked into a little Japanese place in Kensington that did sushi and the usual suspects, but also ochazuke – a little bowl of sushi rice topped with grilled salmon, and a pot of green tea on the side. When the bowl arrives you pour the tea over. I now make this pretty dish as a kind of nutritional reboot, a non-obsessive cleanse when everything else just seems too heavy, too rich, too reduced. In London, when I felt torn from Australia and its proximity to Asia, I came back craving the simple clean food with pickles on the side. Always pickles on the side (see recipe on page 143).

I'd go for evening runs around the gardens, but too much takeaway was killing the sporty and bikini-acceptable figure I'd kept in Sydney. Every time I planned to cook I'd walk into the kitchen and grimace, then dial out for Pizza Express' rather remarkable 'Inferno'.

Give me a moment to talk about this pizza. The Inferno was pepperoni, topped with slivers of roasted capsicum, mozzarella and fresh tomato sauce. All pretty predictable. But with its simplicity came perfection. At this point in London, every cackling group of women out on a hen's night, every huddle of lads out for a good night, every discerning couple in search of 'gourmet' would head to one of a few pizza chains doing a menu containing dough balls and barely a sideways glance at authentic Italian. The best bet was to go for a margherita and hope that the base, at least, held up its side of the bargain with a hint of chew, a decent charring underneath. But mostly, people went for a heavy slick of tandoori sauce, shards of dried chicken swimming in yoghurt, with chopped dried mint added for 'authenticity'. Or, horror, the roasted pumpkin pizza, with dollops of salty curd, described on the menu as 'chèvre'. The Inferno was different. Years later, back in Sydney, Roby and I perfected this pizza, the crunchy exterior of the base giving way to a doughy chew. He found a terracotta tile in the street one day, gave it a wipe down, and the thing became our pizza stone for the Weber on the balcony. I roasted the capsicum and sourced the hottest possible pepperoni, and we labelled the resulting masterstroke The Campden Mansions Inferno. It was hot, sweet, salty, chewy, crispy – perfect pizza (see recipe on page 144).

But in London, takeaway boxes scattered on the coffee table, we'd lean back and groan on the sofa, rub our stomachs and vow to wipe down the benches tomorrow so someone could cook.

One day I slid my hand down the side of the blue velvet sofa and pulled out a mass of short tawny-coloured hair. A clump of something matted. Shuddering, I wondered if someone had given a labrador a fastidious all-over daily brush, depositing the cast-off hair down the side of the cushion like an obsessive hair monopolist. Nobody in our building, the entire Campden Mansions, owned a dog or knew one. This hair had moved in with the sofa, with one of the boys via some other shared house.

I stood in the middle of the room and looked around. The place was revolting. With grime at critical mass, I picked my way through piles of clutter. I put nose to the dust, knees and elbows pressed into the navy-blue-painted, splintered floorboards, and methodically slid my credit card between the sizeable gaps to pull out great thick lines of boy grime. I found patches of living room floor space under dusty black London marathon t-shirts, still salty from the previous year's event.

In a determined domestic purging, I made straight pillars out of crusty *GQ*s and car magazines, and diplomatically slipped the ones with the boobs in them to the bottom of the pile, ignoring stuck-together pages. I grouped grimy pint glasses together and threw out boxer shorts that crackled when folded. I wiped down the massive home-brew beer kit taking up all of the kitchen bench space, stumped by the male penchant for coffee-stained mugs and electric cords that belonged to nothing.

I found a Marmite-smeared plate in the fireplace with a dry sponge stuck to it. I tossed the lot into a garbage bag, less and less discerning in what I was labelling The Great Decluttering of 2004. A crash, another grime-soaked sponge, another black garbage bag filled.

Red wine rings disappeared and the hessian-sack curtain in our bedroom that formed its own dust was pulled down. I tossed out the random brick under the oven. An old bulk bag of rice, which shared the entire bottom shelf of the three-shelf pantry with some toilet paper rolls, was dragged to the pavement. Spurred on by a belief that it was morally, practically and hygienically wrong to live like this, I moved from bafflement to rage to serene self-righteousness. Grimed, sweating, fingernails and nostrils clogged, I came perilously close to throwing myself in the bin.

I hated the kitchen most of all. In the clogged gaps between the oven and cupboards of our London flat, cockroaches were having disgusting orgies, revelling in the sticky sweet grease of stir-fry slops and spilled beer. They were tiny brown critters, not like Sydney's self-respecting beasts that fly into the house on summer nights. These London ones were menacing and tiny, and lived in writhing hordes.

I picked at hardened splotches on the stovetop and scoured at blackened smears. Furry, musty scents were gradually won over by lemon bleach. My eyes stung and my nose ran, a headache loomed in frontal throbs. I filled buckets with hot water and treated the lino in the kitchen like a Turkish bath, dousing and sponging, steaming, scrubbing and beating. It was a fumigation of chlorine and water. Eventually, hours into the purge, surfaces lost their tackiness and, while nothing gleamed exactly, it was spotless.

At a restaurant called Momofuku Seiobo, in Sydney, if you're lucky enough to get a reservation, and then a stool at the kitchen bar where you watch the chefs work, they do it in clear view. After the last pork belly and steamed bun have gone out and the final offering of goat's curd with blackcurrant and mint oil is made, the chefs clean.

If ever I were to pay someone to clean my house, I'd jump straight to out-of-work chefs. These guys may be trained in whisks and tongs, but somehow, that talent has rubbed off onto sponges and mops. They wipe down surfaces and then scrub and wipe again. They'll target one specific square metre of bench and stroke it with a scouring brush for ten minutes. I'd say they were procrastinating, drawing out their clocked hours, except I know how exhausted they must be and how much they want to get out of there; they've already worked hard enough for one shift. I know – I was watching from my pedestal while they made my plate of raw striped trumpeter with fragments of crisp celery and mustard dressing.

When I ran out of things to clean that grey day in London, I cooked. Foordy returned home first to the sparkle.

'It smells nice in here.'

Then falling into the sofa and reaching for the remote, not noticing the mute button was no longer clogged with tomato sauce, he said, 'What shall we do for dinner?'

In my bleach-fragrant London kitchen, I lit the stove with a match and heated up a frying pan. I seasoned three steaks and threw salad greens into a large bowl. I julienned carrot and smashed cucumber with lime and chilli. I tore up mint and coriander leaves, ground lemongrass in a mortar and pestle and made a dressing, mostly of lime juice and fish sauce.

When Roby got home, he did notice. He mock-rubbed his eyes and, not even removing his brown leather man bag, he walked through the apartment like a child on an Easter egg hunt.

'Ooh, look at the walls, look at the space. Look, there's my lost blue shirt!'

I bounced behind him. 'And see the floors? And the bit where you can see the window sill now?'

We flopped backwards onto his wood-framed futon and looked at the ceiling, absolutely exhausted but content now, in a space a little more like home. I called out to Foordy: 'We're eating at the table from now on.'

I brought three plates of my Thai beef salad to the table and Roby grabbed cutlery, opened a bottle of wine.

'It's so clean I feel bad messing it up.'

He knew the family story of Grandma by heart. 'Shall I put newspaper down under Foordy when he eats?'

OCHAZUKE *with* ASSORTED PICKLES

See story on page 137

SERVES 2
PREPARATION 30 minutes,
plus pickling time
COOKING 6 minutes
Start the pickles 3 days ahead

2 x 200 g (7 oz) salmon fillets,
   skin on
sea salt
2 teaspoons olive oil
370 g (13 oz/2 cups) cooked
   Japanese sushi rice
2 teaspoons toasted
   sesame seeds
½ sheet nori, cut into very thin
   strips with scissors
500 ml (17 fl oz/2 cups) hot
   Japanese green tea
1 teaspoon wasabi paste

Assorted pickles
225 ml (7¾ fl oz) water, hot
   but not quite boiling
125 ml (4 fl oz/½ cup) rice
   wine vinegar
115 g (4 oz) sugar
½ teaspoon salt
1–2 Lebanese (short)
   cucumbers, sliced into
   3–4 mm (⅛ in) rounds
6 radishes, quartered
6 golden radishes or baby
   turnips, halved

For the pickles, combine the water, vinegar, sugar and salt in a medium bowl, and stir until the sugar dissolves.

Pack the vegetables into a 1 litre (35 fl oz/4 cup) sterilised jar, pour over the vinegar solution, cover with a lid and refrigerate. Leave for 3 days before eating. The pickles will keep for up to 1 month.

Season the salmon fillets with a pinch or two of sea salt and coat with olive oil. Heat a frying pan until very hot and cook the salmon, skin-side down, for 2–3 minutes, or until the skin is crispy. Turn and cook for a further 2–3 minutes, or until just cooked on the outside and still very pink inside. (Salmon will continue cooking a little once removed from the heat, so do not overcook.) Let it rest for 2 minutes, then break the salmon up into large pieces – you may need a knife to slice the skin.

Divide the rice between two bowls, top with the salmon pieces, then sesame seeds and nori. Pour the hot tea over the rice, and serve the pickles and wasabi on the side.

THE INFERNO

See story on page 138

MAKES 4 x 25 cm
(10 in) pizzas
PREPARATION 30 minutes,
plus 1½ hours proving
COOKING 50 minutes

2 x 400 g (14 oz) tins chopped
 or cherry tomatoes
1 brown onion, peeled
 and halved
2 tablespoons extra
 virgin olive oil, plus extra
 for drizzling
½ teaspoon sea salt
100 g (3½ oz) spicy
 salami, sliced
2 red capsicums (peppers),
 charred and torn into strips
 (see page 24)
375 g (13 oz) buffalo
 mozzarella cheese,
 coarsely torn
1 small handful basil leaves

Pizza base
500 g (1 lb 2 oz) strong '00'
 plain (all-purpose) flour, plus
 extra for dusting
1 teaspoon sea salt
1 x 7 g (¼ oz) sachet
 dried yeast
325 ml (11 fl oz) warm water
2 teaspoons raw (golden)
 caster (superfine) sugar
2 tablespoons extra virgin
 olive oil
50 g (1¾ oz) fine semolina

For the pizza base, sift the flour and salt into a large bowl and make a well in the centre. Combine the yeast, water and sugar in a small bowl and whisk with a fork until the sugar dissolves, then stir in the olive oil. Add the yeast mixture to the flour well and stir with a wooden spoon, gradually bringing in more flour as you stir. Turn the mixture out onto a work surface and knead for 10 minutes, or until elastic and smooth. Put the dough in an oiled bowl, cover with plastic wrap or a damp cloth and put in a warm place for 1–1½ hours, or until doubled in size.

Meanwhile, put the tomatoes in a saucepan with the onion halves, the olive oil and salt, bring to the boil, then reduce the heat and simmer on the lowest heat possible, uncovered, for 30–40 minutes, or until thickened. Break up the cherry tomatoes (if using) during cooking with the back of a wooden spoon. Discard the onion and set the sauce aside to reach room temperature.

While the tomatoes are cooking, preheat the oven to 250°C (500°F) or its highest setting. Put a seasoned pizza stone or heavy baking tray in the lower half of the oven and allow to heat for 45–60 minutes.

Dust the work surface with a little flour. Divide the dough into four pieces and roll into balls using the palms of your hands. (If you don't want to cook all the dough now, break off what you need, cover the remainder with plastic wrap and store in an airtight container in the fridge for up to 1 week.) Knock the air out of each dough ball and spin it on your fingertips, stretching it out as much as possible. Evenly dust four 25 cm (10 in) pizza pans with the semolina and transfer the pizza bases to them, pressing the dough into the edges of the pan.

Quickly smear the top of the pizzas with the tomato sauce, leaving a 1 cm (½ in) border. Scatter over the salami, capsicum and mozzarella, then drizzle with a little more olive oil. Working in batches, slide each pizza onto the hot stone and cook for 8–10 minutes, or until crisp and golden. Scatter with basil and eat immediately.

NOT A GREAT BOWL LICKER

I'm not one for pompous rituals – it bores me. The great aunt who quietly scoffs at the sight of your lopsided framed pictures, or bites her lip when you put milk into the cups *before* the tea: it's trite and tedious. But ask me to leave the washing up until tomorrow, claim the saucepan needs to soak, and I become that very dreary cliché I rail against.

My grandmother has always kept a gorgeous home, a trove of Finnish design and intricate hand-blown glass, an eclectic and immaculate space. When she cooks, she cleans up. And she's never been one of those old ladies with a puddle of dried sauce in the spectacles hanging around her neck. She was raised in a house where things were done properly, as she described to Andrew Denton and Australian television audiences.

'I want you to take me back, if you would, to your mother's kitchen where you say your most vivid memories lie. What would I taste and smell and lick in your mother's kitchen?' said Denton to Margaret.

'It was just marvellous because everything she did, she did so well. Not only that, I'm the youngest of six children, and when a meal was coming on we were all involved…'

'As the youngest, in this communal cooking with the whole family, did you get to lick the bowl? Was that your treat?'

'*No* we never licked the…No. I got to stir the custard and things.'

'Oh, you see that's…' ventured Denton.

Margaret clarified: 'You see, licking the bowls is, it's a fairy story. I mean, I know Nigella Lawson does it. No, I'm not a great bowl licker. {Laughter} I would learn to stir the custard and not let it get caught. I would learn to do things like that and the boys would learn to put the chairs around the table and then somebody would set the table. All of this licking bowls is silly talk.' {Laughter}

'I'm just stuck on this idea of stirring custard because the smell of custard is the best smell in the world, just about,' said Denton. 'How did you resist not going slurp?' {Laughter}

'I knew that there were the better things to come. The whole sitting down at the table was to come. Mother wasn't messy, like she wasn't a great licker either, and she didn't stick her finger…{Laughter} She didn't stick her fingers where they didn't belong. {Laughter} And I don't either.'

But in her thirties, Margaret had other things on her mind. It was time to catch up on her social life, go out to fabulous places with fabulous actors, interior designers and the media. Margaret was working in public relations for the advertising agent J. Walter Thompson in the late 1950s and that meant wooing the press to get media mentions for clients like Kellogg's and Kraft.

'It was a false kind of world,' Margaret says now. 'But we all felt like masters of the universe, saying hello to all kinds of interesting people. You got good at one-liners, the latest gossip. There were no taboos. The only crime was to be middle-of-the-road or boring.'

She learned to live hard, play hard, and burn the candle at both ends. And, from the age of ten, my mother was often left to potter at home on her own. Nobody thought of asking Mum to get a friend around, so she amused herself. Cutting up my grandmother's silk negligée gown to make a dress for her dolls had not gone down well a few years before. So instead, Suzanne took everything out of the fridge, wiped down jars of preserved fruit, and discarded leftover fish stock that had got a bit whiffy. When Margaret and Denis left for another soirée, my mother remade all the beds and put on loads of washing, ironed her own socks. Usual kid stuff.

My mother remembers Margaret searching for things after she had cleaned up.

'Where are the capers, Suzie? Have you thrown them out? How can I make spaghetti puttanesca without capers?'

The small blonde child looked back to her and, brushing her mother's skirt aside with her hand to get to the pantry, she found the dry, salted kind in a bag, and then another jar, pickled. Clearly, she was getting on her mother's nerves with all her cleaning, and was told to go and play outside.

Mum says now she thinks she cleaned so much in an effort to make the house feel a little bit more like home. When your mother is out with your stepfather, whom you neither love nor like, and you've spent years oscillating between boarding school and home, the drive to make a space feel special is palpable.

When she ran out of things to clean, my mother cooked. Bored one morning because Margaret and Denis were sleeping in after a late night out, my mother woke up early and made scones.

'They were terrible,' she remembers now. 'They were hard crumbly things and I couldn't understand why, because I'd followed the instructions. But I was experimenting with it, and I wanted to learn how to do it well.'

A few years later, Margaret returned home late from a cocktail party with a drunken Denis in tow, and a group of friends giggling, singing as they teetered up the path. Once inside, they opened more champagne. This wasn't the era for takeaway kebabs and home-delivered pizza at any hour, so a group of happy friends looking for a late-night something would just have to drink more champagne or starve. They'd talk politics and film and deal with the headache tomorrow.

Having searched for another bottle of champagne in Margaret's fridge, one of her guests walked back into the living room and demanded the floor.

'Tink, tink, tink,' she mocked, as she tapped her glass with her finger. 'Margaret has a wonderful-looking dish in her refrigerator and I think we should all *demand* a taste.'

Puzzled, my grandmother led the entire tipsy group back into the kitchen and swung open the fridge door. An orange cast-iron pot of fragrant coq au vin, pieces of chicken slowly cooked in red wine and mushrooms, little onions tender all the way through, was still warm. The group sat in amazed silence around the table, slicing tender meat from the bone and taking spoonfuls of rich sauce, while their host explained that little Suzanne was into cooking.

WASTE NOT

Seven-year-old Margaret stood on tippy toes and handed the brown-paper-wrapped parcel of meat back to the butcher, telling him that her mother said it would not do.

When Margaret had returned home with her purchase and Isabella unwrapped the butcher's paper to reveal the pieces of meat — thicker at one end than the other and all different sizes — she folded the paper around them again, slipped the package into a woven bag and sent her wee daughter towards the door.

'Now, Margaret, when I sent you down, I didn't expect you to come back with all these funny thicknesses. How am I to cook those? All different shapes and sizes, it's a mess. Before you leave the butcher, you must check what they've given you.'

The butcher took the package from the little girl, who asked him politely to cut the steaks so they all had the same thickness. The butcher nodded to Margaret, cut a new steak and showed it to the pint-sized customer with her perfect black curls, who scanned it and smiled her approval.

I asked my grandmother about this other day. We've always been told this story as a kind of lesson-learned-by-Margaret to benefit us all. But was it true, and did this really impact her as much as she remembers?

'I had to go down and tell the butcher it wasn't good enough. He would groan. I was so embarrassed, I never made the same mistake again,' she said.

'Really? Would you return a steak now?'

'Just the other day, I bought some lamb chops from a good Sydney butcher and they were a big shocking mess. Now, my mother would never have accepted food like that, food we were paying good money for. "Good money" was always the key. Yes, I remembered it. You need good ingredients to cook good food. It's as simple as that. And that includes quality meat that has been butchered well.'

Conversations like this usually spur my grandmother into commentary on quality, driving home the importance of pasture-reared, well-butchered, non-genetically modified, carefully chopped, diced, poached, presented food. And I wonder whether it all stems back to the moment her mother packed her off to the butcher to return the steaks.

I put my spin on it, and put it to her. 'I suppose times were tough. You don't waste food during a depression, you're grateful for being allowed steaks at all.'

'It wasn't about *not wasting*,' she said. 'We didn't talk or think about not wasting food, not throwing out food. You would never think of wasting it. Everything was always used – there was no alternative. That's how my mother got quite fat, because she'd say, "Oh, I'll just eat this up."'

Grandma grew up with that all-important dictum: Use everything! (And use it well.) And based on this common denominator, everything she cooked was the result of a deeply personal and assured approach to food and the value of ingredients. And then she passed this ethos on.

ODDS AND ENDS

'Brains in black butter sauce, please.'

My mother put her birthday order in for the dish she wanted, more than anything else, when she turned fifteen. So my grandmother ordered in the brains at the butcher and they got to work in their kitchen in Sydney's The Rocks. Together they prepared a cerebral concoction my mother has always described as 'a kind of soft pillowy scrambled eggs'. When I was growing up, this story blew my mind.

Another time I heard her giggling at the wooden kitchen bench, her back to me as I approached. I pressed her for the joke and she spun around, holding a foot-long raw beef tongue to her face with one hand so it appeared to dangle from her mouth, her eyes wide and terrifying. With her other hand she made the tip of the tongue move up and down.

'What's wrong darling? Give me a kiss.'

I'd prop myself up on the kitchen bench and marvel as she pulled the skin from the cooked tongue in one piece. She'd slice it like a fillet of beef and serve the tender meat with pommes mousseline and sautéed silverbeet. I was enthralled by the process, the real ingredients, the chemistry, the flavours and textures. I'd swing my feet and ask questions, turn up my nose and eventually taste it and agree: a bit of tongue is alright.

Fergus Henderson changed the world of food with his book *Nose to Tail Eating: A Kind of British Cooking*, giving chefs and cooks across the world permission to follow their hearts, and freely use hearts, lungs, whole heads and gizzards. Suddenly noses and tails were appearing on plates, instead of being hidden inside stocks. As writer, chef and presenter Anthony Bourdain points out in his book *Medium Raw*, Henderson has inspired others to put things on their menus and look at ingredients they might never have thought of had he not done it first. The lone chefs in the heartland of America, England and Australia yearned for a Fergus to come along and inspire them, give them courage. Australian chef Colin Fassnidge, with a handful of others, has that courage. The Sydney chef does tripe hot pot, black pudding, chargrilled lamb's tongue, herb-crusted bone marrow, leaving punters reeling in a heady appreciation of the wobbly bits. Meanwhile, in Spain's San Sebastian, travelling gourmands find razor clams served with blood; heart with chicken, potato and cabbage; and tongue on toast.

Dishes of ugly fish, pig's tails, chicken feet, even kidneys and livers: I love it all. There's something about donning a pair of heels and ordering from a menu that makes eating head cheese – the potentially wonderful jellied flesh from a calf or pig – absolutely fine. Call it pâté de tête and it's all going to be okay. Though most of us are happy enough to eat something *with* a face, eating the *actual* face is a little too real. Preparing that head at home (first step: shave the chin) is another thing altogether.

Eating the whole animal is not only honouring the beast, it's the most practical and sensible thing. As Henderson himself says, eating the entire beast, once you've killed it, is the polite thing to do. We don't have time for squeamish either. Things just won't work out, environmentally and logistically speaking, if we keep throwing away food. Generations before us knew this. Eating the nasty bits of the noble animal is a kind of thrifty necessity, and asking your butcher to order in some chicken feet for stock, livers for parfait, pig's trotters for braising, gizzards and hearts for stuffing, pig's tails for croquettes and marrow for sucking is truly to take part in this delightful, delicious whole-beast renaissance. The French and Vietnamese are experts at using the odds and ends.

Vietnam's pho is a savoury–sweet extraction of beef bones, the marrow gently drawn out, through hours of gentle cooking. The bones themselves are roasted to give the broth an incredible richness and depth of flavour. This soup has been coaxed from the Vietnamese, some say, inspired by the French dish pot au feu. Like Vietnam's pho, the French developed this pot of meat bits and pieces, arguably the most celebrated dish in France, because it honours the tables of rich and poor alike, and is the quintessential family cooking, using low-cost cuts of beef and turning it into something glorious. This dish came about not because the French started off loving the odds and ends of animals, but because they didn't waste a thing.

The French figured out something to do with the chicken's liver, a pig's feet, snails, the cheap cuts and trimmings of animals, because the alternative was to starve. It's one thing being able to decorate a plate with five-hundred-dollar truffles or champagne foam. But the test of a really good cook is being able to turn boiled tongues, tails, bones and cheap root vegetables into something remarkable.

Vietnam's pho draws out the essence of the bones, transforms rigid beef tendon into an unctuous meal. The rice noodles have to be just right, too. Overcooked, not fresh enough, undercooked, anything but perfect, and it's no good. In Hanoi, the soup is made to order, the spiced broth poured over the other ingredients only at the very last moment, so the thinly sliced beef cooks at the table, helped along with a nudge of the customers' chopsticks. The Thai basil, mint and coriander have to be at their most fragrant, most fresh, each bringing a little bitterness and pepper to the mouthful. The pho is a dish of no compromise, despite its humble beginnings. It's proof that cheap can be spectacular and, when made with care and precision and using the very freshest ingredients, dare I say, perfect (see recipe on page 152).

VIETNAMESE PHO

See story on page 151

SERVES 6–8
PREPARATION 15 minutes
COOKING 3 hours

500 g (1 lb 2 oz) beef marrow
  bones, cut into 8–10 cm
  (3¼–4 in) lengths
2 kg (4 lb 8 oz) meaty
  short ribs, cut into 8 cm
  (3¼ in) lengths
750 g (1 lb 10 oz) oxtail, cut
  into joints
2 tablespoons peanut or rice
  bran oil, plus
  1 teaspoon extra
2 large onions, peeled and
  thinly sliced lengthways
6 cloves
4 whole star anise
2 cinnamon sticks
1 teaspoon
  sichuan peppercorns
1 x 8 cm (3¼ in) piece fresh
  ginger, peeled and
  thickly sliced
80 ml (2½ fl oz/⅓ cup) good-
  quality fish sauce, plus extra
  (optional)
2 teaspoons soft brown sugar
sea salt and freshly ground
  black pepper
250 g (9 oz) beef sirloin or
  fillet steak
400 g (145 oz) dried flat Asian
  rice (banh pho) noodles
1 small handful coriander
  (cilantro) sprigs
3 spring onions (scallions),
  thinly sliced, to serve
bean sprouts, to serve
thinly sliced fresh red bird's
  eye chillies, to serve
2 limes, halved, to serve

Put the marrow bones, short ribs and oxtail in a large stockpot and cover with cold water. Bring to the boil over high heat and cook for 5 minutes to remove impurities. Drain, discarding the water, and rinse the meaty bones. Pat the bones dry with paper towel and clean the pot.

Heat half the oil in the same pot and brown the marrow bones, short ribs and oxtail in batches, searing on all sides, for 5–8 minutes, or until well browned. Do not crowd the pot. Transfer each batch to a plate as it is cooked.

Wrap the cloves, star anise, cinnamon and peppercorns in a piece of muslin (cheesecloth) and tie with string.

In the pot, heat the remaining oil over medium–high heat. Add the onion and sauté until golden brown and softened, but not burnt. Add the spice bag, ginger, fish sauce, marrow bones, short ribs, oxtail and sugar to the pan, cover with about 5 litres (170 fl oz/20 cups) of cold water and bring to a simmer over medium–high heat (do not boil). Reduce the heat to low and simmer, skimming off any scum on the surface occasionally, for 2–2½ hours, or until the meat is very tender.

Using tongs, transfer the meat to a board. Discard any bones and membranes, then cut the meat across the grain into 5 cm (2 in) lengths, and shred any remaining meat with your fingers.

Strain the broth through a fine-mesh sieve, discarding the solids. Skim any fat off the top using a large flat spoon, and discard. Season the broth with salt to taste, then pour it back into the cleaned pot. Bring to a gentle simmer – do not boil.

Season the steak with salt and pepper and coat with 1 teaspoon of oil. Heat a small frying pan over high heat and sear the steak for 1 minute on each side, or until brown, but not cooked through; it should still be very rare in the middle. Let rest for 5 minutes, then slice very thinly across the grain. Set aside.

Put the noodles in a large bowl, cover with boiling water and leave for 10 minutes, or until just soft. Drain and divide between bowls. To serve, divide the meat of different cuts (except the steak) between the bowls. Scatter over the coriander, spring onion and bean sprouts, then ladle over the hot stock. Divide the steak between the bowls and offer chillies to scatter and limes for squeezing. Offer extra fish sauce, if liked.

LIVING-ROOM-FLOOR FOOD

True, the benefits of living alone are well known: full access to the phone charger, kingly domain over the bed, the freedom to stand in only knickers in the kitchen spooning hazelnut spread from the jar. The worst thing about breaking up with someone is the sudden reality of dinner for one.

Seven years here and there, in London, Sydney, traipsing through Tokyo, Bali, Vietnam, Paris, our living room, doing everything and usually together – then Roby and I split up. For a month, I was numb, and the month after that, hollowed out by pain and nothingness. After that, I began to mourn the face and the breakfasts and the routines, the rolled-up sleeves, and that specific combination of funny, British, proud, worried, clever, musical and loving that made him perfect to me. After him, there was nothing. To cope, I started going for a run most days and, by the time my clothes were falling off me nearly six months later, I began to wonder what I should have for dinner.

I didn't want to become one of those people who let lack of company get in the way of eating well. But that wasn't easy. Newly single and not yet armed with the special routines and distractions in place, you can amuse yourself in the day, go to work and make plans, but unless you're some kind of serial socialiser you'll end up faced with a table for one. This is not to be confused with 'dining alone' at a restaurant, when you can pretend you're a wild traveller, a widowed heiress or a restaurant reviewer, and you can distract friends from what's really going on with tales of how, finally, you had just a moment to yourself with a glass of red.

When I eat out alone, I have a blast. Taking yourself out for a good meal is not only civilised, it's common sense. It shows a certain independence, but also faith in the power of good company – your own.

A couple of years after Roby and I split up, a different boyfriend and I travelled to San Sebastián, a grand and beautiful city in the Basque country in Spain, a kind of Paris by the seaside, but in holiday mode and with what, I don't think is overstating it to say, is the best food in the world. We'd been wandering around all morning, fuelled by nothing but espressos and churros, and he had gone back to the hotel for his camera. And so it was that I found myself with an hour to spare inside a pintxos bar.

The ceiling groaned with hanging whole legs of jamón, which filled the room with a sweet, nutty scent. A wooden bar stretched the length of the place, displaying the dishes – a sprawl of goat's cheese and sliced jamón on toast fragments, salt cod with piperade, piquillo peppers, frozen icepops of gazpacho, figs in sherry and seared rare beef with umami-rich roasted tomato on a slice of baguette. All the pleasure it was in eating alone, using gestures to translate, happy in my own company. When he returned, I was a bit drunk, full, and so happy. He perched on a stool, sweetly bemused, as I ran through what I'd eaten, how gloriously I'd grazed, plates of it still on display at the bar behind me. I told stories of pomegranate foam on lime-spiked ceviche.

Nobody wants to hear about a fish pie for one. A couple of sausages and a salad do not a story make. Being single made me determined to avoid a number of really depressing scenarios. One of those was eating in front of the television, on the floor at the coffee table, with my legs folded under me, and then pushing the plate aside while I downloaded more episodes of a hospital drama. In this intricate (so far fictional) inevitability, after I ate I'd slide up onto the sofa, and just leave the washing up until tomorrow because, really, who cares? It's a Bridget Jones fate where you end up getting eaten by dogs and it's all too sad.

People who say they love being alone, that they just adore having dinner by themselves every single night, have either not done it enough, have done it for too long, have got so terribly used to it they've forgotten the joy of company, or are lying. Nothing about it is the glory days. That's why dating sites do so well. I just know that when people set up their profiles online, scribing fictions about their tennis-playing prowess, they're balancing a box of Singapore noodles on their lap. They can handle the extra cupboard space and the last word on duvet or sheet. It's eating alone that's the final straw.

Jean-Paul Sartre once said, 'Hell is other people.' I beg to differ (other tourists, when you're travelling, being a notable exception). I'd always been a kind of human relay baton, being passed from parents to a group of friends, before finally hollowing out a place with Roby. I felt like a piece of sports equipment someone had forgotten to take back to the shed with all the other lovely shiny batons.

So here I was. Nobody coming up behind me and slipping their arms around my waist as I sautéed, no pleading for Jamie's tuna basil cinnamon penne and 'stodge', when all I'd made was crunchy vegetable salad. Instead of emphatic debate about whether you should turn the steaks just once, or

Heston's way, where they're tirelessly turned so you're left with a charred exterior and pink medium–rare middle, there was a vacuum. Besides, there was only one steak. Nobody checks whether you've had enough, or want dessert. All the repetitive conversations of the everyday, the nightly grind of making dinner for the family, for the both of you, are eliminated. All that's left are popping word bubbles inside your head, staccato.

'Ice cream in freezer. Better not. Mango. No bother. Another glass of wine. Yep.'

By day I was trekking in national parks, stretching out my arms to the wind, running and running, but by night I curled up on the sofa with a piece of toast and a jar of almond butter.

I'd feared this for some time, for years. For decades? As a child, I'd go up to my parents' bedroom on the top floor of the house, open wide the double doors to their balcony, and finger through the records neatly stored under the sound system. I'd lie on the Persian rug with Dad's massive black headphones around my head, arms stretched out and staring at the ceiling fan. And lying there on the floor, my young heart open wide, I'd get heartbreaking lessons from some of the 1960s' most eloquent on love, loss and loneliness.

The shock of suddenly being single after seven years made dinnertime a bit of an afterthought. I'd work at my computer until after dark and I'd forget to eat. Some nights I had a can of chickpeas mixed in with a can of tuna for dinner, another night a bowl of instant miso soup with spinach leaves in it, added 'for health'. Herbs went limp in the crisper. A regular meal was a couple of sliced cucumbers with a lime and olive oil, a sprinkling of salt. Boiled eggs were good. It wasn't great.

The question of what one person can eat that's genuinely worth making, not taking into account leftovers and not resorting to sandwiches every night, became my version of throwing myself into something. I got better at it. Homemade kimchi with large wobbly cubes of tofu, a ponzu dressing and slivers of cucumber, sesame seeds, became regular dinner fodder. I was making an effort, even though it basically involved combining a bunch of things from jars and packets and bottles, one token item from the crisper. And from this great start, I thought, can I not go still further to reduce the depressing and delirious aspects of eating for one? Can I not, perhaps, make dinnertime a bit more noisy and strident, a bit more neon?

I fell upon the fluorescent, sharp, tangy, hot. A great dollop of gojuchang, that deep-red fermented Korean chilli paste, was folded into a diced handful of sashimi-grade tuna. I overhauled that other single person's sustenance, sushi, and took it up a notch. A mandolin makes short work of cutting anything into julienne, and for a crunch I did long ribbons of carrot, then thinly sliced them into little matchsticks. Chinese cabbage is finely shredded, and the lot is presented in a pretty mound on a plate. The final flourish, in my Korean rendition of a steak tartare, was a single egg yolk (see recipe on page 158). The dish is so damned pretty it's enough to distract any person dining solo from the takeaway menu.

SPICED TUNA TARTARE *with* RICE CRACKERS

See story on page 157

SERVES 2
PREPARATION 15 minutes
COOKING Nil

200 g (7 oz) sashimi-grade
  yellowfin tuna, diced
1 tablespoon gojuchang
  (fermented Korean chilli paste)
½ small carrot, cut into julienne
1 spring onion (scallion), cut
  into julienne
1 teaspoon sesame oil
2 teaspoons toasted
  sesame seeds
2–3 tablespoons vegetable oil
1 x 6–8 cm (2½–3¼ in) piece
  leek, white part only,
  cut into julienne
2–3 Vietnamese sesame
  rice crackers
2 free-range egg yolks
3 radishes, cut into julienne
micro shiso leaves, to serve
  (optional)

In a bowl, combine the tuna, gojuchang, carrot, spring onion, sesame oil and 1 teaspoon of the sesame seeds, and fold together. Refrigerate until ready to serve. (This can be done in advance and kept in the fridge for up to 24 hours – or make a double batch and eat half now, half tomorrow.)

Put a small frying pan over medium–high heat and add the vegetable oil. Once hot, add the leek and fry until golden and crisp. Drain on paper towel.

Microwave the rice crackers, one at a time, on high for 1 minute, or until puffed.

To serve, shape the tuna mixture into a loose ball and divide between two plates. Make an indent in the top of each pile of tuna, and put an egg yolk in each indent. Scatter over the radish, remaining sesame seeds, fried leek and shiso leaves, and serve with the toasted sesame crackers for breaking, scooping and crunching.

tips

Vietnamese sesame rice crackers are available from good Asian grocers. They can also be shallow-fried in rice bran oil in a wok or held over a gas flame to puff, instead of using the microwave.

Use the remaining carrot and leek to make a stock for another time.

ELIZABETH TAYLOR

A year or so later, in March 2011, we all met at a food event, a glamorous gathering at chef Matt Moran's ARIA restaurant, in Sydney. I was already in the city, so I met my mother and Grandma there. Elsewhere, socialites, fashionistas, pretty much everyone else, were mourning the death of Elizabeth Taylor overnight. We'd woken up with the news. Poor Elizabeth Taylor. On the way to the event, Mum picked up Grandma in the car. She opened the door for her and supported her arm and weight while the head of our family navigated her way around the front seat, and Mum asked her how she was.

Grandma replied, 'If Elizabeth Taylor can do it, so can I.'

'Do *what* Mum?' and she waited while Grandma lifted her second leg into the car.

'Die.'

Mum told me the story later in the bathroom at ARIA as we redrew lipstick in our respective mirrors.

'Wow, she is quick,' I laughed.

Margaret was always a follower of fashion and an admirer of grace, always a little impressed by the stars. It made sense that if the younger, elegant, feminine front-runner Elizabeth was doing something extraordinary, she might just want to do it too. Elizabeth Taylor doing something made it acceptable. But, I panicked, this was *dying*.

Had she given up? Had too much time by herself and the exhaustion of being older – tired of the interviews and tired of the food – finally got to her?

'She's just being witty,' Mum reassured me. 'You know how she is.'

I pressed Grandma about it later and she just laughed it off. I tried to put the comment down to a sense of humour that moved from the embarrassingly sexual for a woman in her eighties, to the slightly macabre. But none of it sat that comfortably with me.

With all of us living within walking distance from one another, it's commonplace for us to turn up at each other's places uninvited. We rely heavily on each other and sometimes what's really needed is a cup of milk or a 'wee dram' of whisky and company.

I dropped in on Grandma a couple of weeks after the Elizabeth Taylor incident. I wrapped my arms around her shoulders, holding her for a moment longer than anyone but family would feel comfortable about, breathing her in.

'Katie! How are you, darling?'

And I told her about how I'd been running a lot, how I'd made her scones for friends on the weekend, the usual Grandma chat.

'I was just about to sit down for dinner. Come and sit with me.'

And she turned to finish making her meal for one. I took a peek.

A single Royal Doulton plate sat on her kitchen bench. She took a paring knife and cut the tops and tails from three ruby radishes, sliced them in half and placed them in a pretty tumble on the plate. She picked a small handful of peppery wild arugula from the lettuce spinner in the fridge, trimming the tired ends. She set the leaves in a bowl with extra virgin olive oil and a pinch of sea salt, threw in a few halved cherry tomatoes and tossed it together, then placed it delicately on the plate. A piece of flathead fish had been dusted lightly in plain flour, well seasoned, and had turned golden brown in a pan on the stove, helped along with a knob of butter. She placed the plate on a tray, already dressed with a linen serviette and silver cutlery. There was a little stone pot of sea salt and a glass of water glistened with ice. She cut a wedge from a lemon and positioned it next to the fish, finely chopped fresh parsley a final flourish on the immaculate plate.

Together we moved to 'the front room', a room with a view of Sydney harbour and the universe. The world was golden from here, and it shone right in on this woman, who elegantly sat with me, a serviette over her lap, alert and beautiful. She was every bit as radiant as Ms Taylor ever was. Being alone had done nothing to shake her. Her life was filled with the best things, because she chose to have it that way, she made it that way.

I think of this every time I'm alone, away overseas by myself, or when the chap is on some week-long surf trip with friends. I sit at the table to eat, play music and use a knife as well as a fork. I buy flowers for the house. Flowers make a big difference when you're alone, because there is something else living here except you and the bugs. I eat on the balcony, because there's nothing depressing about eating outside alone. It's not you with nobody to share a meal; it's you, getting a bit of fresh air, eating al fresco. Or I eat by the window, hoping the grace of the world will shine in on me too.

NEW YORK COOK

The first thing I learn at culinary school is this: it's two degrees outside but with wind chill it's more like minus fifteen. The class mimes a collective shiver. Now, how to chop an onion. Our delightful tutor, Madame, is half Julia Child and half Martha Stewart. She holds the onion in place on the board and slices into it down and across in even deliberate slices.

'Now, please,' and she motions us to our own boards, our own knives, then strides around the room. It's her first-things-first way of determining skill in a classroom of moderate home cooks.

I feel we're teetering between it all being terribly exciting, in a culinary education sense, and being a class scattered with nuggets for the domestic ambitions of a 1950s housewife. We learn that sugar cooks (and ruins) raw eggs if you let it sit for too long, but also how to lay the leaves for the niçoise salad out on a platter first to make it more appealing to the eye.

A few months into being newly single, I did one thing any sensible person would do when faced with a flourishing freelance writing career and no beau at home. I went to New York in the dead of winter to attend culinary school. If you can make it there, etcetera.

On New Year's Day, I landed in New York City and ended up in Times Square, looking up at that giant ball, surrounded by New Yorkers and pretzel stands and music, drums, flashing lights – and all I could think was 'How the hell did you end up here?' But in staccato and with blue lips. I picked midtown to stay, not the wisest decision I realise now that I've actually been to New York, but I liked the idea of running in Central Park, plus that Carnegie's sandwich place with the famous Reuben is right there. I also knew that every break I had in my school schedule, I'd be back at MOMA, less than a block away from my hotel. Piles of snow, iced and blackened, stuck cars to pavements. At 10 pm, steam billowed from grates in the pavement and the air froze around me as I queued up outside a cupcake shop.

With a pumpkin cupcake with spiced cinnamon butter cream icing for dinner and a few weeks ahead of me in the greatest city in the world, happiness started to creep in. The first night went like this: Stand in boxer shorts and a singlet under the direct flush of heating, lean against the ceiling-to-floor window with its spectacular view up wintry 54th Street (eating said cupcake), check out the various hotel liquid soaps and make a mini bubble bath in the sink with them, sleep in the centre of the bed for the first time in years. That night the shock of the past months fell away, and I woke up the next day feeling a little more like myself.

There's perfume in the air and the lobby is humming with the slow opening of the double doors, the swift shifting of Louis Vuitton luggage onto the beige plush carpet, and rattle of suitcase wheels on the floor. I pull my jacket collar up to my scarf, which tucks under a woollen beanie, my long hair puffing out over the lot. I look like a merino wool ad. I pull up my gloves and check availability of cash without having to take off said gloves. And then I am outside, away from the sight of the other lone businesses travellers (because who else would visit at this time of year, if they didn't have to), each with their own unfulfilled longings and happier backstories – and New York hits me like a glorious sledgehammer.

I fear that mobility through the city will be limited to a crawl in a cab, but we're halfway down Fifth Avenue before I turn away from the banana-eating cab driver's sound effects and look outside. We fly past frozen Bryant Park and shimmering Sephora, Madison Square Park, and pull up outside the culinary institute.

Straight rows of plates appear on the stainless-steel benches and, one by one, each pupil turns out an omelette. Mine rolls perfectly from the pan: 'Bravo.' Then there is the blanching of beans, the turning out of steaks with immaculate crusts and even, pink centres, then clear stock and clarified butter, shortcrust pastry then puff pastry, then trussing chickens with the deft skills of surgeons, then soufflé omelettes and chocolate soufflés. As the days roll by, we get better and better and, by the end of week two, I'm learning a thing or two, even studying at night and reading ahead to better prepare for the next day's tasks. It's not just how to beat egg whites, but why the proteins do what they do, how long they will keep, how to take the various beating and whipping and sautéing to the perfect point, how to know when it's gone too far. We're in search of perfection. Another student Sarah and I team up, each recognising the other as a worthy partner in a class of mixed ability.

We finely slice a mountain of onions, Sarah and I, churning through the teary process. I rub cold butter through plain flour, then gradually add almost icy water to the mix, turning what looks like breadcrumbs into dough. Sarah reduces the onions further while I roll out the chilled pastry and insert it carefully into a fluted rectangular tin. This recipe was about the last thing I needed to learn how to cook. Not because I had done it before, but because I had my own pissaladière expert back in Sydney, in my mother, raring to go for any picnic, boat trip, afternoon tea or any occasion that calls for this simple French tart of sweet onion and tomato, a hashtag of salty anchovies and olives on top. The onions take on a melting quality that turns them almost to caramel, and my mother's masterstroke is the buttery pastry underneath, a touch of ground cinnamon, and cooked to a golden flaky crispy end (see recipe on page 168). This tart demands perfectly cooked pastry. At home I roll mine out into a kind of spontaneous puddle shape and blind bake it first. A little underdone and it's the same kind of raw, insipid mess that has turned many off quiche lorraine. Real men don't eat undercooked pastry.

We pour a rich chocolate cream into another pre-baked shortcrust shell, another layer of almost black chocolate glaze over the top. It's good in a kind of very sweet and sticky wet way, the shiny top and smoothness of the ganache a test of our culinary prowess in class. We do a version studded with freeze-dried raspberries, which add a tart kick to the bittersweet dessert. But still, I turn to my mother's own version of the chocolate tart, her thinly rolled pastry. Eggs and sugar are beaten into submission over a saucepan of simmering water until thick, forming luscious ribbons of almost a zabaglione consistency, a velvety band running from the spoon when lifted from the bowl. Melted chocolate is whisked into the egg mixture, and a little flour gently folded through at the end. It's almost foaming chocolate, still dense but light enough to pour like thick lava from the bowl. It's baked and served still wobbly. Mum's tart remains my dinner party delivery of I've-made-an-effort, and it's easy to add to it for the occasion. On Valentine's Day, I add a kick of hot chilli powder to the chocolate, or serve it with a light cardamom cream for spooning over. It's the sort of tart that has everyone begging for the recipe (see recipe on page 171). I didn't need culinary school for that.

After class, Sarah took me to a little hidden burger place behind the curtain with only a neon picture of a burger as signage, where autograph-penned walls and order-at-the-counter are the bar's signatures. And one day we walked to the Pearl Oyster Bar in Cornelia Street, where Maine's signature sandwich, the lobster roll, is a slightly sweet and soft bun stuffed and piled up with that tender and firm meat laden with creamy mayonnaise, snips of chives. A stack of matchstick fries comes on the side.

With all the lobster rolls, burgers, fries, spiced pumpkin cupcakes and one massive fresh pretzel bought from a stand on the side of the road, and despite all the culinary enlightenment of the cooking school, one thing became the epitome of my lone journey to New York. And it wasn't even American. The tartine, that open-faced sandwich, had hit some kind of zeitgeist in the city at the precise moment that I was there. The French invented the elegant bite, which encompasses layers of things on a single slice of bread, and the Scandinavians perfected it with their smørrebrød. New York had put its particular tilt on it and I went a little mad for them. The one thing that wrecks a sandwich for me is the very thing that makes it a sandwich: the bread. Not the existence of it, because otherwise it would be a salad, but the amount of it. Stumbling upon this open-faced invention with its assortment of perfect toppings was, for me, akin to the Earl of Sandwich's inevitable delight when he found his own pièce de résistance.

Chopped egg appeared on slices of rye with slivers of anchovy and capers, thinly sliced radishes and cornichon. Avocado came smashed with smoked mozzarella, cannellini beans materialised with housemade tomato chutney and sprouts, each on their own slice of chewy, soft, dense, sticky, crusted walnut bread, spelt or five-grain that held it all together. I realise I'm talking about sandwiches – and in a book that is basically trying to aim a little higher. But the ordinariness, the everydayness of the sandwich is what makes it extraordinary when done well.

As with so many things, though, it was the first taste that got me hooked. I was still jetlagged and basically in need of dinner – but at 8 am. I found a sunny café near the hotel that was some kind of throwback to the rural American ideal, but with Martha Stewart styling. Bouquets of corn decorated the rustic tables. There were massive bare-brick walls and long oak tables, jars of honey and those squirtable bear honeys, and large windows that looked out to the winter only to offset the various yellows and sunny lighting, the warming homeliness of it all inside. Chalkboards described farro porridge with rhubarb compote, leg ham and cheese omelettes, cobb salads and rustic tuna niçoise.

A chirpy waitress brought over a tartine, topped with thin ribbons of cucumber and a spiced cured salmon gravlax. The salmon was almost transparent in its perfect cure, a silken curl spiked with aniseed, fenugreek, cumin and salt. It was a Greek interpretation of cured salmon, or a salmon version of the famed pastourma, or pastirma. In the original, beef is salted, washed, then the blood and salt squeezed out to form the resulting dense charcuterie. It's prepared with a crushed cumin, fenugreek, garlic and hot paprika rub, and finished with a thorough air-drying. There are variations in Syria, Lebanon, Turkey and Greece, and in Egypt it's served for breakfast with eggs. The tartine was sweet and fragrant, with a silky texture, a few pearls of salmon roe to add a fishy salty pop to each mouthful.

Home again, I battled with my suitcase on the stairs to my Balmain apartment, opened the windows to let in the summer Sydney air. I could hear seagulls and magpies, cicadas and the whirring of someone's whipper snipper, the bush cutter, in a nearby garden. A couple of days later, my friend Meg came over and I told her about one catastrophic date with a New York baseball player, the shopping, the elaborate trips trying to work out the New York subway, the city's obsession with cupcakes.

'That would never happen here,' we agreed.

She's the kind of friend who inevitably makes the water you're drinking come out of your nose from laughing suddenly. The best kind of friend, really. I handed her a plate to balance on her lap while we curled on my sofa. A tartine topped with my version of the salmon pastourma (see recipe on page 173): ribbons of cucumber and pink peppercorns, the salmon itself cured in ouzo, sugar and salt, with a gentle balance of cumin and fenugreek, smoked paprika. We squeezed lemon over.

'See, this is why you needed to go to New York,' she says. 'To learn this stuff, for me.'

'Yep, I'll make a t-shirt,' I say: 'I flew all the way to New York and all I got was this rather fabulous sandwich.'

PISSALADIÈRE

See story on page 164

SERVES 6–8
PREPARATION 20 minutes,
plus 45 minutes chilling
COOKING 1 hour 25 minutes

300 g (10½ oz/2 cups) plain
   (all-purpose) flour
½ teaspoon baking powder
½ teaspoon ground cinnamon
150 g (5½ oz) butter, diced
1 x 45 g (1¾ oz) tin anchovy
   fillets in oil, well drained
100 g (3½ oz/½ cup) small
   black olives
olive oil, for drizzling
baby basil leaves, to serve

Topping
1 kg (2 lb 4 oz) brown onions,
   thinly sliced
125 ml (4 fl oz/½ cup) olive oil
3 large garlic cloves
1 x 400 g (14 oz) tin chopped
   tomatoes or 1 kg (2 lb 4 oz)
   ripe tomatoes, peeled,
   seeded and diced
1 small fresh bay leaf
1 sprig thyme or marjoram
freshly ground black pepper

Combine the flour, baking powder, cinnamon and butter in a food processor and pulse for 15–20 seconds, or longer if necessary, until the mixture resembles fine breadcrumbs. Add 80 ml (2½ fl oz/⅓ cup) of water and process for a further 20–30 seconds, or until the mixture starts to cling together. Turn onto a floured surface and knead lightly into a smooth ball. Pat into a thick round, wrap in plastic wrap and chill for 30 minutes.

For the topping, put the onion and oil in a medium saucepan and cook slowly over a gentle heat for about 15 minutes, or until the onion is soft and pulpy, but not brown. Add the garlic and cook for a further 5 minutes. Add the tomato and herbs and continue cooking until the mixture is reduced to a thick pulp. Remove the herbs and season with pepper.

Roll the pastry out on a floured board and trim to a large rectangle or oval. Transfer to a lightly oiled baking tray, prick gently all over with a fork and chill for 15 minutes.

Preheat the oven to 190°C (375°F).

Lay a piece of baking paper over the base, add baking beads or dried pulses and blind bake for 10–15 minutes. Remove the paper and beads or pulses and leave the pastry to cool slightly.

Increase the oven temperature to 200°C (400°F). Spread the onion topping evenly over the pastry base. Arrange the anchovy fillets over the topping, scatter with olives, drizzle lightly with olive oil and bake for about 25 minutes, or until the crust is golden.

Scatter with basil leaves and serve warm or at room temperature.

tip

You can also cook the pastry in a large 25 cm (10 in) fluted flan (tart) tin, if you prefer. Or you can use bought shortcrust pastry – just follow the packet instructions.

CHOCOLATE CHILLI TART

See story on page 164

SERVES 8–10
PREPARATION 40 minutes,
plus 1 hour resting and
15 minutes chilling
COOKING 1 hour

340 g (11¾ oz) plain
 (all-purpose) flour
1 pinch of sea salt
150 g (5½ oz)
 unsalted butter, diced
90 g (3¼ oz/¾ cup) icing
 (confectioners') sugar
2 free-range eggs,
 lightly whisked
cocoa powder, for dusting

Filling
150 g (5½ oz) dark chocolate,
 finely chopped
125 g (4½ oz)
 unsalted butter, diced
1 teaspoon good-quality
 chilli powder, plus extra
 for dusting
5 free-range eggs
220 g (7¾ oz/1 cup) caster
 (superfine) sugar
75 g (2¾ oz/½ cup) plain
 (all-purpose) flour, sifted

Sift the flour and salt into a large mixing bowl. Make a well in the centre, add the butter and pinch with floured fingers to form pea-sized pieces. Add the sugar and eggs to the well, mix to combine, then gradually draw in the flour until you have a rough dough. Knead a few times, just until it becomes smooth, then press into a flat disc, cover with plastic wrap and refrigerate for 1 hour, or until firm enough to roll out.

Roll the pastry out on a lightly floured piece of baking paper until 3 mm (⅛ in) thick and about 35 cm (14 in) in diameter. Use a rolling pin to transfer the pastry to a 28 cm (11¼ in) round fluted flan (tart) tin. Ease the pastry into the tin, taking care not to stretch it, as this will cause it to shrink. Press into the fluted edges. Roll the rolling pin over the tin edges to remove the excess pastry. (Wrap and keep excess pastry in the freezer for another use.) Chill the pastry base in the freezer for 15 minutes, or in the fridge for 30 minutes–1 hour.

Preheat the oven to 190°C (375°F).

Line the pastry base with baking paper and pour in some baking beads or dried pulses. Blind bake the pastry for 10–15 minutes, then remove the paper and beads or pulses and bake for another 10 minutes, or until golden. Remove from the oven and set aside.

Reduce the oven temperature to 150°C (300°F).

For the filling, combine the chocolate and butter in a heatproof bowl that fits snugly over a saucepan of simmering water, stirring gently until melted. Stir in the chilli powder and taste, adding a little more chilli if liked. Set aside.

Put the eggs and sugar in a heatproof bowl that fits snugly over a large saucepan of simmering water, and whisk with hand-held electric beaters for 10 minutes, or until thick and ribbons form when the beaters are lifted.

Whisk the chocolate mixture into the egg mixture, then whisk in the flour. Pour the mixture into the pastry case and bake for 15–18 minutes, or until the filling is just set, but still a little wobbly.

Dust with cocoa and chilli powder. Cut into wedges and serve at room temperature.

SALMON PASTOURMA WITH FENUGREEK *and* CUCUMBER

See story on page 166

SERVES 6–8 as an entrée
PREPARATION 30 minutes,
plus 36 hours to cure
COOKING 2 minutes
Start this recipe 36 hours
ahead

½ teaspoon cumin seeds
½ teaspoon fenugreek
¼ teaspoon smoked paprika
2 tablespoons salt, plus extra,
   to taste
2 teaspoons brown sugar
2 tablespoons ouzo
500 g (1 lb 2 oz) centre-cut
   piece of salmon or trout,
   skin on, bones removed
250 g (9 oz) baby cucumbers or
   Lebanese (short) cucumbers
1 French shallot, halved and
   thinly sliced lengthways
2 tablespoons baby flat-
   leaf (Italian) parsley leaves
   (or regular parsley leaves,
   coarsely chopped)
1 tablespoon extra virgin olive
   oil, plus extra for drizzling
juice of ½ lemon
2 tablespoons salmon roe
1 teaspoon pink peppercorns,
   coarsely crushed
sliced sourdough, toasted,
   to serve

Toast the cumin and fenugreek in a dry saucepan over low heat until aromatic, then grind in a mortar and pestle with the paprika, salt and brown sugar. Add the ouzo and mix to form a paste. Rub the paste into the salmon, put in an airtight container or plastic snap-lock bag and refrigerate for 36 hours, to cure.

Thinly slice the cucumbers lengthways into ribbons, using a mandolin. In a bowl, combine the cucumber, shallot, parsley, olive oil, lemon juice and a pinch of salt. Set aside until needed.

Pat the salmon dry with paper towel. Thinly slice on an angle, removing the flesh from the skin. Place on a serving platter. Arrange the cucumber salad over the salmon, scatter over the salmon roe and pink peppercorns and drizzle with extra olive oil. Serve with toasted sourdough.

tip

Pink peppercorns are available from good grocers or delicatessens.

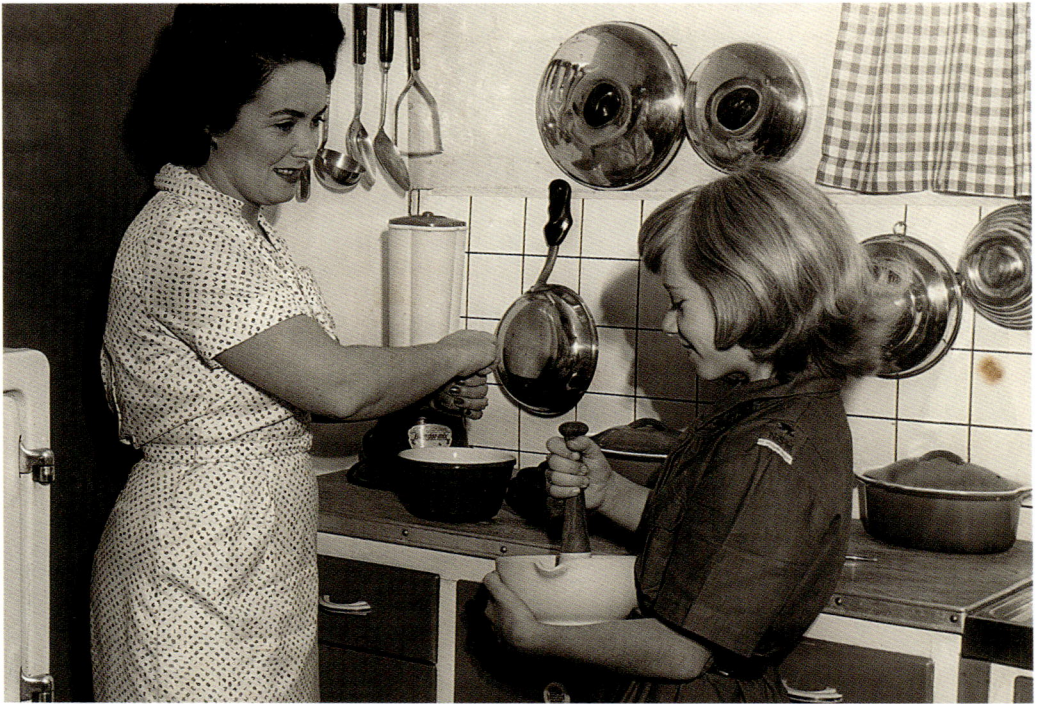

Above: Margaret and Suzanne (in her Brownies uniform) in their kitchen in Essex Street, The Rocks, 1959; below left: Margaret poses for a Tupperware advertisement, 1963; below right: Suzanne and Margaret cooking for an advertisement, 1964.

BROWN BREAD ROLLS AND OTHER STORIES

'The job interview was not the ordeal I had been expecting,' my grandmother tells me.

She entered the editor's office at *Woman* magazine and was immediately put at ease. Forgoing the elaborate curriculum vitae, the internship stint in the research department at a newspaper, the nail-biting writing test set against other journalistic hopefuls, Margaret was asked one question.

'How are your brown bread rolls?'

'Yes, I'm very good at brown bread rolls,' Margaret told interviewer, Elizabeth Riddell.

'You've got the job.'

Since the merger of Associated Newspapers, publishers of *The Sun* and a raft of periodicals, and its mighty peer, John Fairfax and Sons, publishers of *The Sydney Morning Herald*, the newly formed board of directors met once a month in the executive dining room at the *Sun* office in Elizabeth Street. The executives liked freshly baked brown bread rolls for lunch. And so, on the strength of her bread rolls, Margaret's career as a food writer began. That was it, she tells me now, the moment that launched a lifetime of writing about food in magazines and newspapers and then cookery books. All of it came on the back of her brown bread rolls.

Margaret's office was on the top floor, at one end of a large, imposing, parquet-floored, highly polished dining room that held a large colonial cedar table to seat twenty. She inherited a pretty, waif-like assistant called Maureen Bull – later to become Maureen Simpson – who longed for dimples on her elbows, just like Margaret's.

'She got them soon enough,' Grandma tells me, chuckling. 'And more, as the force of good food did its job.'

Maureen would, one day, become a rather notable commentator on food for ABC radio, delivering her culinary truisms to a hungry audience of Australians. But first, she had a course to do. She enrolled in the same course at the East Sydney Technical College that Margaret had just completed. Although, in Margaret's own case, it had started rather crudely, she thought.

So basic was the course that she felt compelled to pull her teacher, Chef Weinberg, aside.

'Chef,' she ventured. 'Look, all I've done so far is make soup.'

'Ah, yes,' he replied. 'But your soup is getting better.'

'For one year, I seemed to do nothing by chop vegetables, and here I was telling the readers of *Woman* how to cook,' she tells me.

Margaret and Maureen made the bread rolls for the board luncheons, as well as elegant soups, fillets of beef, tournedos with béarnaise sauce, and proper English puddings. Together the duo could produce any meal with the refinement of haute cuisine in the classical manner of French master Auguste Escoffier.

Margaret was in love. With the food. She penned an article for *Woman* magazine with the headline 'Some say French is the language of love, I say it's the language of the kitchen'. She was addicted, and when she wasn't learning something from Chef or writing French recipes for the magazine, she was reading and practising. Again and again she repeated recipes, making the perfect omelette, a clean, sparkling consommé, a perfect soufflé, high and light, and a béchamel sauce that was as smooth as satin, as rich as velvet.

After the war, well-heeled Australians began to travel. Suddenly the island was not a place from which only the very privileged, or soldiers, ventured. Europe, Britain, even Asia, became holiday destinations. With duck à la presse from the Tour d'Argent in Paris in their bellies and hearts, Australians returned home wanting to recreate what they had eaten. The term 'haute cuisine' was thrown about at dinner parties, and everyone wanted a piece of it. Learning about salads from the Latin Quarter and pork and veal terrine from France's country towns engendered a new eagerness around food experimentation in Australia. And Margaret, in the pages of *Woman* magazine, would help these eager home cooks do it.

Margaret read books such as *Larousse Gastronomique*, she spoke to chefs in restaurants. Even now, if you take Margaret to a decent restaurant, you'll find she disappears off into the kitchen. I once waited by the exit with her jacket and bag when she disappeared at the end of a meal only to re-emerge from the kitchen chatting to two gorgeous chefs in their whites. She goes in to thank them, to be amongst the (mostly) men; it's the habit of a woman who is eternally interested in the tricks of the trade and who has based a career on knowing those tricks, repeating and perfecting them, then channelling that insight to the vast and intrigued faction of Australian home cooks.

In her pages for the magazine – written, incidentally, under the by-line

Ann Maxwell – Margaret tried to break new ground. She offered recipes and ideas for cocktails – how to make and serve the perfect dry martini; she wrote articles such as 'When the boss comes to dinner' and 'A French dinner party'. She talked her readers through six-course affairs.

'It was hard work for the hostess,' she admits now, 'but it was what everyone wanted to do.'

She had them starting preparation five days in advance and explained, in intricate detail, how and when to serve the hors d'oeuvres, how to keep the garden neat, the husband respectable, and the preference for a long hostess gown. Australian hostesses lapped it up, making their dinner parties a little more perfect with the help of their discerning and well-read guide.

Margaret held dinner parties, too, practising on her guests and refining recipes. In the 1950s, she tells me now, everyone was intent on having a good time. They were bored with the gloom of the war, the rationing. The liberal and artistic, intellectual crowd turned up to Margaret's elaborate dinner parties in fancy dress.

'We were mad about dressing up,' she says.

Nymphs and shepherds, cartoon characters, Arabian nights – no theatrical or literary cornerstone was left unturned as the imaginative friends dressed up and turned up. Margaret built culinary themes around the fancy dress, introducing Mongolian hot pots to a gathering at which guests wore tea-cosy hats with their conservative suits.

At one of these parties, Margaret found herself in the ladies' toilet with Mandrake the Magician, complete with top hat, tails and a fine moustache. When not in fancy dress, Mandrake was one of Sydney's early female leading lawyers. She cornered Margaret when she saw her.

'I want you to understand there is really nothing between me and Denis. We are just good friends.'

My grandmother burst out laughing, having thought nothing of it, before. She was one of Margaret and Denis' best friends. But more and more, these assurances from female friends and acquaintances continued.

'There is nothing between me and Denis, we're just friends.'

Margaret's laughter began to wear thin.

HARD WORK

FREELANCER

I'm sitting on a chair in a suburban food court in Chatswood in 2010, arguably one of a few epicentres of Sydney's Asian food scene, tearing apart crisp-fried chicken in a bowl of Vietnamese noodle soup with my chopsticks. With the tangled coriander sprigs and mint leaves, long handmade noodles and the hot stock, it's getting messy. In my other hand, I'm holding a tissue from a box that's set on the sticky wooden table. My colleagues, Aaron and a British chap I call Bingley, as in Jane Austen, similarly struggle, each of us trying to maintain some work-appropriate manners and dignity in the lunch hour we have available.

I'm tied up in an editor role in a business magazine, a job that I love because it's editing, but that's the main thing to recommend it. Bingley is talking about blogging. I'm sceptical. A friend of his, Kristin Hove, was doing it, and so was a friend of hers in Oslo, and it was basically a way to catalogue photographs and whatever else you wanted. He'd been talking about this for a few days and, sitting next to me at work, he'd ping over a new blog to prove his point.

'Like a food diary, but online? Does anyone read it?' I say.

I'd started a blog a few years earlier, but it was a silly stream of keepsakes, of things I'd written for magazines and newspapers, mixed up with a new rug or lamp I liked. 'Let's see.'

I lean over the table to look at his phone. He scans through Kristin's images, for which she bakes things, pretty healthy loaves and beetroot with a mixed grain salad, all of which beg to be baked and made for the aesthetic loveliness of it all, and photographs them.

'You can cook, Miss Gibbs,' he says. 'You should do this.'

Aaron nods while he slurps noodles from his giant bowl.

'Oh no, she's already doing it,' I say. 'No need for another out there.'

That evening after work, in the rain, I drove Bingley to where his car was parked.

'Maybe I'd like to do a travel one,' I say. 'A travel blog.'

I pull the car up in front of his.

'I could travel around Spain and to Istanbul, shoot the food markets in Marrakesh and eat baklava in the Greek Islands. Can that be a job? Would people pay for that? I want to go to Hong Kong and just do a dumpling blog. Is that a thing?'

'Maybe not,' he said. 'But you're a writer. Do that anyway. But get paid. Why don't you do that?'

'Food writing?' I shrugged. 'There's like a handful of writers in Sydney already and I've been writing about lawyers and finance, and what it's like working in a London school. The best writers in the world all want to end up writing about food and travel. It's the best possible job.'

'Miss Gibbs, you could do that.'

He turns to open the car door, steps out and gets completely drenched. But before he slams the door shut, he leans in, drips of water running down his face, his olive skin. He squints and a smile stretches across his face.

'Pick me up some baklava, okay?'

I logged into the Wordpress account I'd opened a couple of years earlier, on which I'd last posted some some pictures from Tokyo. In the time since I had started my Wordpress account, others had refined the blogging process into a discerning and inspiring masterstroke. I'd done a post on the fact that I'd just subedited Margaret Fulton's upcoming Christmas cookbook, while others stepped into forests and took photographs of pine mushrooms, told evocative tales of sautéing and domestic godliness. If I was going to do this, I had to lift my game.

With a vacuum still at home that had a Roby-shaped black hole in it, even four months later, I started blogging. I shunned the television for the computer screen at nights, I took photographs of a friend's roast pork one weekend, and when the chef Giovanni Pilu did a photo shoot at Mum's place for *BBC Good Food* magazine, where she was food director, I took pictures of his pink grapefruit and Aperol cocktail. When Bingley's friend, Kristin, and I met up in Manly for a photo date, when I baked muffins, when I made alphabet soup, when I saw Portobello mushrooms at the market, I took photographs and I wrote about it. Blogging became a practice run, a means to experiment with words. And just to write. I edited and I wrote, every day. And when I wasn't cooking or eating or taking photographs of food, I was reading *Australian Gourmet Traveller*, *New York* magazine, the *The New Yorker*, London's *The Times*, the restaurant reviews in the *LA Times*, the best food writing in the world. I read constantly.

The clock was ticking on the interminable routine of turning up every day to produce insights into the ceaseless grind of the business world. I wanted to get home to my blog. In the day, sitting next to each other, Bingley and I carved out time to talk about food, mainly. His happy face every morning became the main reason I wanted to go into the office. A friendship was developing amongst the manila folders and crumb-scattered keyboards, the bowls of Vietnamese noodle soup and my growing awareness that he made me hopeful, even happy. He also made his girlfriend happy.

Buoyed by a glass or two of red wine and a case of career limbo, plus a rather vital plan to avoid the terrible stagnation that had flattened me years before, I sent an email to a former journalism lecturer at the University of Technology, whom I'd had for my Masters. In his class I'd done pretty well, scored mostly high distinctions. He was also a senior editor at *The Sydney Morning Herald*, so I mentioned I'd like to write for him, or his newspaper, and if anything cropped up that specifically needed a former *Evening Standard* journalist with a penchant for food and travel, and a rather serious background in business journalism, I was just the man to write it. A week later, the editor of the newspaper's food and wine supplement emailed me: would I like to write for her?

Freelancing, as a job, means getting out of bed, showered and into real clothes before 8 am. Otherwise, after you check your emails in your underwear, singlet and Ugg boots, make a second coffee and then have a shower, it's 11.10 am. For the rest of the day you're in a confused mess of sleep-in-your-eyes and craving an arrive-at-work coffee but you've already had the quota. Plus, you're always at work. It's all downhill and, next thing, it's 4.50 pm and all you've done is unload the dishwasher, read a few emails and made that third coffee. The effective freelancer puts rules in place and Meg (who has meanwhile carved out a career writing for *GQ* magazine and a string of prestigious others) will back me up here. No television: not in the background, not on mute, not ever. No midday naps. No alcohol before 5.30 pm. No cleaning after 9 am, not even to wipe down the bathroom mirror. Do nothing that you wouldn't do in an office with colleagues. Break any of these rules and you fall into a strange flexibility that means no time is 'off' time and all time is 'medium' time. It's never really 'on' time. And that's not going to get you good commissions. Ugg boots are okay if you're otherwise dressed.

My by-lines appeared on stories about how licorice was suddenly a thing, on where to find the best cannoli in Sydney, and on how the barbecue was humble no more. I flew to Kangaroo Island to write about a rare breed animal farmer and when I got there I also did a story on the island's historic colony of Ligurian bees, and another on the rising reputation of the place as a kind of gourmet escape for discerning foodies. I pitched stories to other editors at the newspaper: a sampling of bars and restaurants in Venice for the travel section, a story on European rail travel. I travelled and wrote, ate and took photographs – and I was being paid to do it.

The food writer Jill Dupleix miraculously got me onto *The Sydney Morning Herald's Good Cafe Guide*, which she edited. Armed with a list of about twenty-five cafés, the job involved traipsing around Sydney with a thirst for the black stuff, to make notes on flavour profiles and to check out the food while I was there. A rigorous ranking system ensured fair marks and, frankly, it was hard to get it wrong. Every caffeine hit was a reminder of what I was doing, a happy jolt that I was a food writer now.

Heading out the door one morning to review a string of cafés in Surry Hills, and thus radically under-dosed on coffee in preparation, I opened my front door and there was a boy standing in front of me. I hadn't seen him in five months.

'Miss Gibbs, I have something to tell you.'

THE LAKE HOUSE SCHOOL

Margaret's name was called over the loud speaker and the hotel conference room filled with applause; little spotlights beamed all over the room to signal 'Award, award!' She rose to her feet. Somebody held her forearm as she made her way slowly to the stage, a woman in her mid-eighties. She took her lifetime achievement award and returned to her table after a modest, slightly random speech about how she spent her life exploring and learning. It had the room laughing.

'I learned how to make hamburgers out of mincemeat from women in America, then I learned how to make pastries filled with mincemeat from women in Morocco, and I learned how to make dishes with mincemeat in Spain. So, when they asked me to do a cookbook, *101 Ways with Mincemeat*, I could do it!'

Somebody handed her a glass of champagne.

'Congratulations, Margaret, it's so deserved.'

Throughout the evening others took turns to speak with her, kneeling down so she didn't have to stand, holding her hand, rubbing her arm.

'Congratulations, Margaret.'

And: 'Margaret, I had to come to say hello. My mother gave me your first cookbook in 1971 and I still have it. The lemon delicious page is splattered and I still do your béarnaise sauce. I love it, so thank you.'

As others joined her at the table she began to really feel that perhaps it was a lifetime of achievement.

Someone from the food industry, seated at her table, leaned over just as she took the first sip of champagne.

'The thing is, Margaret,' he said, 'you did well, but you didn't have any competition. It was easier for you.'

As a protective granddaughter, I still bridle with fury at this thoughtless, ill-informed comment.

Certainly, when Margaret did it, there were not so many celebrity chefs jostling for another book deal, a television spot, and the world in which she worked was not so obsessively foodie, where every intern with a whisk is vying for a food column, *your* food column. But the path was not easy just because there was less competition. Women didn't do what she was doing. She didn't have much competition because nobody had dared, nobody else sacrificed precisely what she did and followed precisely that path.

There was no path to follow, at least not in Australia, and especially not for women. Competition gives you something against which to measure yourself, something to emulate and make your own. And Margaret didn't have that. She had to make it up as she went along. Nobody offers the budding food writer career advice – follow Margaret Fulton – because what she did and how she got there was completely mad, a series of disasters and missteps, unfathomable hard work and dedication, with many lessons learned in the hardest ways. Much better to start a blog or a social media account and hope that some publisher picks up on your sass. She was never a chef, working tirelessly in a professional kitchen, hoping that a book deal would come along. So yes, she didn't have any competition as we know competition now. But that didn't make things easier.

She did love forging that lonely, thrilling path, however.

The first major sacrifice came soon after she moved into Essex Street in The Rocks. Suzanne, my Mum, was only four years old, and she sat on the bed crying as Grandma packed her bags. Margaret promised that it would not be for long and that they would see each other all the time. With no husband on hand, no childcare, no single-parent support, Margaret had to make a living. So she sent my mother to boarding school, a place called Lake House School just outside Sydney. My mother was there for five years.

The life of the school appealed to Grandma. When we ask about it now, she says she loved the idea of the liberal education it offered. Lake House School was modelled on a progressive school in Scotland called the Steiner School; as well as the usual school subjects, students were taught drama, arts and crafts and, in Grandma's words, 'many life skills that would make them capable, self-sufficient adults'. It was 1954, and my four-year-old mother was less concerned about life skills than she was about not being with her only parent. The initial separation was brutal.

'It was traumatic,' says Grandma.

The school insisted on an initial clean break of four weeks, so the child could settle in without the distraction of parents, or mother. It was hard for Suzanne and it was hard for Margaret. Grandma would have claimed her daughter back in a heartbeat, but she believed Suzanne was better off there than in any environment that she could offer.

After the initial black embargo, Suzanne spent most weekends at home with her mum in Essex Street. On Saturday mornings, they walked to Sydney's Paddy's Market in Chinatown. The bargains irresistible, the two of them carted back their hoard in a taxi. A case of iceberg lettuce bought for a shilling, a case of tomatoes for two shillings, oranges, apples, pineapples 'all for a song', Grandma says now. They bought smoked sausages, salamis, hams and pickles from new migrants from Europe, and Margaret begged details on technique and pork. The pair dropped into a specialty pork butcher who supplied many of the Chinese restaurants in the area. He minced pork neck for Margaret and wrapped large sheets of pork fat in butcher's paper for lining terrines.

Grandma says my mother hated being dragged around the markets at the age of five, six, seven, eight.

'The knocks and smells that I found fascinating, that stirred my soul, were a horrid confusion to her.'

But it was this early contact with food that eventually hooked my mother into the same profession. Not only was she by her mother's side (and therefore in bliss), but she was confronted with, and gradually amazed by, the horrid smells, the glorious smoked meats and pillars of fruit and vegetables. She remembers my grandmother collecting a bouquet of globe artichokes, their long stems and prickly leaves, asking the stall owner to wrap them in newspaper so she wouldn't get spiked. Later that day, Grandma produced a whole lamb shoulder, a large thing from a well-developed creature. She rubbed it with spices and squished it into a large pot with a lid, adjusting bones and joints to make it fit. She cooked it in the oven for hours while she preened the artichokes, using a spoon to scoop out the rough chokes, chopping off the spiky ends with a large knife, cutting off the tough stalks. After all the grooming and discarding, the outer leaves in a pile on the side, Margaret sautéed the artichokes in onion, adding a splash of wine to the hot pan so steam enveloped my mother's face as she peered over the bench. It was chemistry and magic, and when they sat down to eat the spice-rubbed, slow-roasted lamb (see recipe on page 188) after a painfully long wait, Suzanne felt proud and included.

Silk stockings make your legs look better, but they also make you feel better, Margaret thought. And so it was in silk stockings and what was technically Christian Dior (designed by Dior, stitched by Margaret) that she went to Melbourne to meet with Kraft Foods as part of her job at *Woman* magazine. And they paid off, the stockings and Dior. After meeting Margaret Fulton, the head honcho at advertising giant J. Walter Thompson hooked her up with a gig.

'There's a girl our organisation could use,' said Deke Coleman.

'It changed my life,' says Margaret.

The job came at an opportune time, my grandma says, 'because I was being sexually harassed, if that's what you call it nowadays, by one of my male bosses at *Woman*.' When I push her on the story, she winces.

'I didn't like it, and nor did the fellow's girlfriend, who also worked there. So I left.'

J. Walter Thompson was the world's top advertising agency in 1955, with the biggest accounts: Kellogg's, Kraft and, for a short time, Coca-Cola. Margaret was made an account executive. Back then this was about as high as you could get without being a director, and there were few women in these lofty positions – it was just Margaret and the men. She labelled her sole account the Money for Jam account, which basically involved pushing Queensland's sugar on the population, inciting a post-war sweet tooth. The Colonial Sugar Refining company (CSR) and the agency came up with a ploy: the more jam people ate, the more sugar they would eat.

Margaret's scones were called on again, and she also came up with recipes for the queen of puddings, an elaborate version of a baked bread custard that involves a creamy base topped with jam and then a layer of meringue. Australians would get their sugar fix. When the school holidays rolled around, and Money for Jam was still Margaret's big account, she invited a friend from the press to attend a cooking demonstration by her sister Jean at David Jones department store, where Jean had a job dolloping jam on homemade biscuits to help out her sister's account. The photographer latched onto a boy eating a warm scone piled up with cream and jam, and someone put a smear of jam on his cheek. The next day, *The Sun* newspaper ran on its cover a full-page picture of the boy and the headline: JAM. The exececs liked this Margaret.

With Money for Jam, Margaret had to make it count. She wrote all the copy, envisaged how the campaign would look with artwork, planned the budget and media buying and general marketing, as well as being the client contact. Negotiating and counselling, squeezing the best work out of the best people, calming them when the client wasn't happy, convincing the client that the pitch would work: Margaret was under constant pressure in the name of the burgeoning flurry of food advertising in Australia.

In 1956, Sydney collectively switched on their televisions to find channel TCN-9, and other stations soon followed. Despite her executive status at

the advertising agency, Margaret appeared on the broadcasts, pouring Rice
Bubbles, Cornflakes, All-Bran and Special K into bowls, cheerily making
chocolate crackles while corn waved in the breeze in the studio window
behind her (cue crew crouching under the windowsill waving greenery).
Take after take she tilted the boxes, showing Australians how crispy their
breakfasts could be. There's a family rumour that Grandma came up with
the 'Snap, crackle, pop' slogan that we came to know and love with our
morning box of routine cereal but, as my father says: 'Never let the truth
get in the way of a good story.' Being 'bright and bouncy' was what the
television was about. Grandma says, 'Not the hardest job in the world.'

In 1960, with ten-year-old Suzanne back in Essex Street – home, finally,
from boarding school – Margaret's days in the high-flying, hard-living,
hard-working ad world came to an end. On one all-nighter, doing an
advertisement for Rice Bubbles, Margaret took a call from her long-time
friend Sally Baker, who said *Woman's Day* was asking for her.

SLOW-ROASTED HARISSA LAMB SHOULDER *with* SAUTÉED ARTICHOKES

See story on page 185

SERVES 4–6
PREPARATION 40 minutes, plus 2 hours marinating
COOKING 3 hours

1 x 1 kg (2 lb 4 oz) boneless lamb shoulder
1 red onion, peeled and cut into wedges
8–10 garlic cloves, smashed
8–10 small globe artichokes
juice of ½ lemon
60 ml (2 fl oz/¼ cup) extra virgin olive oil
2 brown onions, thinly sliced lengthways
125 ml (4 fl oz/½ cup) white wine or verjuice
500 ml (17 fl oz/2 cups) homemade vegetable stock
1 handful mint leaves
seeds from ½ pomegranate

Harissa
1 teaspoon coriander seeds, toasted
1 teaspoon cumin seeds, toasted
4 garlic cloves, coarsely chopped
4 dried ancho chillies, seeded and soaked
3 fresh long red chillies, seeded
1 teaspoon sweet paprika
juice and zest of 1 lemon
1 tablespoon red wine vinegar
2 tablespoons olive oil
½ teaspoon sea salt

For the harissa, grind the seeds in a mortar and pestle. Transfer to the bowl of a small food processor with the garlic, chillies, paprika and lemon zest and process to form a thick paste. Mix in the lemon juice, vinegar, oil and salt, adjusting the quantities to suit your taste. Store in a jar in the fridge for up to 1 week.

Put the lamb, skin-side down, on a work surface, and rub 3–4 tablespoons of the harissa all over the meat, working it in well. Roll up the meat lengthways and tie at intervals with kitchen string. Leave it to stand, covered, at room temperature for 1–2 hours, or refrigerate overnight, for the flavours to develop fully.

Preheat the oven to 160°C (315°F).

Bring the lamb to room temperature, if refrigerated. Put 125 ml (4 fl oz/½ cup) of water in a roasting tin, add the red onion and garlic and place the lamb on top. Cover the dish with foil or a lid and roast for 2–2½ hours, or until the lamb is tender. Remove the foil and roast for a further 30 minutes. Remove from the oven and set aside to rest.

Meanwhile, prepare the artichokes. Peel back the tough outer leaves, trim about 3 cm (1¼ in) from the tops and discard. Trim the stems to 8–10 cm (3¼–4 in) long, then use a vegetable peeler to remove the tough, stringy, outer stem, revealing the tender white part. Halve the artichokes lengthways, then scoop out the choke with a spoon and discard, along with any spiky internal leaves. Put the artichokes in a bowl of water and squeeze in the lemon juice. Set aside.

Heat the oil in a large frying pan over medium–low heat, add the brown onion and sauté until tender. Add the drained artichokes and wine, simmer for a few minutes to burn off the alcohol, then add the stock. Cover with a round of baking paper to fit inside the frying pan, pressing it down a little to let the artichokes steam slightly. Reduce heat to low and sauté for 15–20 minutes, or until the artichoke hearts are tender when pierced with a knife.

Serve the lamb on a platter with artichokes, and scatter with mint leaves and pomegranate seeds.

THE KNIFE IS MIGHTIER THAN THE PEN

No industry is more deserving of the 'blood, sweat and tears' tag than the professional kitchen. Probably fitting too are the ones about 'burn, baby, burn' and 'my life as a dog', and something like 'fifty shades of black and blue'. That last one is all about secret desires, long sweaty nights, sadism and bodily fluids in the professional kitchen.

Eating constantly, jotting down notes, calling up chefs, analysing food on plates, became my expertise. And as a food writer and specifically a food reviewer for Fairfax mainly, I saw first hand what chefs do, how hard it is. I loved being on this side of the kitchen – knowing what it takes to get that dish in front of diners, knowing what made it good, or bad, but not actually being in the buzz, rush, exhaustion of the professional kitchen myself. My new job: eat, speak to chefs, farmers and producers, and write. I loved it.

Through all their different styles and passions, hopes, disappointments and failures, chefs and cooks all agree on one thing. Whether you're Ferran Adrià in Spain, perfecting texture, making potato air or liquid-centred olives, or some guy deep-frying waffles at a carnival, it's bloody hard work.

If you want to be a chef, you need to be prepared to bleed, burn and perform surgery on a pigeon's carcass, fifty pigeons' carcasses, inside an hour. You need to be fine with spending three hours with a potato peeler in your hand, or being beaten up by thistles and spikes as you pare back two hundred baby artichokes, hands blackened and sore. You need to be okay about doing that every day and on Saturday nights, while your friends are out drinking shots, for five years. You need to say 'yes' to every gruelling piece of prep work available, and be grateful for the chance to do it. You'll be running up and down stairs in excruciating heat, making hundreds of deep knee-bends a day to reach inside waist-high refrigerators, carrying boxes loaded with ingredients and stretching under a heat lamp to fine-tune a pigeon's pirouette on a plate.

Roads to success as a professional chef are paved with tears, fierce competition, egos and verbal abuse. Night after night you slice onions, cut celery and carrots into brunoise, perfect your batonnet – a 'little stick' knife-cut, which is a little (but not a whole lot) larger than a matchstick, smaller than a baton. Get it wrong and you have to start all over again. Then, every shift, when you're exhausted and shaking, your stomach aching and your feet swollen, you have to clean. Someone else is there to do the dishes, sure, but it's those beleaguered individuals in the kitchen who have to scrub the floors, the benches, the inside burnt-salmon-scented, grimy bits under the stove.

The writer and television host Anthony Bourdain once told me and ten or so others over dinner in Sydney that cooking is much harder than writing. He has no commiserations for the writer who sits in the comfort of their own home, tapping on a computer and complaining of the painstaking hardship of putting words on the page.

'Maybe you're just a better writer than you are a cook,' I said to him afterwards, half joking, which is about the meanest thing you can say to a person who used to be a chef.

For a man who used to work in the kitchens of Les Halles, who admires his chef compatriots' skills and who had dedicated his career to the work of the world's top cooks, this might have pricked just a little. It may be true but, still, it was mean. He gave me a kind of surprised eyebrow–raise.

'Ha. Yeah, maybe.'

And then he offered to sign my book anyway, drawing the end of his name up my forearm with a black Texta like a big flirt. It was my favourite, no, my only fan experience. I'd say 'celebrity experience', but I've had thousands of those. This was the only time I was a fan in the celebrity scenario. And I reacted to the pressure of it by being mean. Better than being a screaming girl about it, perhaps.

Actually, I agree with him. Cooking is much harder than writing. People who don't do both, or can't do either, imagine they're completely different processes, one physical and the other intellectual. This is not true. Yes, cooking is physical, but it's also intellectually gruelling. Like writing, cooking makes heavy demands on technical skills. It requires the ability to unfailingly call on years of experience and practice, to repeat yet again the licorice crumb or the almond fondant. Plus, while a writer has full access to the delete button, for the cook 'delete' means starting over, and that costs money. Overcook the lamb or char the pine nuts, because you were too busy nestling the chervil sprig into the perfect curl of linguini, and someone has to pay for that – which means you have to pay for that. Maybe not financially, but definitely in some way.

Good chefs also expand their repertoire, calling on their tranche of skills to create new dishes, and that requires the ability to intelligently weigh up which processes work together, which flavour profiles will turn into culinary epiphanies. They're not just throwing ingredients together, and the good ones are not just copying each other. Sure, they borrow. They travel, they explore, they decipher ingredients on a plate across the globe, and then they transform and experiment, overhaul and redo in their own kitchens. That's not a physical job; that's a creative and intellectual one. For every gruelling late night or early morning spent pushing blanched parsley through a sieve or reducing a vat of stock, there is the added pressure of being ahead of your game creatively. Being a little bit quicker and a little bit cleverer than your competitor is the make-or-break for many chefs.

They thrive under the weight of the reviewers, the hats, the diners, each other, Australian chef Matt Moran once told me in an interview. 'Chefs feel the pressure in the kitchen their whole lives. A chef who has worked in that high-pressured environment can handle anything. That's our life. We love the adrenaline rush. We love the competitiveness.'

Chefs need to see into the future, too. And that can put a strain on the bonce. When the orders come through to the kitchen, all at 7.43 pm, chefs have to time the wagyu to come out at exactly the same time as the blue-eye trevalla, or else risk your – the diner's – vitriol on some online review site. And they're doing that with thirty tables. They have to time your last mouthful of tongue pastrami with yuzu mayonnaise and know the cured bonito should be plated ready and the black sausage gently warmed through for when the entrees drop on table four. Can you even conceive of cooking twenty-three identical plates of trevalla in one night, each to come out at precisely the same time as another one, two, six dishes, depending on the table, one after the other, after the next, for fourteen hours straight, for forty-seven covers? Each of the pieces of fish immaculately cooked, seasoned, and presented on a plate without a smudged thumbprint? And even more pressure if you have a chef's hat (or Michelin Star, depending where in the world you are), because to lose one of those is death. Can you imagine the pressure? The very idea of it makes me panicky. Or maybe I'm just a better writer than I am a cook.

WOMAN'S DAY

Mrs Bull held one of Margaret's old sheets between her fingers, tugged at a single thread running through the centre, and then ripped it in half. She got to work on the fabric with scissors, cutting it in to long strips. My mother sat on the floor, running the ribbons along the floor as though teasing a cat. Then, with swift fingers, Mrs Bull twisted my mother's long and thick damp blonde hair into knots around the fabric.

'There you are, darling. Tomorrow you'll be Shirley Temple.'

The mother of Maureen Simpson, formerly Maureen Bull, the dimpled-elbow envier at *Woman* magazine, now spent the odd afternoon minding Suzanne while Margaret was at work or away, becoming a kind of surrogate mother. And Denis was there too. Margaret's father disapproved of this awkward union, definitely not man and wife.

'Why doesn't he go to his own home and look after his mother, while I look after Margaret,' Alexander asked Jean, I'm told.

When my mother returned from boarding school to Essex Street to live full-time with her mother and her grandfather, Margaret decided it was inappropriate to have Denis living there too. Denis worked to win Alexander over, taking him to his local pub, the Newcastle, introducing him to his friends and lining up double rums with schooner chasers at the bar, a testosterone-fuelled wager of who was the man. Alexander, the sturdy rounded Scot, easily stood his ground.

Alexander spent days walking down to Circular Quay to watch the overseas liners embark and disembark. He treated himself to a dozen oysters at the Sorrento fish café at the Quay or smoked kippers at the nearest McIlrath's, an old-fashioned grocer. He took them home, wrapped in paper, and poached and then grilled them. When Margaret came home after work, Alexander fell on the family with stories of his day. Every day, through summer and winter, he walked to the Domain Baths, now the Andrew (Boy) Charlton swimming pool, to take his daily dose of salt water. This kept him fit, Grandma says now, 'as well as his steady diet of whisky and oatmeal porridge'.

Although her life was unconventional at the time, being improper was not something Margaret craved. Even though she wore trousers to pick up my mother from school, not like all the other smart mothers who wore nice skirts, Mum thought. And even though she'd worn blue at her wedding and sought a career led by men, she didn't set out to be shocking. So, she finally divorced Trevor and married Denis. That is about as romantic as the story gets at my place.

My mother wanted to be part of it. A rose by any other name would smell as sweet, but she nevertheless wanted to change her name from her father Trevor's last name, Price, to Denis' name, Doonan. She's since told me that she wished now she had taken Fulton. Margaret never changed her name, and it was my grandmother she really wanted to be closer to. Meanwhile, Margaret worked.

Elizabeth Taylor and Richard Burton were in Rome making love, news and the epic film *Cleopatra* (which Elizabeth Taylor herself described as 'surely the most bizarre piece of entertainment ever perpetuated'), and so Margaret jumped at the idea to do a *Cleopatra* cookbook, a pull-out in the *Woman's Day*. She went into research mode, coming up with recipes for Persian chicken, where the bird is cooked in orange juice and served with white rice and orange saffron rice, garnished with candied orange rind and vegetable date kebabs. It was a daring thing for a magazine to do that time, even for a *Cleopatra* issue.

More in line with current thinking was an issue that showed a full-bleed photograph of thirty lamingtons on the cover, with the irresistible headline 'Margaret Fulton gives recipes for fetes' and 'How to run a lamington drive'. Margaret presented the Persian chicken on her mother's ornate Scottish silver fruit stand and thought that if nobody made the dish, at least they could admire the beautiful pictures (see the original *The Margaret Fulton Cookbook* for a peek). How wrong she was. *Woman's Day* readers were ecstatic, and Persian rice chicken became a dinner-party craze.

Writing her own recipes and having the space to do it gave her the chance to call on dishes her own mother had made for her. Isabella made kedgeree for her children, using a Scotch haddock. Years later, Margaret cooked the dish using fresh Tasmanian salmon. In the 1980s, it cropped up in another magazine with her by-line, this time with canned red salmon. But in its original form, the smoked fish would be poached in milk or water, then flaked and tossed through just-cooked basmati rice. It features a couple of hard-boiled eggs and cayenne pepper. I have since reinvented the wheel, yet again, using soft-boiled eggs and garam masala, a knob of grated ginger and, as well as the smoked fish of my great-grandmother, I include my own grandmother's home version, with fresh salmon, as well as turmeric, coriander and finely chopped parsley. I love it packed with different ingredients and textures, and serve it in the middle of the table for everyone to help themselves (see recipe on page 199). Canned salmon doesn't make an appearance.

Australian women wanted to know how to use mince meat, that thrifty option of ground-up, less popular cuts, and so Margaret turned out another book as part of *Woman's Day – 101 Ways with Mincemeat*.

'I knew about dolmas, koftas and meatballs as they made them in Sweden and Denmark, Italy, Greece, India, Morocco and Indonesia,' she recalls. 'We also included smoked Chinese meatballs and Königsberger klopse, meatballs in lemon caper sauce.'

An 'Australian dish' also appeared in this book, the oddly named porcupines, which were meatballs with rice, cooked in tomato soup; the rice swells up to little porcupine quills out of the rounded meatball. It seems to me a good opportunity was missed to name them after the Australian native animal the echidna, but children loved them anyway.

Readers wrote in asking for recipes too. Chicken with apricot sauce, that dish that won't die and for which Margaret never actually wrote the recipe, cropped up every now and then. The best request came years later, in the form of a fax.

'Dear Margaret, Greetings from Davis Station Antarctica…'

The writers were twenty-five men holed up, wintering at the station. They had arrived in December and so had seen in a white Christmas and a white New Year, and their on-crew chef Selwyn Saunders, from Bunbury in Western Australia, cooked for the shivering team.

'Selwyn is an excellent chef who takes a great deal of pride in his presentations,' the fax continued. 'As you can imagine, there are some foods that are unavailable, that we miss, which is the reason for this letter. We're missing crumpets! What we wouldn't do for a nice hot crumpet, dripping with butter and honey! Selwyn assures me that there is a recipe for crumpets. Could you feel for the sanity of 25 expeditioners and locate a delicious recipe? We're sorry we don't get the magazine delivered, but what newsagent would come down here! Yours, Shayne Phelps, 1993 Plant Inspector, Davis Station Antarctica.'

Margaret faxed back the recipe for crumpets (see recipe on page 200).

The food team at the magazine visited readers' kitchens, and readers visited the magazine's kitchens. Once, a Chinese woman flew from Hong

Kong to Sydney to learn how to make the truly Australian sponge sandwich from Margaret Fulton herself. Another time, Margaret met another Hong Kong local at the airport, cooking queen of the city, Rebecca Hsu Hui Min, the daughter of wealthy and powerful merchants in Peking who fled to Hong Kong after the communists came to power in China.

I press Grandma for more information on Rebecca, who visited Australia years later and who moved in with Margaret in her house in Balmain. Many years after that, she was killed in a restaurant fire. Rebecca wrote cookbooks on Cantonese food and arranged for young Chinese boys to move to Hong Kong to train as cooks. When she travelled, she travelled like royalty. Stymied by Australian Customs, Rebecca waited for the *Woman's Day* crew to rescue her, to help her bring in the hoard of knives, choppers and woks, cases of clothes, shoes, jewellery and wigs she carted with her.

Rebecca taught Margaret how to cook Chinese food. When Margaret visited her in Hong Kong, she was shown 'the rich life of the rich Oriental'. A boyfriend gave Rebecca a gold-plated piano and she sang along to it – in a funny squeaky voice, Margaret thought. Rebecca brought her own recipes into the magazine, including a chicken salad with spicy sesame dressing. This became one of my favourite meals when growing up, and I'd beg Mum for 'Rebecca's chicken'. I have tweaked the recipe over the years (see recipe on page 202).

Flying first class to Spain with a group of olive oil producers, Margaret began to see some truth in the Sydney journalists' mantra: 'Join *Woman's Day* and see the world.' Escorted from five-star hotels to bull fights, which she dreaded and loathed, then through olive groves all over Spain to coastal villages where saffron is grown, she learned that travel makes the cook. At one coastal village she was so excited about the price of the saffron that she began to stock up on the orange-coloured stigmas. There are only three stigmas inside each saffron crocus flower, and it takes about half a million of these filaments to make one kilogram of saffron. Margaret bought up big; from individual stallholders and little shops, from people selling their wares by the side of the road. She couldn't resist the price. As they left the village, her guide turned to her.

'You have bought the saffron supply for an entire year for the people of this village.'

Margaret was horrified by her greed, and the idea that these people would have to eat saffron-free paella for the next twelve months.

Margaret during a cooking demonstration, 1965

SPICED KEDGEREE

See story on page 195

SERVES 4–6
PREPARATION 20 minutes
COOKING 40 minutes

200 g (7 oz) smoked haddock
 or smoked mackerel
200 g (7 oz/1 cup) basmati rice
4 free-range eggs,
 at room temperature
300 g (10½ oz) salmon fillet,
 skinned, bones removed
sea salt and freshly ground
 black pepper
2 tablespoons rice bran oil
50 g (1¾ oz) butter
2 brown onions,
 finely chopped
3 garlic cloves, finely chopped
1½ teaspoons curry powder
 or garam masala
1 x 3 cm (1¼ in) piece fresh
 ginger, peeled and
 finely grated
1 fresh long red chilli, finely
 sliced (seeds removed, if you
 want to reduce the heat)
90 g (3¼ oz/1 bunch) coriander
 (cilantro), leaves picked,
 stalks finely chopped
2–3 lemons
1 teaspoon ground turmeric
100 g (3½ oz/1 small bunch)
 flat-leaf (Italian) parsley,
 leaves and half the stalks
 finely chopped

Put the smoked haddock or mackerel in a shallow pan with enough water to cover. Bring to the boil, then reduce the heat, cover and simmer for about 5 minutes, or until cooked through. Remove from the pan and leave until cool enough to handle. Remove the skin from the fish, flake into chunks and set aside.

Boil the rice in water according to the directions on the packet, then drain, rinse under cold water and set aside.

Meanwhile, in a medium saucepan, cover the eggs with cold water, bring to a simmer and cook for 6 minutes, then drain and put in a bowl of iced water until cool. Peel the eggs and break gently into large pieces with your hands. Set aside.

To cook the salmon, heat a small frying pan over medium heat. Season the fish with salt and pepper, then drizzle over half the oil to coat. Pan-fry the fish for 2 minutes, or until golden brown, then turn over and cook for a further 1–2 minutes, until just cooked but still pink in the middle. Set aside on a board to rest.

Heat a large frying pan over medium heat, add the butter and remaining oil and cook the onions for 10 minutes or until soft. Add the garlic, curry powder, ginger and chilli and reduce the heat to medium–low. Add the coriander stalks and sauté gently until tender.

Add the cooked rice to the pan and fold together. Reduce the heat to low, squeeze over the juice of 1 lemon, then fold in the turmeric and flaked smoked fish. Carefully fold in half the eggs, half the coriander leaves and half the parsley. Scatter over the remaining eggs. Add more lemon juice and pepper, if liked, then cover and cook gently for about 5 minutes, or until warmed through.

To serve, divide the rice mixture between plates or shallow bowls. Break the salmon into 3–4 cm (1¼–1½ in) pieces over the rice and scatter over the remaining coriander and parsley. Cut the remaining lemon into wedges or cheeks and serve in a small dish.

tip

You can find smoked haddock, the traditional kedgeree ingredient, in good delicatessens or fishmongers. But a hot-smoked trout is an accessible option too; buy it whole and then skin and debone it, a task that's easier than it sounds. Be careful not to salt the dish until after you've added the smoked fish, which can be very salty.

CRUMPETS

See story on page 195

MAKES 10
PREPARATION 10 minutes,
plus 1 hour rising
COOKING 20 minutes

2 x 7 g (¼ oz) sachets
    dried yeast
875 ml (30 fl oz/3½ cups) milk,
    warmed to about 36°C
    (97°F), plus extra, if needed
450 g (1 lb/3 cups) plain
    (all-purpose) flour
½ teaspoon sea salt
1 tablespoon caster
    (superfine) sugar
butter, for greasing, plus extra,
    to serve
honey, to serve

Dissolve the yeast in 60 ml (2 fl oz/¼ cup) of the warm milk in a small bowl.

Mix together the flour, salt and sugar in a large bowl. Make a well in the dry ingredients and pour in the yeast mixture with the rest of the milk. Mix with a wooden spoon, starting in the middle and gradually drawing in the remaining flour as you mix, to form a batter. Add a little more warm milk, if needed. Set aside in a warm place for 45–60 minutes, or until a little frothy.

Heat a large frying pan over medium–high heat. Add a tiny knob of butter to grease the pan, and place two or three heavily greased metal egg or crumpet rings, about 10 cm (4 in) diameter and 2 cm (¾ in) deep, in the pan, allowing them to heat up.

Pour in about 125 ml (4 fl oz/½ cup) of batter, or enough to fill each ring. Cook for 3–4 minutes, or until bubbles form on the surface and the batter begins to set, then carefully turn the rings over with a spatula and cook for 2 minutes. Alternatively, place them under a hot grill (broiler) to cook the top.

Keep the cooked crumpets warm in a low oven while you cook the remaining batter.

Serve with butter and honey.

CHICKEN SALAD *with* SPICY SESAME DRESSING

See story on page 196

SERVES 4, as a light lunch
PREPARATION 20 minutes
COOKING 25 minutes

125 ml (4 fl oz/½ cup)
  shaoxing rice wine
2 garlic cloves, thinly sliced
1 x 6 cm (2½ in) piece fresh
  ginger, peeled and
  thickly sliced
150 g (5½ oz/½ bunch) spring
  onions (scallions), green part
  trimmed and reserved, white
  part finely sliced diagonally
400 g (14 oz) free-range,
  organic chicken breast
¼ Chinese cabbage (wong
  bok), finely shredded
2 Lebanese (short) cucumbers,
  halved lengthways, thinly
  sliced diagonally
1 handful (½ cup) coriander
  (cilantro) leaves
1 tablespoon toasted black
  sesame seeds

Spicy sesame dressing
1 teaspoon chilli flakes
1 x 2–3 cm (¾–1¼ in) piece
  fresh ginger, peeled and
  finely grated
1 garlic clove, finely chopped
3 tablespoons tamari
1 tablespoon brown rice
  vinegar (or black vinegar)
1 tablespoon sesame paste
½ teaspoon sesame oil
juice of ½ lemon

Combine the shaoxing wine, garlic, ginger and the green ends of the spring onions in a medium saucepan with 750 ml (26 fl oz/3 cups) of water and bring to the boil over medium–high heat. Add the chicken and simmer for 2 minutes, then remove the pan from the heat and let the chicken stand in the liquid for 20 minutes.

Meanwhile, for the spicy sesame dressing, grind the chilli flakes in a mortar and pestle, then whisk together with the remaining ingredients, using a fork. Set aside.

Using your fingers, pull the chicken into bite-sized pieces, and put in a bowl with the sliced spring onion, cabbage, cucumber and half the coriander. Add the dressing, toss to combine and transfer to a serving plate or bowl.

Sprinkle the remaining coriander and sesame seeds over the top to serve.

tip

Sesame paste can be found at Asian grocers. Alternatively, you can use tahini.

202

A VERSION OF PERFECT

I'm slotting pork belly into a recipe, or building a recipe around pork belly, not just because I've been eating the delicious cut for three days straight in various guises – slow-cooked in a Chinese master stock, brined and roasted, and smoked and cured in a kind of maple salt glaze – but because it's on trend. The people want it. And what the people want…

Somehow, the planets aligned, or the hard work paid off, and I was handed my own recipe page in a prestigious Sydney weekend pull-out. I took it seriously. I scanned every recipe book I had, and then ransacked my mother's veritable library of cookbooks, flicking through them and red-flagging inspiration when I found it. When I ate out I made notes in a little book, scribbling about presentation and flavour combinations, the thin lengthways mandolin cut of raw Brussels sprouts, whether hazelnuts really worked in that dish.

Pork belly was appearing on tables everywhere, and so I cooked three or four interpretations of the perfect roast, working on crackling and cooking times, using David Chang's brine and Kylie Kwong's marinade, but with ginger and no star anise, then tweaking the sesame oil and using no pre-brining. Cooking longer, basting more frequently, pairing it with a shredded Chinese cabbage salad and then with my homemade kimchi. I did it sliced and pan-seared and tucked into tacos, a squirt of Japanese mayonnaise the final flourish. Bingley and I had pork belly three days a week for two weeks as I tested and made perfect.

He arrived at my place and peered in the oven.

'Pork belly? Are you kidding? I mean yum, but seriously, again?'

He wrapped his arms around me, kissed my forehead and face and neck.

'God, I have it tough.'

Part of the job of a recipe columnist or food editor in a magazine is being acutely aware of which dishes are popular right now, or which recipes will be swiftly turned out in kitchens everywhere and embraced as the next big thing, or at least the next dinner.

We follow trends and chefs, picking up on new techniques and ingredients in favour. And magazines, with all their lusty imagery and inspiration, are doing everything they can to provide just the right recipes this month, so you will invest your money in the magazine next month, too. For the cook who wants to stay ahead of the Joneses next door, this is definitely money well spent. For what price inspiration?

Magazines and newspapers, with their prolific turnover and that whole today's-news-yesterday's-fish-and-chips-wrapper thing, can stay in tune with what's cooking, literally, much more easily. The production time of a cookbook makes it much harder to hit the nail on the head. By March, the manuscript is filed so you have a stocking-filler for December, and that lead time means the author has to predict what you're going to want to cook a year later, or at least be so inspiring that you're not going to resist.

There's no more poignant reminder of what we used to eat – and what is definitely out of favour – than an ancient cookbook. Flick through pages of trout in aspic and jellied eels and remember just how fickle we are. From meat in cans to cheese fondue, pineapple-glazed ham and apricot chicken: as the years pass, trends take with them gastronomic hostages. Sometimes, we get them back, clinging on to sticky date pudding, for example, and sometimes we just let them go, move on to better things.

If we took stock of our endangered culinary species and remembered those iconic foods you just don't see anymore, we might be more selective about what we choose to eat. How many of us shed a tear over chicken and mushroom vol-au-vents? Steak and kidney pudding, an upturned pudding bowl of lard-heavy dough, filled with rich lumps of gravy-laden meat, came and went. Nobody does tropical flummery any more.

And boula, of course, was tossed to the kerb. My grandmother writes in one of her original cookbooks about this soup, made from canned turtle soup, cream, brandy and curry powder. She never tried it on me, but for readers in the late 1960s, the ghastly concoction was recommended as a 'favourite from other lands'. Some dishes are as famous as they are fantastical. So, one day's turtle soup could be tomorrow's macaron.

Who are the gatekeepers of this culinary wasteland? Who lets seafood fettuccini salad and oyster chiffonade wander in, tails between their legs? Why is gazpacho retained as the happy ritual of our summer favour, while vichyssoise rarely gets a look in? It can't be about deliciousness, or otherwise we'd finally move on from cupcakes.

We often see nouvelle touches on old recipes, pleasing renditions of classics with tweaks for modern tastes. Jamie Oliver won't let stuffed mushrooms die, but at least he does them with ricotta and golden parmesan topping. A gastronomic preservationist, he single-handedly keeps pasta bakes, kedgeree and shepherd's pie in vogue. Otherwise, these comforting culinary rocks might have been lost with the handwritten cookbooks of our grandmothers, missed and longed for by nostalgic stodge-hunters.

Sometimes, dishes hang around simply because they're so good. For every forgotten pot of jellied eel, a firm savoury wobble of bony fishy bits, there's something that stands the test of erratic tastes and bloggers' fevers. Or we look through those old cookbooks and decide a dish deserves a comeback. The lemon delicious captured our pudding-loving hearts and still we make that self-saucing citrus-iness. The recipe appears in my grandmother's first cookbook, *The Margaret Fulton Cookbook*, on a page with four other desserts. The lemon meringue pie, like the lemon delicious, remains in our favour, of course, that pastry base filled with lemon cream, involving egg yolks, lemons, sugar and plain flour, and then topped with light meringue and baked.

But who, since that book was first published in 1968, has made the eggnog tart? I imagine women tackling it at home when the book first came out, filling the pastry base with the gelatine-thickened custard, chilling it until set, and then topping the tart with whipped cream and grated nutmeg. And how many of us remember the canary pudding, a plain steamed pudding of creamed butter (or margarine), milk, a little lemon, eggs and sugar, which is served on a platter with 'warmed jam' spooned over. It's served hot, with custard. I've done the chocolate version she offers in the book as a variation, without the jam, and it's a perfect, light and puddingish pudding, perfect for 'wintry days', as she says. The final dessert, a sultana pudding, is another steamed, incredibly sweet concoction, but in 1968, when our teeth loved sugar, it probably went down a treat at dinner parties. However, it's lemon delicious and lemon meringue pie that we coo over when they appear on dinner tables still.

The pork belly, finally, was done. It was perfect. To me, anyway – taking into account what readers would reasonably be willing to tackle on a Sunday. It was a version of perfect. So many pork bellies were eaten in the making of this column (see recipe on page 208).

A note on pork: I ask my butcher to deal with nipples. Sorry to bring this up. It's embarrassing to ask and just as horrifying to notice, but it's better than having to snip them off with scissors yourself. Don't let that turn you off, either. It's an animal, and if you forget that, you don't deserve to be eating it at all. The butcher is your gastronomic friend, the person who will deliver you from those supermarkets that don't tell you how the creature was raised, what it ate and, therefore, what you're really eating. Chefs will baulk at this cutting-off-the-nipples business. Just eat the bloody nipples, I hear them murmur in my nightmares of insecurity. But I can't. There are two things in this world I will not eat. One of them is caraway seeds, which send shivers over my body just thinking about them. If I bite into one I will be turned off food for the day. And I don't eat nipples. While you're there, at the butcher, ask him (usually, him) to get his Stanley knife to the skin and score it across in 1 cm slices, so you don't have to plunder the toolshed when you get home. A knife, this time, won't cut it.

I turned up to the photographer's house with my scored and marinated pork belly, the kimchi I'd had slowly agitating and turning, rich and stinky but still fresh, for two weeks, marvelling at its fermenting perfection on my bench top. While the pig cooked in this foreign kitchen, I turned to another well-rehearsed recipe, and dolloped orange-spiked ricotta batter into almost-smoking oil, watched as my tilt on the donut turned golden. These perfect, aromatic donuts were tumbled onto a plate, and the photographer and I lifted chocolate sauce from the spoon onto the table to 'mess it up'. The belly still cooking, we sat outside and dipped a donut each into the chocolate. Steam burst from the sides and the slightly liquid centres oozed into our mouths, our lips sugary (see recipe on page 211).

'Oh my God,' she said, smiling. 'We have it tough.'

ROAST PORK BOSSAM
with KIMCHI

See story on page 206

SERVES 4–6
PREPARATION 40 minutes,
plus marinating overnight
COOKING 1 hour 20 minutes,
plus 20 minutes resting
Start the kimchi at least
2 days ahead

1 x 1.5 kg (3 lb 5 oz) piece
    free-range pork belly
2 garlic cloves, chopped
3 tablespoons soft
    brown sugar
80 ml (2½ fl oz/⅓ cup)
    soy sauce
1 teaspoon freshly ground
    white pepper
2 teaspoons sea salt flakes
2 tablespoons toasted
    sesame seeds
12 baby cos (romaine) lettuce
    leaves, to serve

Kimchi

1 small Chinese cabbage
    (wong bok), outer
    leaves discarded
1½ tablespoons sea salt flakes
110 g (3¾ oz/½ cup) sugar,
    plus 2 tablespoons extra
2 garlic cloves, finely chopped
1 x 2 cm (¾ in) piece fresh
    ginger, peeled and
    finely chopped
1 tablespoon dried chilli flakes
80 ml (2½ fl oz/⅓ cup) light
    soy sauce
60 ml (2 fl oz/¼ cup) good-
    quality fish sauce
2 red Asian shallots, finely sliced
1 large carrot, cut into julienne

For the kimchi, cut the cabbage lengthways into four pieces, then into 2.5 cm (1 in) wide pieces. In a large bowl, combine the cabbage, salt and sugar and toss together well. Let stand in the fridge overnight.

In a large bowl, combine the garlic, ginger, chilli, soy sauce, fish sauce and 2 tablespoons sugar. Add the shallots and carrot and mix well. Drain the cabbage and add it to the bowl, then toss well to combine.

Pack the kimchi into an 800 ml (28 fl oz) jar that seals with a lid. Refrigerate for at least 2 days to enhance the flavours. Kimchi will be at its best at 2 weeks.

Score the pork skin in lines 1 cm (½ in) apart crossways, or ask your butcher to do this for you.

In a glass or ceramic dish that will fit the pork, combine the garlic, brown sugar, soy and pepper. Put the pork in the marinade, being careful to keep the skin clean and dry. Cover with plastic wrap and marinate in the fridge for at least 3 hours, or overnight.

Bring the pork to room temperature and pat the skin dry with paper towel.

Preheat the oven to 220°C (425°F). Transfer the pork to a roasting tin (discarding the marinade), sprinkle the skin with the salt flakes and roast for 30 minutes or until the skin starts to blister. Reduce the oven temperature to 180°C (350°F) and roast for a further 30 minutes.

Turn the oven grill (broiler) to high and cook the pork for a further 20 minutes, or until the skin is crackled and blistered. Watch to make sure it doesn't burn.

Let the meat rest for 20 minutes, then carve along the score lines. Arrange the meat on a serving platter and sprinkle with toasted sesame seeds. Serve the kimchi alongside, accompanied by lettuce leaves to wrap the meat and kimchi in.

ORANGE AND RICOTTA DONUTS *with* CHOCOLATE SAUCE

See story on page 207

MAKES 12
PREPARATION 15 minutes
plus 1 hour chilling
COOKING 20 minutes

300 g (10½ oz) ricotta
   cheese, drained
55 g (2 oz/¼ cup) caster
   (superfine) sugar
1 tablespoon grated
   orange zest
2 tablespoons fresh
   orange juice
grated zest of 1 lemon
1 free-range egg and
   1 free-range egg yolk,
   lightly whisked
75 g (2¾ oz/½ cup) plain
   (all-purpose) flour
2 tablespoons
   cornflour (cornstarch)
1½ teaspoons baking powder
up to 2 litres (70 fl oz/8 cups)
   rice bran oil
icing (confectioners') sugar,
   for dusting
hot Chocolate Sauce
   (see page 26), to serve

Combine the ricotta, sugar, orange zest, orange juice, lemon zest, egg and egg yolk in a bowl. Sift in the flour, cornflour and baking powder and stir to combine, but don't overwork. Cover and refrigerate for 1 hour.

Pour the oil into a small heavy-based saucepan to a depth of about 6 cm (2½ in) and heat to 180°C (350°F). To test the temperature of the oil, sprinkle in some flour. If it sizzles, it is ready. Use two dessertspoons to shape the mixture into quenelles or balls, and deep-fry in batches of two or three for about 2 minutes, or until golden. Drain on paper towel and dust with icing sugar.

Serve warm, dusted with icing sugar and drizzled with hot chocolate sauce.

tip

You can reuse the oil once. Just wait until it's completely cool and then transfer to a clean bottle.

FOOD DUDE

A certain breed of food enthusiast is taking over our kitchens and our dinner talk. He's getting worked up about konro barbecues and cuts of porchetta that can only be sourced on the other side of town. He is the food dude, an excited foodist ordering heirloom seeds online, culturing his own butter, while his sous vide machine takes up half the bench. And I went and fell head and feet first, all in, completely in love with one of them.

Two suitcases sit propped open on a hotel bed and Bingley and I are packing again, after only just unpacking. A couple of weeks before, we'd left Sydney with suitcases neatly sorted, various shoes in cloth bags, and t-shirts and a faded denim shirt or two folded properly so the buttons face upwards, but now everything is a tumbled mess of underwear and t-shirts I never wore and there's only one sneaker in my bag. I'm sacrificing the shoe for another chance to fit in a few plates of dumplings at the cheapest Michelin Star restaurant in the world. Bingley lifts up the corner of the king-sized bed so I can peer underneath for the shoe.

'Forget it, it's not worth a couple of those dumplings.'

We had a few hours to get to the airport and I didn't want to spend it looking for a shoe.

'I love your priorities,' he says.

He's wearing a white towel around his waist and he turns to lean against the ceiling-to-floor windows looking out to Hong Kong, to the massive skyline. He checks out the sprawling city, propped on the harbour like a futuristic utopia that grew rough around the edges, muddied up by pollution and waning grey architecture. I'm sitting on the bed, and turn around to check out his arms, hands propped on his waist, and his back; the magic formed by a lifetime of surfing.

'I love this view,' I say.

He turns around, does that massive smile that knocked me out in my car nearly a year before, and approaches the bed.

'Forget the dumplings.'

'I love *your* priorities,' I say, grabbing my jacket. 'Meet you in the lobby.'

We had lined up at the hole-in-the-wall eatery a few days before. This place has the grubbiest entrance, the longest queue, the most American tourists, the smallest breathing space, the steamiest kitchen, the swiftest delivery of buns and dumplings, no question, the flakiest slightly sweet and crumbly barbecue pork buns, for two unsuspecting tourists – an Aussie and a Brit – who thought they knew what a pork bun was until they turned up here and became so obsessed with the things that it basically overturned their entire Spain–Norway–England–Ireland–Hong Kong whirlwind of a trip into That–Trip–with–the–Buns.

After the pork buns come dumplings and, years later, I learned how to replicate these morsels from a dumpling expert. A high-protein flour is mixed with regular flour and kneaded with hot water to develop a tacky consistency, like a wet pasta dough but sticky. They roll a ball the size of a small walnut, place it on a board and thwack it with the flat of a cleaver, or 'chopper', and then drag it along a bit to form a perfect circular thin disc. They drop a spoonful of prawn and vibrant green snow peas into the middle, and fold it over to form a dimpled crescent moon.

Everything is made fresh, here in our hole-in-the-wall, cooked to order. So when the waiter takes our little filled-out form with ticked boxes into the kitchen, it's then and only then that the whacking, dolloping and inevitable steaming in those bamboo steamers happens. Then we eat them. The full process, from shaping to down-the-trap, is about nine-and-a-half minutes. That is what they should mean when they say fresh dumplings, because everything else, once you've had this, is fraud. The waiter brings over those little lard-pastry custard tarts I'd grown up with, but the custard more wobbly, less sweet, the pastry more crumbly, a kind of dissolving-crust situation. They almost fold in half under the pressure of being lifted and you have to put the lot in your mouth, silken and crumbly. It's like biscuits dipped in hot English breakfast tea; quickly into the mouth it must go before the lot disintegrates into a messy disaster, and quickly it disappears down the throat. It's exhilarating fun, like a game of cat and mouse but with custard and biscuits (see recipe on page 217).

Travel with Bingley: it had definitely turned into one of those pleasantly intoxicated dreams of following our stomachs through the air-conditioned mega malls and the stench of tiny back streets, past women squatting by the pavement selling a pile of what appear to be rags, to find the place with the crabs with the chicken oil (the spider crabs are cracked into large fragments and in a puddle of pink French-buttery sauce are dots of oil, tasting like the crispy skin of a roast chicken). We go in search of mind-blowing food. We'd followed my impeccable food-oriented research to a Japanese ramen place, then we kind of threw away a few hours, lying in a central park that has flamingos, reading magazines and blocking out the sun in ours eyes with a book. There, lying on the luminous green grass of Hong Kong's most watered gardens, I caught myself thinking: 'I could stay with this person. I'd like to commit to this person and not wonder how good it might be with somebody else every time a beautiful, funny Brit walks into my life. I think I'd actually *like* to do that. And maybe, no matter how many things overturn and destroy me, no matter the hurdles and glorious head-spinning successes, I'd like this person to be beside me. I don't *need* him to be, because I can handle it and love it by myself as well, but I think I would *like* it if he were.'

We head back to the hotel to pick up our bags, the final walk; not hand in hand so much, because Hong Kong has a way of drawing your other half into the crowd, which slips between you with the sweaty rush of a city always on their phones, or looking at the screen and never where they're going. We'd walked back to the hotel the night before, our last official night before the return home to routine and perfect pillows and clean clothes, after yet another day of eating. And just as I was groaning and complaining to Bingley of broken stomach and general fatness, I joined the end of another queue to yet another culinary escapade and found myself ordering a plastic glass of some sweet concoction involving coffee, tapioca and soy milk, with pieces of jelly floating within. The straw is so wide you can gulp the drink, but then a wobbly bit will hit you in the back of the throat or bump into your teeth and you have to stop and chew for a moment, as if given a piece of well-worn bubblegum, mid-sip. It's alarming, having these pieces in your drink, but while at first horrified by the shock of the gulp, I grow to love it a couple of blocks down the road.

Months later, I found these bubble pearls in an Asian supermarket in Sydney, also called black boba pearls. They're not unlike tapioca, but they're larger and chewier and, I suspect, even less digestible. I do an adult tilt on the bubble tea, but using Sydney's obsession with the espresso martini (a martini it is not, but vodka it does have), and shake and pour two frothy drinks into a tall glass each for Bingley and me (see recipe on page 218).

Mostly I do the cooking. I'm freelancing from home, so it makes sense, but Bingley steps in with grand plans that require a weekend of slow cooking and prep, and yet another day of tidying up. He doesn't see cooking as the routine of putting dinner on the table, but rather as a scientific experiment to channel his creative energy.

I wrote a story for my food column on the problem of the burgeoning food dude or, less flatteringly, the doodie. It's not just a term for males who cook, I wrote. Food dudes go further. It describes a particular kind of food buff whose characteristics are intrinsically male. Food dudes up the ante on home gastronomy. While some of us are fine with a seared piece of salmon and salad on a Tuesday night, they're building an outdoor oven in the garden or cooking a whole pig on the spit on the balcony, taking on projects that involve the food-dude trifecta: nose-to-tail, fire and Boy Scout know-how. A food dude doesn't do these things because he is an exhibitionist. It's an intricate obsessive hobby, akin to building a model train. It's hands-on, requires tools and tinkering, is time-consuming, not terribly practical, but annoyingly impressive (even though dinner will never be ready in time).

Like his predecessor, the foodie, the doodie gets obsessive. These are guys who invite you over for dinner, only to have you wait five hours for the sous vide lamb to finish gurgling in the corner: 'So evenly cooked!'

You're too tired to care. They own Fergus Henderson's *The Complete Nose to Tail*, they read A A Gill and Frank Bruni (without plans to go to New York). To them, Bourdain is a rock star. David Chang is close to godliness. They can sustain a remarkably long conversation about knives. They know about the maillard reaction, and remind you about it every time you cook a steak. We'd call them food bores, except half of it is fascinating.

Food dudes are culinary nerds in the way that hipsters are urban geeks: they're happy being who they are, would never identify themselves with the label, and they are taste-makers. They pick up on a niche and pickling, or cooking your meat in a fire pit is a thing. The food dude trawls through chefs' suppliers online, comparing blow torches and mandolins, ordering in Silpat baking mats and gnocchi boards, bannetons and Rigamonti passata churners. He owns a Thermomix, or has looked into getting one, and can't focus on anything you say to him until he finds his microplane. Food dudes are everywhere. There may be one in your kitchen now. There's definitely one in mine.

CHINESE EGG CUSTARD TARTS

See story on page 213

MAKES 12 tarts
PREPARATION 40 minutes,
plus 1 hour 30 minutes chilling
COOKING 30 minutes

6 free-range egg yolks
100 g (3½ oz) caster
  (superfine) sugar
150 ml (5 fl oz) thin
  (pouring) cream
125 ml (4 fl oz/½ cup) milk
1 vanilla bean, halved
  lengthways and
  seeds scraped

Pastry
340 g (11¾ oz) plain
  (all-purpose) flour
1 large pinch of sea salt
150 g (5½ oz) unsalted butter,
  softened slightly, diced
30 g (1 oz/¼ cup) icing
  (confectioners') sugar
2 free-range eggs,
  lightly whisked

For the pastry, combine the flour and salt in a food processor, then add the butter, a few cubes at a time, pulsing after each addition. Add the sugar and pulse until the mixture resembles breadcrumbs. Add the egg and process until it forms a dough. Bring the dough together on a work surface, pat into a flat disc and wrap in plastic wrap. Rest in the fridge for at least 1 hour.

Preheat the oven to 190°C (375°F).

Roll out the pastry on a lightly floured board to 3–4 mm (about ⅛ in) thick. Using an 8 or 9 cm (3¼ or 3½ in) cutter, cut out twelve rounds, re-rolling and cutting any remaining pastry as necessary. Put pastry rounds in a twelve-hole standard (60 ml/⅓ cup) muffin tin. Prick the bases lightly three or four times and chill for about 30 minutes in the fridge, or 15–20 minutes in the freezer, until firm.

Bake the tart cases for 8–10 minutes, or until the pastry is just set but still pale. Remove from the oven and set aside. Reduce the oven temperature to 180°C (350°F).

Lightly whisk the egg yolks, sugar, cream, milk and vanilla in a jug until combined. Pour into the pastry shells, leaving at least 5 mm (¼ in) at the top so the custard doesn't spill over during cooking. Bake for 12–15 minutes, or until the filling is just set but still a little wobbly in the centre. Let the tarts cool slightly, then serve.

tip

You can use store-bought shortcrust pastry as an alternative: roll out and bake the tart shells according to the packet instructions, then proceed with the recipe as above.

ESPRESSO MARTINI BUBBLE TEA

See story on page 214

SERVES 2
PREPARATION 10 minutes
COOKING 15 minutes, plus
15 minutes sitting time

60 g (2¼ oz/½ cup) dried black
   boba pearls (large tapioca)
90 ml (3 fl oz) vodka
50 ml (1¾ fl oz) Kahlua
90 ml (3 fl oz) prepared
   espresso coffee
500 ml (17 fl oz/2 cups)
   cold-pressed almond milk
1 tablespoon sweetened
   condensed milk
ice, for shaking and serving

Bring 750 ml (26 fl oz/3 cups) of water to the boil in a medium saucepan over high heat. Add the boba pearls, reduce the heat to low and simmer, stirring occasionally, for 12–15 minutes, or until the pearls are just tender. Remove from the heat and let sit, covered, for a further 12–15 minutes, then drain.

Pour the remaining ingredients into a cocktail shaker and shake vigorously until frothy. Pour into the glasses with extra ice, if desired, and divide the boba between the glasses.

tip

If you want to cook the boba pearls ahead of time, follow the instructions above and then transfer the drained boba to a sugar syrup to prevent them becoming hard. To make the syrup, bring 125 ml (4 fl oz/½ cup) water to the boil over medium–high heat, stir in 60 ml (2 fl oz/¼ cup) honey and ½ teaspoon vanilla extract, then remove from the heat and set aside to cool. Store in an airtight container in the fridge until ready to use. Strain the boba from the sugar syrup before use.

THE MARGARET FULTON COOKBOOK

'I bought that sofa and lay flat on it for a month,' Grandma tells me.

'I'd just finished my first book, and with the money I bought this. I needed it to collapse. I bought it in the lying down position.'

We are standing in my living room, looking down at the sofa. It is forty-odd years old but she has cared for it. It has dark wooden legs and is close to the ground. My father had helped us cart it to my apartment and there, in the middle of the room, we took turns sitting in it, standing up again, peering under it to check springs, twisting the legs and weighing up sturdiness.

'I liked it because I could sit back in it while my feet touched the ground.'

I look down at her wee legs, her straight trousers tailored to fit her father's Scottish genes, little suede camel-coloured flats and pulled-up socks just hidden.

'But I was so tired after finishing that book, *The Margaret Fulton Cookbook*, I just lay across the sofa for a month. I had a whisky, and just lay down, toes to the ceiling, for a month.'

She always refers to the book in its full title. *The Margaret Fulton Cookbook.*

Margaret had wanted to make a book that her daughter, now seventeen, could manage, and dishes that her father the Scot would like. She called on the soups of her mother, barley into Scotch broth, rice into a chicken soup.

'What else?' she thought.

She sat down with a typewriter and hundreds of blank pages.

'What do I do about all these blank pages?' she asked my mother. 'I'm going to be here at home all the time, like a lodger.'

Suzanne, a stunning, skinny blonde, pocket-sized like her mother and completely cute and funny, shrugged it off.

'I'll cook, Mum, you write.'

She said the same thing to me in 2012, when I sat down to write a book of my own. This was my first solo cookbook, and I undertook the task with a kind of all-in attitude.

'I'll cook, darling.'

For weeks she signed up for meals: Thai fish cakes served in lettuce cups with noodles, bowls of pot au feu, beef ribs done in her pressure cooker – she too was writing an amazing book using the greatest gadget for the modern kitchen of the time-poor cook, the pressure cooker. I'd turn up, frazzled, hair dishevelled, and eat her soothing, perfect dinners, taking leftovers for lunch the next day. It was her twenty-somethingth cookbook and it was only my second. To be clear: she could certainly handle the pressure.

Margaret got her London-based book editor Joan Clibbon, publisher with Paul Hamlyn, on the phone to ask her which market she should write for. It was 1967, so the phone call had to count.

'Write the book for yourself, Margaret. Write the book you want to write.'

Did that mean like a Victorian or Edwardian woman would write, Margaret wondered. Details of her own household, her journals, so to speak – menus, recipes and small details from her family and her cook?

'That's right,' answered Joan. 'Write it for yourself, for your family.'

Paul Hamlyn did his research on what Australia wanted on a trip to the island in the early 1960s. He returned to London with a plan: to publish books that sold the most copies. In the 1960s that meant big, thick books with photographs on most pages, many of them in colour, packed with information on one of two subjects: gardening and cooking. So, to launch the Australian arm of the massive publishing house, they approached two household names: horticulturalist and photographer Stirling Macoboy and recipe columnist and obsessive foodist Margaret Fulton.

She started at the beginning, moving through green goddess dressing and spiced beetroot salad to crème caramel and crème anglaise or 'stirred custard'. The book should have recipes to use eggs, she thought: so, omelettes and a soufflé, and sauce recipes, from a rich béchamel to a buttery hollandaise, a mayonnaise. She tested every recipe three times and in some cases more, making notes on each recipe and tweaking, tweaking. Suzanne and her grandpa, and Denis, groaned in their chairs at the table as Margaret tested orange sherbert and filet de boeuf en croute, simmered cucumbers and crusted carrots, cabbage wedges and Swedish meatballs, corned beef and aberdeen sausage – a steamed, then roasted, concoction of minced bacon, steak, breadcrumbs, tomato sauce, nutmeg and egg.

She included recipes she had found on her travels.

'I had been introduced to the best cooks of the place or country, and there was always a great exchange of recipes,' Grandma says. 'I would taste their pilaus and biryanis and learn how to cook them. Indian ghee rice was a revelation, so perfumed, so different.'

The recipe went into the book and, nearly fifty years later, she still makes it for herself or a crowd.

I have a copy of this first book, with my grandmother's initial notes and edits, tweaks that would later be applied for future editions. She writes next to the recipe for apple strudel: 'A very good country cook gave me this recipe' and 'it may be necessary to curve it on pan', referring to the way the dessert sits in a 'Swiss roll tin'.

Modern edits extinguish these quaint details. We now just use a baking tray. But this cookbook gives me insight into my own grandmother's life perhaps more than the stories of her job at *Woman's Day*, more than the frivolous escapades and champagne-addled nights. I can see her gliding around the kitchen, black hair tied up, apron around her waist, stirring pots and testing for seasoning, cooking carbonnade of beef or green beans lyonnaise.

I love that she recommends serving the chicken livers in cream with 'hot buttered noodles' – which I assume is spaghetti – done with butter, sprinkled with paprika and garnished with a sprig of parsley. Now antiquated, it's these details that offer an insight, not only into the way our grandparents or parents ate, but what was amazing to them, what was new. A recipe for chicken liver risotto was eventually edited out of *The Margaret Fulton Cookbook*, probably for the best. But I love my original version, with the scribblings of a cook who has spent a lifetime in the kitchen.

One night in 1967 while working on the book at home, she received a phone call from a man she'd met in London three years before, Michael McKeag. He had chatted her up at a party. The British actor was in Sydney to do a television series, and had taken a house in Whale Beach. Margaret worked days at *Woman's Day* and nights on the book, but allowed herself Saturday evenings off. Denis was overseas for several months to see his family in London, so she joined Michael at the movies, theatre, for dinner, one Saturday night after the next.

'All this gadding about was perhaps not what one would call proper behaviour for a married woman,' she says now. 'I was doing what comes naturally. I was forty-two and having a second bite at the cherry of youth.'

Michael thought Denis was short-changing Margaret, and told her so. But when she saw a newspaper article about two Bluebell girls fighting over Michael, knew he'd had a string of the famous Parisian dancers as girlfriends, she figured he'd just be another Denis in disguise.

'I didn't want to take on a real professional in the Valentino stakes. And I really didn't want to work the marriage mill further, having learned the lessons of a faithless, fruitless relationship. "Good luck to them," I said to myself at the time. Men could bugger off as far as I was concerned.'

Her husband returned and the couple resumed their old routine, Margaret working hard and Denis playing very hard. She wondered what had kept Denis in London so long.

'Not that it mattered. I had waved goodbye to Michael, yes, but I also waved goodbye to Denis emotionally. Denis had waved goodbye to me long ago.'

Before the book was published, Margaret thought to herself: 'Won't it be nice, if I'm feeling blue or unsure of myself, to go into Angus & Robertson's or Dymocks bookshops, look up at the cookery books, see my book on the shelves, and then, silently addressing the shoppers, say, "Maybe you don't know it, but I wrote one of those books."'

When the book came out in 1968, the queues wrapped from Dymocks, around the corner of the block. Hamlyn was optimistic and published 60,000 copies in the first print run, a coup for a first-time author.

'Little did I know my face would get plastered all over the place. People knew me and, although I didn't know them, would greet me in the street as though I was their best friend,' she recalls.

Maybe it's because I grew up with a grandmother who was better known than most grandmothers but, if I'm honest, the fame part is not the interesting part to me. Whenever people talk about fame as though it's something to be coveted, I tell them this story. Soon after the book came out, Margaret ducked into the women's restroom while out at a restaurant. A little light-headed she walked into the cubicle and closed the door. A moment later, the door swung open and the intruding woman shrieked. Grandma squealed and the woman apologised, closing the door behind her. Trousers down by her ankles, Margaret relaxed again. Then she heard on the other side of the door:

'Oh! That was Margaret Fulton!'

The door swung open again and the same woman stood by the door.

'Oh, Margaret Fulton! I am such a fan. I adore your book; it has changed my life. I cook the Cantonese roast duck and my husband says I'm a better cook now than I've ever been.'

She beamed at Margaret, the woman who had overhauled her domestic life with a sweep of culinary know-how.

'Oh, well, thank you so much,' my grandma replied. 'But listen,' and she gestured to the cubicle walls around her, 'would you mind terribly if we speak further outside the toilet?'

The woman froze. Had she just…? Her mouth opened and her eyes widened, and Grandma thought the woman would collapse or be sick or burst into tears.

'Never mind,' she reassured her. 'Close the door and I'll be with you in a moment.'

The woman closed the door and slunk away, never to be seen again.

When first royalty cheque arrived Margaret's closest friends were staggered by the amount.

'Now you can buy a new fridge.'

Previously she had used an ice chest, which involved a visit from the ice man two or three times a week. He tramped through the house leaving a trail of drips from the heavy block of ice he carted in and dropped into the ice compartment in the top of the wooden cabinet. Each morning Margaret would empty the tray of water underneath. But she loved the way the cool air that filtered its way from the melting ice kept her milk and butter just right. Eventually she would be forced to trade it in for a small refrigerator, but not yet.

'Oh, for heaven's sake,' she countered. 'Is this what I've been working for? If success is a new fridge, who needs it?'

Instead, she bought a curlew. The large ceramic bird sits in pride of place in her dining room. It's the beaded Finnish centrepiece to our New Year's feasts, the thing she walks past every day still and gets more pleasure from than any other material thing. The ceramicist Birger Kaipiainen made the piece from thousands of tiny beads, and inside is a ceramic clock.

'I was flying with the birds, investigating new places, new foods, a new paradise,' she tells me. 'I thought, if ever I had enough money, I would buy Birger's curlew. Well, after my book, I did have enough money.'

She also bought the sofa.

With that money Grandma also did one of the most important things she ever did. Now nineteen, Suzanne began to wonder how she was ever going to leave home.

'How was I going to say to Mum, "I'm ready to go now"?' she told me recently. 'I wasn't about to support myself.'

Grandma acknowledged to my mother that she, Margaret, was a very strong-willed person, and that she thought it best if her daughter was allowed to blossom and find herself, find her own strength. So she paid for Suzanne to go to London to attend the Cordon Bleu cooking school.

'It was the best thing she could have done for me.'

Also, my mother was miserable living with her stepfather Denis, longing for change and the chance to escape from his bullying, his fighting, his ego. She too flew with the birds – but on a ship, to London.

Mum boarded the cruise liner to London, by herself. She had wanted to fly.

'At the time, flying and going by boat cost almost the same,' she says. 'But I had this image of myself arriving on a plane, wearing a hat and coat. For some reason I thought yellow and black would be a smart combination. I had a picture of me turning around to the plane and waving.'

But Margaret insisted she go by sea, and so she found herself in a cabin with three other girls.

'The marvellous thing about youth is that ignorance is largely bliss,' my mum tells me. 'You don't realise the magnitude of what you're doing. I'd left a boyfriend, in fact, I'd left two. I couldn't really figure out which one I wanted. As soon as I got over this – after about an hour – and started chatting to the other girls in the bunk, we had a ball on that month-long voyage.'

LONDON CALLING

Suzanne is beating butter in an electric mixer so it turns creamy and white, then slowly adds the sugar. Her Cordon Bleu teacher leans in, nodding.

'Very good, Suzanne. It's rare to find a pupil who doesn't have bad habits to unlearn. Very good indeed.'

My mother, still nineteen, was a star student, and was in heaven in the sprawling kitchen, cooking all day, turning out perfect roast chickens and puff pastry and meringues.

'I discovered I had a knack for it,' she tells me now. 'I should have been more interested in science at school. I found I had a talent for the science of it, putting things together.'

She'd scooped a buddy, Adie, on the ship to London, and moved in with her and another Australian girl, Barbie. Yet another, Jannie Brown, would arrive later. The apartment was a cramped, London-typical hole on Dennington Park Road on the Bakerloo Line in West Hampstead. Suzanne usually did the cooking, a win for the others until she started getting really experimental. One day Barbie walked into the kitchen after a day in the office, shed her skirt and jersey in the warmth of the house.

'Good evening, Suzie, what are you cooking?'

Mum turned around, holding a chicken foot up to Barbie's face, pulling the tendon at the cut-off end so the foot opened and closed like a claw.

'This, Barbie. Have a little nibble.'

Barbie screamed and Mum chased her out the front door, down the stairs, Barbie in only her underpants and shirt. The door to the apartment below theirs opened and a dashing dark-haired boy stuck his head out.

'What's going on here?'

They all burst out laughing. And that is how the Australian girls met the New Zealand boys downstairs.

Jannie Brown arrived from Melbourne, matching my mother in tiny stature, 1960s-appropriate skinniness, amazing beauty and sense of humour, but Jannie had dark brown curls to my mother's thick-as-anything blonde mop (a trait my sister and I would later inherit). The girls got ready for a party, Mum in a white lace and silk almost see-through nightie she decided she could totally get away with. Jannie set up the ironing board and put her head sideways on it while my Mum stood beside her, reluctantly ironing her friend's beautiful curls dead straight. They slipped downstairs having been invited by the boys for drinks.

'I think it was probably a cup of tea,' Mum tells me now, 'or an instant coffee, which we drank back then.'

'I thought there were four of you,' Barbie piped up, doing the maths and hoping there would be one for her.

'Ah yes, Robert Gibbs. He's at a concert.'

The girls questioned their New Zealand counterparts. 'A concert? By himself?'

'Yes, he's into classical music. It's Mahler, I think.'

Suzanne presented a double-layered almond meringue cake, filled with chocolate butter cream, which she had brought home from her cooking school. Someone cut into the cake, layers of crisp and chew, the silken butter cream making it rich and soft and luxurious. Then, a key in the door. Adie jumped to welcome him.

'You must be Robert Gibbs.'

All the girls leaned and stretched towards the door to see.

Mum tells me now: 'He was tall, with shoulder-length dark hair, and was wearing a hand-knitted Aran jersey that had stretched in length, so it was well below his belt. And he wore corduroy flares. He had a huge smile. I can still see him standing there.'

Robert was introduced to the girls, one by one, and then to the gateau on the table.

'Suzanne made it,' said David Israel, one of the boys. 'She's a Cordon Bleu cook.'

'A Cordon Bleu cook? Really?' said my dad.

Back home in their own flat, the girls gathered around the heater, all swooning over David Israel. They giggled and teased Barbie, and wondered which boy Suzanne liked. Jannie interrupted.

'Girls, girls. You may all like David Israel but let me tell you something. One of those boys is by far the best.'

The girls leaned in.

'That Robert Gibbs.'

'Robert Gibbs? Really?'

Over the following weeks, my mother began to see that, yes, there was something rather wonderful about that Robert Gibbs.

On 6 June 1969, twenty-three-year-old Robert left his parents' home in Howick, New Zealand, and flew to England. He had an air ticket to England and three hundred New Zealand dollars. Long haul wasn't really a thing then, so the airline stopped over in Sydney, then Darwin, Hong Kong and finally in Tokyo, where he got off the plane.

He ate ramen in Tokyo and then caught the bullet train to Osaka, making friends on the way with local Japanese tourists wanting to practise their English.

'I didn't have much money so I would go into a little place for some noodles and a stir-fried number. Whatever was cheap.'

The food was not like in New Zealand. In Japan breakfast was 'a bowl of rice, soup, and a raw egg in its shell', he tells me now. He cracked the raw egg over the hot steamed rice and ate that with miso soup on the side.

'The idea of doing that in New Zealand in 1969 would be a total shock,' he says.

Back in Auckland, my grandmother Marion, my father's mother, had left his dinner on a pot of hot water twice a week. He warmed it when he returned from night school, where he was studying to be a draftsman and saving money to travel to England.

His mother did all the cooking for the six children growing up. Corned beef with onion white sauce, lamb stews, Irish stews, roast lamb, and sweet and sour steak, which involved steak pieces in a stew with a vinegar kick, all arrived at the table, immaculately set with laundered linen every meal. She did lemon delicious pudding and sometimes pancakes. My father, the youngest of the siblings, loved her golden syrup dumplings, and fried bananas. Marion made bread rolls from scratch, and tied the dough into little knots before she baked them. She made blancmange – that creamy-white jelly dessert – in a rabbit mould. She pickled and preserved, growing everything herself in their bountiful garden. As a child visiting my grandmother Marion and grandad Norm, I used to be fascinated by the 'wrigglers', or mosquito larvae, which found their way into the water tank and into my glass of water.

'Don't be fussy,' I was told.

From Tokyo Dad caught a flight into Moscow, the Soviet Union. He hitched his way across Europe, pitching his A-frame tent by the side of the road, in forests and national parks where possible. In Asia he stayed in youth hostels, choosing the dorm room and rolling up his sleeping bag early in the morning to avoid the usual rowdy crowds.

In Zurich he found a public restroom inside a hotel, and as he walked in he saw a man in front of him, a shocking skinny frame and clothes draped over his bones. His hair was dark, to his shoulders, and collarbones projected from above his chest.

'Somebody needs to buy that fellow a meal,' he thought to himself.

He walked forward, and the man walked towards him. And then my father stopped: it was his own reflection. He bought that guy a meal.

In Zurich he hitched his way to Venice and then up into Austria, until he ran out of money. In Austria he only had a few shillings so needed to find a meal that could last him a couple of days. He found a bakery and invested in a loaf of rye bread, which he stuffed into his backpack. When he found a park to rest, shrug his massive canvas khaki backpack from his shoulders, he pulled out the loaf and tore off the end. As the crusty wedge approached his mouth he could smell it: caraway seeds. My father and I share an intense loathing of this seed. Why anyone would add the detestable stuff to their sauerkraut or their loaf of rye is beyond us. I find it so abominable I cannot eat it, will not. But in 1968, with no money to buy another loaf of bread, my poor dad suffered the seeds.

A year later he would return to climb to the top of the Matterhorn successfully, but right now he was too cash-strapped. He arrived at Heathrow and immediately went to New Zealand House, home of the New Zealand High Commission. If you arrived there in 1969 with nothing to your name you could still get a meal of roast lamb, roast potatoes, peas and beans, gravy.

'I ate it all. I just sat there, eating this meal,' he says.

He flicked through a little A4 lined book in the High Commission in which people could write in accommodation-wanted notices, when another man came in and asked for the book.

'You'll have to wait for this chap to finish looking,' the attendant said.

'No, I want to put something in,' replied the man.

'I'll take it,' said my father.

He didn't want to spend any money on a hotel. The guy was heading out to work on an oil rig in the North Sea, but said he'd have to call his friend David Israel with the spare room in the apartment, to check it was okay to give the room away immediately. So he phoned David Israel.

'I have this Kiwi here; he wants to stay in the flat right now. Can he stay there tonight?'

On the other end of the phone, David asked, 'Well, what's he like?'

'What are you like?' asked the oil rigger man.

'I'm fantastic,' said my dad.

'He's fantastic.'

'Oh,' said David Israel. 'We'd better have him then.'

There were two bedrooms, a couple of chaps in each. It was August 1969.

My dad had a job at an architectural firm in Green Park, where he was a draftsman. Some senior person at the firm liked to have fresh eccles cakes in the boardroom meetings, so the various employees would take turns picking them up from Fortnum & Mason, the department store. Dad used to buy extras and bring them back for Mum when they started dating.

'They had perfect buttery, flaky pastry, not overwrought with too many ingredients,' Mum remembers.

The two used to collect them from Fortnum's on the weekend, and take them back to the apartment to have with tea.

'I realise this is what we had at school,' Suzanne told Robert at the time. 'We used to call them fly cemeteries. But these are way better.'

A year and a Cordon Bleu diploma later, Suzanne was approached by the very woman who conceived the original coronation chicken recipe for

Elizabeth II, Rosemary Hume, who offered her a job as the pastry chef in the Cordon Bleu restaurant kitchen. Rosemary promised Suzanne an ongoing education, working under an experienced pastry chef.

'Even though it was only fifteen pounds a week, I thought "Yippee, I'll learn so much!" But in three weeks she went and left me, saying she thought I could handle it from there on in. I had to make all the afternoon teas and desserts for the entire restaurant.'

Suzanne had a commercial Hobart mixer to whip up huge batches of butter cream, and the layered meringue cake filled with butter cream became one of the most popular desserts on the menu. That butter cream appeared again and again at the Cordon Bleu, to fill cakes and decorate cakes.

'This is really how we turned a cake into a gateau,' says my mum. 'It made them very special-looking.'

Baking paper, that non-stick kitchen paper, didn't exist in 1969 – it came out much later, in the 1980s. So Suzanne had to grease and flour greaseproof paper or baking trays, learning how to lift the baked and delicate meringue from the paper without breaking it. It's this skill, that lightness of touch, that kept me entranced in the kitchen during my entire childhood. A few years later my mother turned to this recipe again, for her wedding. She made a layered almond meringue cake and filled it with layers of whipped cream in which she swirled dark chocolate sauce. I've tweaked it with hazelnuts (see recipe on page 232).

Despite having a year at the school behind her, Suzanne hit a steep learning curve. One Saturday night, she was working late and the chefs asked her to take twelve chickens out of the freezer to defrost. As she switched out all the lights, she took the chickens out of the freezer. On Monday morning when the chefs arrived at work they were hit by a terrible overpowering stink that had permeated the entire restaurant.

'Suzanne! The chickens!'

They had asked her to take them out of the freezer, 'but they should have asked me to transfer them to the fridge'. They wanted her to pay for them.

'You don't pay me enough to pay for the chickens,' said the immovable nineteen-year-old.

Another time, a waiter came into the kitchen to tell Suzanne that a noble couple in the restaurant wanted to see her.

'It's about your cake.'

He looked worried. My mother was terrified.

'I was shaking in my clogs; we all wore clogs back then. I wondered what terrible disaster had happened.'

She walked into the restaurant and stood by the customers' table as they presented one of her rings, which had been baked in the mixture with the cake. But when they saw the diminutive girl from Australia, looking like a child in her chef's uniform, obviously forlorn, their hearts melted. They softened – and invited her to stay on their estate in Scotland. She never took up their offer, but it made up for the terror she'd been through.

My parents took trips around England, sailing in the middle of winter with Jannie, David Israel, Barbie and Adie. A friend of Robert's, a photographer who shot for all the English magazines, asked Suzanne to model for him in Brighton for a shoot about the area. There's a picture of her standing by the seaside wearing a long woollen skirt and tucked-in white shirt, a fat blonde bob framing her little face, digging a fork into a tub. Behind her, the stall advertises jellied eels and potted shrimps, fish and chips, all the early 1970s best seaside foodstuffs.

'I couldn't resist a new culinary treat. I love to try new things, so I had the jellied eels,' she tells me now. 'But something went very wrong.'

She made her way back to London shadowed by terrible waves of sickness. Home in bed she couldn't stop picturing the jellied eels. 'I lay there, so sick, and I couldn't stop picturing the tiny bits of eel and the bones all coated in aspic. And every time I thought of it, I'd rush to the bathroom. I should have had the potted shrimp.' (See recipe on page 235.)

Margaret took the fast route to London, and flew in at the end of 1969 to promote her new *The Margaret Fulton Cookbook*. She visited Suzanne and her friends in their new apartment in Abbey Road (*the* Abbey Road). A boy called Robert Gibbs was often about and, one morning, he called Margaret from the lobby of her hotel while she was having tea and breakfast in bed, asking if he could come up. He stood beside the bed, Margaret propped up by a few pillows, toast balancing on her breast, and asked for Suzanne's hand in marriage. Margaret was taken aback.

'Does Suzanne know how you feel?'

'Their love was like that,' my grandma says now. 'Solid but not showy.'

The pair was planning to marry when they returned to Australia.

HAZELNUT MERINGUE COFFEE CRÈME LAYER CAKE

See story on page 230

SERVES 10–12
PREPARATION 35 minutes
COOKING 45 minutes

150 g (5½ oz/⅔ cup) caster
   (superfine) sugar
140 g (5 oz/1¼ cups)
   hazelnut meal
5 free-range egg whites
icing (confectioners') sugar,
   for dusting

Coffee crème
110 g (3¾ oz/½ cup) sugar
90 ml (3 fl oz/3 shots)
   espresso coffee
1 teaspoon ground cardamom
5 free-range egg yolks
250 g (9 oz) unsalted
   butter, softened slightly
   and diced

Preheat the oven to 180°C (350°F). Mark a 20 cm (8 in) circle on three pieces of baking paper and place on three baking trays.

Reserve 55 g (2 oz/ cup) of the sugar and sift the remainder with the hazelnut meal.

Whisk the egg whites in an electric mixer until soft peaks form. Gradually add the reserved sugar and beat until the mixture is thick and glossy. Fold in the sifted sugar and hazelnut mixture quickly and lightly.

Divide the mixture into three equal portions and spread each portion neatly on a baking paper circle, to form three meringue rounds (you can also use a piping bag to do this – start from the middle and gradually spiral out to the edge of the circle).

Bake the meringue rounds for 20–25 minutes, or until slightly firm to the touch. Remove to wire racks to cool completely. If making the meringue ahead, cool and store in airtight containers for up to 1 week.

For the coffee crème, dissolve the sugar in the coffee in a small saucepan over a very low heat, then bring to a simmer for about 10 minutes, or until the syrup falls in a thread from the spoon – if you have a sugar thermometer, it should register 112°C (234°F). Turn off the heat and stir in the cardamom.

In an electric mixer, beat the egg yolks for 1 minute. With the motor running, gradually add the hot syrup in a very slow stream. Continue beating for 3 minutes, then add one cube of butter at a time with the motor still running. Beat until all the butter is thoroughly incorporated and the crème is light, fluffy and silky. Chill in the fridge for about 10 minutes to firm up a little.

To assemble the cake, spread the coffee crème evenly, about 1–2 cm (½–¾ in) thick, on top of two of the meringue rounds with a small spatula (you may have some coffee crème left over). Lay one of the topped meringues on top of the other, then top with the final un-topped meringue. To serve, dust with icing sugar and cut into wedges.

POTTED SHRIMPS

See story on page 231

SERVES 2
PREPARATION 10 minutes,
plus chilling/setting overnight
COOKING 5 minutes
Start this recipe 2 days ahead

300 g (10½ oz) peeled
   raw prawns (shrimp)
¼ teaspoon freshly
   ground nutmeg
½ teaspoon sea salt
freshly ground black pepper
1 tablespoon lemon juice
1 teaspoon anchovy paste or
   2 anchovy fillets, mashed
baby cress, to serve
toasted sliced baguette,
   to serve

Clarified butter
500 g (1 lb 2 oz) butter

For the clarified butter, put the butter in a medium saucepan and melt very slowly over low heat, being careful not to let it boil or burn at all. When the butter has separated into a clear yellow layer and a milky layer underneath, put the saucepan in the fridge and leave it overnight.

Next day, remove the solid mass from the top of the saucepan – this is the clarified butter. Discard the milky layer and use paper towel to wipe any milky residue from the clarified butter.

Melt the clarified butter in a clean saucepan over low heat. Pour into a clean jar with a lid and store in the fridge for 3–6 months, using as required.

Keep six prawns whole and cut the remaining prawns into four to six pieces each.

Put a deep-sided pan over medium heat, add 200 g (7 oz) of the clarified butter and melt gently. Add the prawns (chopped and whole), nutmeg, salt and pepper, lemon juice and anchovy paste to the pan. When the prawns start to change colour, turn off the heat immediately – it is important not to overcook them.

Put the whole prawns into the base of two 150 ml (5 fl oz) dariole or timbale moulds, then pack in the chopped prawns loosely. Pour over the clarified butter from the pan. Tap the moulds firmly to dislodge any air bubbles. Refrigerate, uncovered, overnight to set.

To serve, rub the outside of the moulds with a hot damp cloth and ease out onto a plate. Sprinkle with baby cress and serve at room temperature with hot toast. Once the outer clarified butter seal is broken, the potted shrimp will keep for 1–2 days in the fridge.

tip

You can substitute the same weight of crab meat for the prawns, if preferred.

FARM GIRL

Chef came into the kitchen with a bucket and placed it on the bench in front of me. Solemn, he gave me a nod, 'Thanks, Gibbsie,' and walked out again. Alone in the kitchen, I tried to hold back tears. I had bumped out of my freelance career momentarily to pursue an opportunity in television.

I picked up the end of my long denim apron to wipe my face, and held my breath as I leaned against the kitchen bench.

'Get it together.'

It was early morning, seven or eight o'clock. I was two dishes into Episode Four on a food show, in which I was playing background prep, food researcher and general prop person, the invisible cook and behind-the-scenes kitchen human. The show's set was a gorgeous weatherboard cottage near Narooma on the far south coast of New South Wales. It was painted dove grey and set off the ground, surrounded by rock boulders and national park – an Australian rural idyll. I was two months in, living away from home and from Bingley. I knew I had exactly eight weeks and four days to go. Right now, I had to deal with these bloody birds that the chef – who was also the host of the show – had moments before killed.

An hour earlier, I had said my goodbyes to the feathered beings. Not exactly spring chickens, the two black Australorps had been acquired in Season One of the show, the year before. Scrappy, nervous birds, the girls had stopped laying months before and were enjoying an idyllic retirement from productivity, in the company of a duck. They grazed on pasture and every night, by the time I left the cottage, they had propped themselves on a wooden perch inside their coop. I'd peer in and say goodnight.

It was not my closeness or some kind of bond with the birds that had me welling up. I struggled with the animals-as-pets actually being animals-as-farm-creatures distinction, and grappled with the animals-have-to-be-productive-to-be-worthwhile-and-therefore-alive issue. What got me here was shock at the speed with which two creatures can be scratching around in some straw, lifting a wing so they can twist around and give themselves a little nibble in the armpit, bossing their companion around as to who gets the pumpkin seeds that I gave them as a last meal – to being two perfectly plucked and roastable chickens on a bench. I was way too urban for this.

This is not a story about how I had to deal with blood and sweat, despite my tears; the chef did everything. He picked up the birds from their coop, held them neatly under his arm and kept them calm as he carried them to an old trestle table under a tree. He held them down, one at a time, and knocked their necks into a wooden shaft, a kind of blunt cleaver designed to break the spine and render the nervous system ineffective. Turning them upside down into the open-ended cones as they wrestled rhythmically with nerves, he slit their throats with the swift move of a knife. He dunked them in a large saucepan of boiling water set on the trestle, and easily stripped the feathers from their pink naked backs and under their wings where he, too, had once seen them scratching. Then he cleavered off their feet and heads, made a slit in their backsides and pulled out their insides, tucked in loose skin, and lay them in a cold water bath. He turned them from chickens into dinner.

When he brought them to the kitchen, I saw it all on his face. Determined, sure and justified, but also so hard. I was annoyed at myself and pulled it together, though not quite fast enough to elude the show's director, who wandered into the kitchen, asked how I was, and unwittingly spurred on another wobbly-voiced bubble.

'Sorry, I'm not becoming a farm girl as quickly as I'd hoped…'

Horrified, I picked up the birds with my hands, poured the water from their cavities, transferred them into a smaller container, wrapped the lot in plastic and found room in the fridge for them. Then I turned back to making a salt-crust pastry to wrap another Australorp I'd acquired the day before from a local farmer for the food shoot. Here's one I prepared earlier…

My entire adult life I'd been ordering up death over the counter. I'd taken the lives of pigs, cows and chickens with a nod of my head to the butcher. So the creatures weren't actually killed in front of me but, nonetheless, I'd collaborated in the dealing of lives. This is what people mean when they say to people who rail against death, or turn away at the sight of a cattle truck: 'You like steak, don't you?'

There's something naïve – no, worse – irresponsible, about eating meat but refusing to look death in the face. In all the cryovacking and plastic wrapping, we've somehow lost that connection, and I felt guilty for my urban, blinkered ways. I loved this work, cooking and telling food stories for television.

There were prep days and shoot days and, scattered on indiscriminate days, weekends, slipped between shooting blocks, falling rarely on the actual weekend. I'd drive five hours to Sydney for two nights about once a month, then back again. Other times, my tiny plane would sputter just over an hour north, skimming the clouds up the coast, past Gerroa and Wollongong and the Bulli escarpment. The stunning national parks back onto the coast along much of this stretch, dark green and apparently endless. I'd follow the land all the way, head pressed to the window, looking out for a nice little wave tickling its way into shore, counting how many minutes until I'd see *him*. Moments after the plane took off, the captain announced we'd be landing, and the stewardess interrupted my daydreaming.

'Coffee or tea, Madam? A sweet or savoury snack?'

After the first couple of weeks away, still feeling very green, I'd arrive home with horror stories and tales of paradise, both encapsulating the rural idyll. After one of my late-night drives home, Bingley put a plate in front of me at the table and sat down beside me. I was frazzled on nutrition-free car snacks and too many wasabi peas. Onto the plate he spooned ricotta tortellini he'd made himself, turning egg wonton wrappers into bite-sized parcels stuffed with whipped citrus-spiked ricotta and herbs, just a spoonful or two of brown butter sauce, some crispy fried sage leaves. He makes these ahead and freezes them before cooking. Then, when we need some last-thought meal or a comforting welcome home from the bush, they're there in their oozing perfection (see recipe on page 240).

I regaled and horrified him in equal measure. Leaning on the table, his beautiful head in his elbow nook, he was tired from summoning up a meal at eleven o'clock for his buzzing, exhausted girl. I'd brought home a bottle of homemade ginger beer, a farm souvenir, and peered into the brew, still amazed at my own home-and-hearth domesticity. He sat with me and smiled, relieved to have me home for a moment. I told him about our new baby goats – half milk-producing Saanen, half good-eating Boer. He heard how I'd climb over the barbed wire to shortcut a paddock, pass the pigs on the way, and visit the goats. The crew and I would feed them pieces of toast as a treat (their mouths widen around the toast as they try to eat it whole. Honestly, it's hilarious).

I brought home stories, too, of 'recces' to the dairy cow cattle yards, where two-week-old male dairy calves – mainly Jersey and Friesian – are auctioned off for twelve to thirty dollars a piece, to be turned into mince. Or they're sold off in portioned packets to countries where white veal is socially acceptable.

Shivering, terrified, hungry, the animals – a little larger in height than a labrador – bunch together. Like knobbly-kneed Bambis, their wide eyes are caked in tears. The farmers can't afford to let their milk-producing mothers feed them; we need their milk in our tea and porridge. And they can't afford the two-hundred-and-fifty-odd dollars it takes to raise a baby calf to full size, when nobody buys dairy meat. When milking cows have to give birth about once a year to keep producing milk, what can farmers do about the terrible potluck of gender? Newborn females add to the milking quota: win. But newborn males are sometimes shot on the spot and buried on the farm: lose. Or they're carted to cattle sales, an expensive feat for farmers, a terrible, terrible waste in every regard.

I pleaded with Bingley, as though he could change it all. Everyone wants to eat Angus beef. You don't see Jersey or Friesian steaks for sale in Australia, but you should. I have never had a better standing rib roast than the one I cooked from our own Jersey one-year-old veal. I may have stood up at this point in the conversation. I mimed carving the beef, described the buttery, tender meat. Smallholders should buy these little steers, bottle-feed them from their own milking cows, and then sell them off at a year old as the best-quality beef you can find, at a premium price, or just eat them themselves. Or maybe everyone needs to stop drinking milk? I didn't know the answer. I was frustrated. Bingley rubbed his eyes and then my back and told me to get to bed, rest.

'Tomorrow will be better.

RICOTTA TORTELLINI *with* MARJORAM BURNT BUTTER

See story on page 238

SERVES 4
PREPARATION 30 minutes
COOKING 10 minutes

50 g (1¾ oz/¼ cup)
   fine semolina
24 square wonton wrappers
1 free-range egg,
   lightly whisked
100 g (3½ oz) unsalted butter,
   chilled, chopped
4 garlic cloves, thinly sliced
2 tablespoons marjoram leaves
   and sprigs
sea salt and freshly ground
   black pepper
grated Parmigiano Reggiano
   cheese, to serve

Ricotta filling
1 free-range egg,
   lightly whisked
250 g (9 oz) ricotta cheese
1 tablespoon grated
   Parmigiano Reggiano cheese
¼ teaspoon freshly
   grated nutmeg
1 tablespoon extra virgin
   olive oil
sea salt and freshly ground
   black pepper

For the ricotta filling, mix all the ingredients in a bowl until well combined. Season well with salt and pepper.

Sprinkle a baking tray with the semolina.

Place the wonton wrappers on a bench and brush the edge of each one with beaten egg using a pastry brush. Put 1 heaped teaspoonful of filling in the centre of each square and fold over diagonally to form a triangle. Brush a little more egg on two corners of each one and twist around your finger so they come together in a tortellini shape. Press the ends together and seal. Place on the prepared tray.

Melt the butter in a frying pan over medium–high heat, add the garlic and cook for 4 minutes, or until golden. Stir through the marjoram, letting it crisp a little, and season with salt and pepper to taste. The butter should now be nut-brown, but not burnt. Transfer to a heatproof bowl and reserve the pan.

Add a large pinch of sea salt to a large saucepan of water and bring to the boil. Add the tortellini and cook for 2 minutes, lift out with a slotted spoon to drain, then transfer to the reserved saucepan. Return the burnt butter to the pan and toss briefly over low heat to coat the tortellini in the butter.

Divide the tortellini between four plates, drizzle over the burnt butter and serve with a sprinkling of Parmigiano.

tip

Whole nutmeg, freshly grated over the tortellini just as it is served, really intensifies the flavour of this dish.

COMING HOME

She didn't stop at one. Even after the vast *Encyclopedia of Food and Cookery* came out she kept going, on to *Superb Restaurant Dishes*, again with the publisher Paul Hamlyn. Margaret travelled for book tours and research, and to line up yet another book.

In London, the publisher's personal chauffeur picked her up from the airport in a green Rolls Royce, drove her to some smart hotel where she'd find chilled champagne and bouquets in her room. From her suite at the Royal Garden Hotel overlooking Kensington Palace she put new binoculars, bought on a stopover in Singapore, to good use: spotting Princess Diana as she slipped from her car and Prince Charles as he walked his dog.

'I watched the young princes William and Harry with their mother, going off to Harry's first day at kindergarten,' she says.

London inspired her, she loved it. Lunching at the Connaught could grow on a person. She called in to the British cook and writer Elizabeth David's Belgravia kitchenware store. Someone once said that the famous cook had inner elegance, but when Margaret read that description in a newspaper she threw it aside.

'What a load of tripe.'

When she actually saw Elizabeth David, she read between the lines.

'She had soup stains down her twinset and her teeth were stained from all the red wine she loved so much. Still, her eyes beamed with intelligence, her face declared a passion for living life to its fullest.'

With Suzanne in London and Denis off on his frequent escapades, my grandmother wanted a place to come home to, somewhere that was her own. With the economic downturn in 1969, and some cash in her pockets from the sale of a house she'd kept in Palm Beach, as well as the success of her first book, she bought a house for twenty-eight thousand dollars on the Balmain peninsula: a sandstone semi-detached that stretched all the way to the harbour and a little boatshed. The house was long and dark, the rooms were small and mean, but she could fish off her own seawall, see the city lights and hear the gulls nesting on Goat Island right in front. Fisherman came during the night to haul little harbour prawns, and Margaret went to sleep on her first night there hearing the fishermen's calls.

Margaret in her Balmain home in 1983 with her latest book

LOVE

DRIFTING

My six-year-old sister and I are drifting further and further out to sea. We're trying to turn back, but we're not getting far.

'Who knows where we're heading?' I say.

I turn to her, then, in mock terror: 'Maybe nowhere, ever again.'

She looks at me, horrified.

'Kate! Try harder!'

We nod at each other, we'll try harder. We both look down at our legs, stretch our feet out, and pedal like hell. We edge closer to the shore and further away from the United States, or whatever land mass comes next in the sea beside Hawaii. I spot Grandma in her swimsuit on the shore, a fifty-something in a stretchy black one-piece, Michael lying next to her, both more golden than they'd been at breakfast: rotisserie humans on Waikiki.

'There! Get their attention!'

We both jump to our feet on the heavy plastic floating contraption that Grandma and Michael put us on to entertain us while they get a bit of sun. We yell and wave. 'Grandma! Michael! Grandma!'

Our grandmother sits up in the sand as if woken suddenly from a perfect dream, adjusts her rattan sun visor and big tortoiseshell shades. Seeing us, basically a dot in the distance, she puts her hand to her mouth and with the other gives Michael a slow-motion tap on his back. He jumps to his feet and puts his hands to his head, then bolts towards a hire place doling out windsurfers, floating bikes and surfboards to unassuming children whose parents need a break.

'Let's just sit,' I say to Louise, as though we had a choice.

Michael and his floating bike crew arrive at breakneck speed, then he transfers across, sits between my sister and me and pedals us back to shore. Louise and I slip either side of Grandma lying in the sand, exhausted. With the scent of coconut oil, a hint of Michael's Gitanes cigarettes and summer in the towel beside her, we recover. Michael walks back up the beach, having paid for two sets of hire, and the four of us head home to the Pink Flamingo hotel to get ready for dinner.

'Mike was the quintessential hedonist,' Grandma says now.

In other words, he was completely dedicated to the doctrine of pleasure. With him by her side, Margaret learned to find pleasure in indulgence.

'Michael taught your grandmother how to spend her money,' my mum once said.

At the time I thought this was a dig at him, but now I realise she meant Michael showed her how to explore, live, enjoy things, items, travel, without guilt. Mostly, he showed her how to travel his way. Michael came into our lives in 1980. As far as I was concerned, as a three-year-old oblivious to history, he was a permanent fixture and therefore family. He was the other half of Grandma, the sixth member of our immediate family.

Michael behaved in a very Noel Cowardish manner. He held a sterling silver cigarette holder in his elegant hand, it seemed all the time.

'I loved the smell of those Gitanes and was spellbound at the way he smoked them,' says Margaret.

She was impressed by his acting past and flicked through press cuttings of his earlier career.

'Why did you give up acting?' she asked him.

'I didn't give up acting. It gave me up,' he said.

The pair worked ten months of the year and travelled for two.

'To a hedonist, travel implies first class and nothing else,' Margaret says.

Michael was a production chief in the film industry and knew how to get good deals with airlines and hotels. He did it for the stars and he did it for Margaret. He'd make friends with airlines and hotels. He wasn't interested in airline food but he knew Margaret was. His requirements involved French champagne and beluga caviar for breakfast, lunch or supper. He favoured Qantas because it had an arrangement with the Plaza Hotel in New York, where he took her early in their relationship.

'Mike got drunk, quite drunk on the flight to New York. Limitless bottles of French champagne with only the odd spoonful of caviar made sure of that. Mike was obnoxious and I was furious,' she says. 'I thought, "Never again will I travel with this man."'

But a limousine picked them up at the airport in New York and took them through the suburbs and over Brooklyn Bridge. Margaret looked out the window to the skyline of the Chrysler Building, the bright navy-blue sky of New York in the evening. They arrived at the Plaza, dotted with golden lights and filled with sophisticated New Yorkers and other world travellers. Margaret fell in love. Their luggage was taken from them in a gilded trolley and a desk clerk checked the booking for their room.

'A double bed or twin beds?' he asked.

'Mike's back-of-the-theatre-reaching voice roared out: "Of course a double bed! We do everything together!"'

Minutes later, they were in a yellow taxi, then they were being ushered into the Virginia Theatre on Broadway just as the lights were being lowered for the show *On Your Toes*. The pair sat down and the band struck up, playing 'See the Pretty Apple, Top of the Tree', 'It's Got to be Love' and 'There's a Small Hotel' – all songs from Margaret's childhood. Margaret was still furious.

'I muttered mad things to myself: "He's done it this time" and then, "Never again".'

Michael sobered up, Margaret cooled down. After the show, they walked to the restaurant Sardi's, then passed Lindy's – the restaurant that created the cheesecake whose recipe Margaret had used at Johnnie Walker's Bistro – on the way back to the Plaza.

If Louise or I disappeared when we were growing up, my parents always figured that we'd gone to Grandma's house, a few doors down the street. If she wasn't home, we'd slip in through the dog door. We'd play with the dolls' house with its intricate ceramic thumbnail-sized plates and tea sets that the palm-sized dolls could drink and dine from. My sister and I spent hours setting matchbox-sized tables, bartering a minuscule roast dinner complete with peas for a large gateau decorated with cherries, pressing the faces of the velvet-clad dolls into a whole ceramic cabbage.

'Ooh yum, this is so delicious!'

We'd curl up in the hallway, walking the dolls up the walls, in our own little world.

Grandma cooked dinner and Michael sat in the sunroom overlooking the harbour, reading *The Sydney Morning Herald*. He once bought my sister and me a five-foot-tall camel from FA Schwartz in New York and we'd sit between the humps and pretend to be Lawrence of Arabia.

We squished beside them while they sat down for grilled lamb chops, rare in the middle with a deep-brown crust, fried halved tomatoes and potato purée that had been beaten with butter. And HP Sauce.

'Why do you like that sauce, Michael? Is it tomato sauce?'

He sliced the fatty tail off his chop end (the best bit), dipped it in the sauce on his plate and handed his fork to me. I squinted as the vinegary tomato-based sauce, sweet with dates and spice, kicked my throat.

Michael decided that my sister and I needed to be introduced to a bit of fantasy, so he packed us up in 1984 and took us to the United States. Stopping in Hawaii on the way, we met a macaw bird that appeared on the show *Magnum*, fed the dolphins at Sea World (learned that when you feed dolphins it's annoying to rinse your hands in the water every time you handle a fish: 'Just wash them at the end, Louise'), discovered dinner-plate-sized waffles piled up with strawberries and whipped cream. Then, in Disneyland, we met Donald Duck and learned that Michael made the best haunted-house-riding companion in the world.

He had a constant desire to travel. The moment he returned from one trip with Margaret, he'd be planning the next. One year they went cruising on the Nile with the curator of the Egypt section of the British Museum. They went to Nepal, where they shot tigers (with their cameras); they travelled on elephants through the jungle, and came face-to-face with a one-horned rhinoceros. They went to Venice. Michael picked up the international edition of the *New York Herald Tribune* and settled in St Mark's Square with a coffee, followed by a beer for him and a Campari for her. Another year they stayed for a month at a hotel on the Grand Canal, right next to Harry's Bar where the famous Bellini – prosecco and fresh white peach pulp – became a daily staple.

They had the money for restaurants and champagne, beluga caviar. Margaret made the odd cheese soufflé, an occasional caesar salad and his favourite huevos rancheros, for which he had acquired a taste in Mexico City while he was there filming for the Olympic Games. Michael only knew about three kinds of food when Margaret met him and so it continued: the classic dishes served in the top restaurants that he had frequented as a young star, baked beans on toast (which he could make), and a roast lamb dinner. And he liked chips, so she invested in a chip fryer.

Michael commented one day that Margaret didn't read regularly, especially for an author.

'When would I have the time?' she asked him.

'Fulfilling a seven-book contract, walking the beagles, cooking little meals for us both, breaking off for our happy hour at six every evening, throwing the odd big party for Mike, sitting on the lounge holding hands – I was a very busy girl. Burning the candle at both ends isn't for the faint-hearted, or for the bookish,' she says now.

'I knew the joys of companionship,' she adds. 'I could snuggle up to my love, Michael, and drift off to sleep knowing that tomorrow was going to be another good day. For the first time in my life I knew what true companionship could be. I knew how life shared with someone – a special someone, the right person – could be.'

THE PERSON WHO MAKES THE FIRE

A ute rattled past me on the Narooma to Tilba highway, my commute to work. The sky was black and pink; it got up with me in shocking colours while I pulled on my faded blue denim and Blundstones at 4.30 am, stretched out against the sky, over the dams and national park, the river, the bridge, the turn-off to Mystery Bay, four hours south of Sydney.

I opened the windows every morning and the wind roared into my bouncy four-wheel drive that the production company had given me for this four-month stint away. I woke up in the air, soaked in oxygen and eucalyptus. I was grateful to be here with the morning. I had yanked myself away from Bingley and my burgeoning freelance work and opportunities, from freebies and glittering nights at Sydney bar openings. But I loved this, being away, doing *something*. I stopped at the first gate to the farm: out of the car, motor running, open the gate, shift the car forward, close the gate, drive up the hill over the tawny dust to the next gate; repeat.

I looked for snakes directly under me, not in front of me, just as Bill, a local Aborigine from Bermagui, told me to do one day while we were filming. He poked at a small fire he built with a stick, picked up a handful of dried leaves and threw them in.

'The person who makes the fire owns the fire, has responsibility for the fire. Nobody else feeds the fire.'

He added a few twigs to the flames.

'It's like feeding the devil, a bad spirit. The person who builds the fire is responsible for it. Nobody else.'

I thought of him and shut the gate, noticing a hint of smoke in the summer morning air. I was happy, exhausted, grilled to the bone. In those first months I was wired to point of collapse every day – but so happy.

'This is my fire, I built it, I'm responsible for it.'

At a long table in the middle of the set kitchen – the only room inside the house that viewers actually see – the show's host and chef, the director, series producer and I mooted ideas around mushrooms. We had a tangle of large oyster mushrooms and a bundle of fresh shiitakes coming via some local talent who grew his own. Others were bringing home-brewed beer, rhubarb sparkling wine, a couple of rabbits, and we'd had more goat's milk. It was our task to work recipes into the next two episodes that we'd film over the coming three or so weeks. As recipe developer and prep cook on the show, it was key to my job that these recipes were spot-on, a balance of accessible and inspirational and, most important of all, highlighting local produce and real, sustainable, whole ingredients.

I'd railed against the monumental global shift towards fast, fat-laden, highly processed food in my writing for years. At home I cooked meals from scratch and developed recipes in my books and columns to urge people to do the same. So when I talked through slow-cooked polenta – grating raw pumpkin into the mixture as it cooks, so it develops a kind of sweet, caramelised nuttiness, topped with sautéed mushrooms, ginger julienne, loads of butter – things fell into place. I described outdoor-oven roasted quince, cooked in cinnamon syrup and verjuice, with goat's milk panna cotta and shaved fresh carob over the top.

'The stonemason on the hill has carob, turning black in pods, nearly ready. How can we get that in there?' the producer says.

The host, a chef, got up from the meeting every twenty minutes or so to check a massive vat of roasted veal bones simmering with caramelised garlic and onions, carrots he had pulled out of the earth that morning.

I borrowed a pumpkin from the garden and roasted it for me and Jodes, my beautiful, tall, freckled flatmate for the season. Sometimes it was cucumbers, other times zucchini; a real garden is all about dealing with the glut. This was our chance to be healthy, come back fitter and slimmer. I cooked quinoa and tossed it in a large shallow dish with pepita seeds and sunflower seeds, threw in the pieces of roasted pumpkin with pomegranate seeds and goat's cheese that we'd made the week before. The dish has become my go-to vegetarian reboot, even if the goats themselves aren't always on hand to milk (see recipe on page 254).

We dreamed up recipes. When lilly pillies, that native Australian berry not unlike a crab apple, punched into bloom on a tree on the farm, the chef and I gathered notepads and our brains to think up the best ways to use them. They're not particularly flavourful, but their bright-pink colour and slightly spongy, crispy texture works on a salad of shredded duck confit, crumbled ricotta and native plants such as samphire: a crunchy, sweet, rich and salty entrée. The chef and I looked up at the giant tree, then he grabbed the trunk and shook it, and down rained thousands of the little hard berries on our heads. I smashed up a bucket of lilly pillies, painstakingly removing every single stone, discarding blackened fruit, leaves, twigs, bugs. Combined with yeast – sourced from a brewing store in nearby Cobargo, where the owners have painted over the former Bank of Wales sign at the entrance to read Bank of Ales – and water, lemon juice and sugar, the mixture sat and bubbled, fermented, turned from berries on a tree into bright-pink bottles of sparkling wine. The chef repeated the process a couple of weeks later, shaking down the tree and turning out more bottles of this stuff for viewers – and us.

I tried this at home, not with lilly pillies but with whatever fruit, vegetable, in-season thing I had in great supply. I smashed up raw rhubarb when I bought bundles of it at a farmers' market. When the gallon jar was full of pink sticks and bubbling champagne, I filled a jar of vodka with the leftover rhubarb. The vegetable flavours the vodka and, in a few weeks, you're topping up shots of pink clear vodka with soda water, a squeeze of fresh lime. Try this at home (see recipe on page 256). Using the same techniques as we did on the farm, I now have a constant supply of slightly alcoholic ginger beer at home. The mixture slowly ferments, eating up the sugar and steeping ginger deeper into the brew. It's a serious competitor for the lilly pilly (see recipe on page 259).

The flies were always bad come eleven o'clock. Remnants of the old dairy farm survived – an old milking shed, a couple of silos and acres of kikuyu pasture. Neighbours' Jersey and Friesian 'milkers' grazed and by the house two beautiful black pregnant sows snorted and watched out for me carrying over buckets of scraps. Seeing me approach they'd canter towards me, then snort and jostle for food, shoving each other out of the way until it was gone. They'd turn their noses to the air, sniffing for more offerings, then trot back to their little shed. But they brought with them flies – blasted lazy swarming flies that stuck on our arms and dive-bombed our eyeballs, got tangled in our hair, walked on our lips.

The kitchen screen door slammed every few minutes as crew members wandered in and out, rinsing their coffee cups and washing their hands. The screen door slammed shut again, they were gone, and a few more flies were in. I'd go into a dream as I buttered a pudding dish. I measured out my days with tablespoons.

After work, outside shooting blocks, the crew and I took our Toyota convoy to nearby Narooma, stopped into some pub and ended up at one of our houses. A few times, as the bottles of wine on the dining room table emptied, we'd dance in the living room, ending up in collapsed laughing piles on the kitchen floor.

There's a phrase I like: 'I am thankful for the nights that turned into mornings, friends that turned into family, and dreams that turned into reality.' That is how I feel about these months.

Guards down and exhaustion taking its toll, we all did all sorts of stupid things. I loved the crew. I loved their company. When I was freelancing alone in my living room in Balmain, before I knew them, it was them I missed. A kind of perforated human-shaped void had been cut out of my day when I stopped working in an office. I tried to remember that when I had my hand up the backside of a freshly plucked chicken.

When things got hectic in the kitchen on food shoot days, I'd stand quite literally over the stove for fifteen hours, two or three days in a row. Leesh, the runner, was washing up and she'd been doing it all day while I cooked. We tiptoed around the prep kitchen while the producer, director, camera assistant, two cameramen, 'soundo' and host made television in the set kitchen next door. I tried to sauté onions in silence while she scraped crusty bits off frying pans, rinsing on mute lest we ruin a scene next door. We were both hot and bothered, but spent most of the day giggling and whispering, telling stories of former boyfriends, my life in Sydney and her former life in Tasmania. We wore heavy Blundstones all day, obligatory on-set farm wear, insurance against snakes, barbed wire, heavy machinery, and hot coal pits on the lawn I'd made when testing outdoor recipes. Hard yakka is what the heavy boots were made for, and hard it was.

'Gah, my swollen feet are bloody killing me,' I moaned to Leesha.

'Well, if you want to work in TV…'

Actually, I was here for the cooking and the food, to remember where food came from, not for the television specifically. But everyone else was. Everyone else skittered from show to show, freelancing and being picked up for four- or five-month stints. Their skills were in researching and finding talent, developing stories. While I'd carved out a career freelancing via story commissions that could take a few days, they'd done it based on jobs, month-long posts that might fall close to home or just as easily in Papua New Guinea or Tilba Tilba.

If you couldn't handle the pressure, you definitely wouldn't survive.

'How would *you* like to be the gimp?' a fed-up camera assistant barked at the host on one long hot day of shooting.

The crew looked away, stunned, embarrassed.

'I've been the gimp mate. We all have,' replied the host.

The TV dream died for that camera assistant, who bowed out soon after.

It was true; everyone had been the gimp. The host had worked in professional kitchens in Tasmania and Melbourne; others had been posted to faraway places as a camera assistant or had plugged away as data loggers, essentially entering everyone's research results into a computer all day long. Sometimes, when I scraped out handfuls of dead flies and cherry pips from the plughole with my fingers, I felt like the gimp. I was fine with that.

Then I'd talk through the salt-crust chicken idea with the host, or harvest cucumbers from the garden with a paring knife for my own lunch, visit a local honey producer and bee expert who wore actual denim overalls rolled up, and remember that it was my fire, I'd made it. And I was thankful that a dream I'd always had, had turned into reality.

SEEDED QUINOA WITH ROAST PUMPKIN, POMEGRANATE *and* GOAT'S CHEESE

See story on page 251

SERVES 4–6
PREPARATION 30 minutes
COOKING 40 minutes

350 g (12 oz) pumpkin (winter squash), such as butternut or Kent, peeled and diced
1 red onion, cut into 6 wedges
1 garlic bulb, unpeeled, cut in half crossways
60 ml (2 fl oz/¼ cup) extra virgin olive oil
sea salt and freshly ground black pepper
40 g (1½ oz/¼ cup) pepitas (pumpkin seeds)
150 g (5½ oz/¾ cup) quinoa, rinsed well
180 g (6½ oz/¾ cup) pearl barley, rinsed well
40 g (1½ oz/1 cup) chopped coriander (cilantro)
1 large handful mint leaves, torn
seeds from 1 pomegranate
juice of 1 lemon
120 g (4¼ oz) ashed goat's cheese
2 tablespoons pomegranate molasses, to serve (optional)

Preheat the oven to 220°C (425°F).

Scatter the pumpkin and onion in a shallow baking tray and nestle the garlic halves in-between so they're not too exposed. Drizzle over 1 tablespoon of the olive oil, season with salt and pepper, and toss together to coat. Bake for about 20 minutes, or until tender and caramelised.

Meanwhile, soak the pepitas in a bowl of cold water for 20 minutes, then drain.

Put the quinoa in a saucepan with 375 ml (13 fl oz/1½ cups) of water and a large pinch of salt and bring to the boil. Reduce the heat, cover and cook for 12–15 minutes, or until all the liquid is absorbed. When it is ready, the quinoa should look like little spirals. Turn off the heat and let it sit for 5 minutes with the lid on, then fluff with a fork.

Put the barley in a saucepan and cover generously with cold water. Bring to the boil, then lower the heat, cover and cook for 30–40 minutes, or until the barley is tender. Drain thoroughly.

In a large bowl, combine the quinoa, barley, pepitas, coriander, mint, half the pomegranate seeds, the pumpkin, onion, garlic, lemon juice and remaining olive oil. Break up the onion and toss well to combine. Season to taste.

Transfer the mixture to a serving plate or large shallow bowl, scatter over the remaining pomegranate seeds, crumble over the goat's cheese and drizzle with pomegranate molasses, if using.

tip

Pomegranate molasses is available from large supermarkets, good grocers and delicatessens. It is delicious but very high in sugar, and it is perfectly acceptable to omit it.

RHUBARB VODKA

See story on page 251

MAKES About 1.6 litres
PREPARATION 20 minutes,
plus 24 hours macerating and
3 weeks maturing

5 stalks rhubarb (use the
    reddest ones you can find)
3 heaped tablespoons caster
    (superfine) sugar
1 litre (35 fl oz/4 cups) vodka
peeled rind of ½ lemon
1 cinnamon stick (optional)
ice, to serve
soda water (club soda),
    to serve

Chop the rhubarb into 2 cm (¾ in) lengths, then smash using a mortar and pestle (or put into a large plastic snap-lock bag and bash with a rolling pin). Put the rhubarb and any juice into a 2 litre (70 fl oz/8 cup) jar with a tight-fitting lid, pour in the sugar, seal and shake to combine. Leave to macerate at room temperature for at least 24 hours.

Add the vodka, lemon rind and cinnamon to the jar, stir with a wooden spoon to combine, and leave the jar in a cool, dark place for 3 weeks. Shake gently every day or so.

When the vodka is very pink, give it a taste test. If the rhubarb flavour is strong enough, strain it through a muslin- (cheesecloth-) lined sieve into a bowl. Use a funnel to transfer the liquid to a sterilised bottle. (Alternatively, if you'd like a stronger rhubarb flavour, leave the rhubarb mixture for another week.)

Leave the strained vodka for at least 1 more week before drinking, to allow the flavours to develop further.

To serve, add one shot to a glass filled with ice and top up with soda water.

tip

The longer you leave the vodka muddling with the rhubarb, the stronger the taste will be.

REAL GINGER BEER

See story on page 252

MAKES About 2 litres
PREPARATION 20 minutes,
plus 48 hours fermentation
COOKING 5 minutes

1 x 5 cm (2 in) piece
    fresh ginger
250 ml (9 fl oz/1 cup)
    filtered water
165 g (5¾ oz/¾ cup) sugar,
    plus extra, to taste
⅛ teaspoon fine sea salt
juice of 2–3 lemons (about
    100 ml/3½ fl oz), plus
    extra to taste
⅛ teaspoon dried
    champagne yeast
ice, to serve

Peel and finely grate the ginger to make about
2 tablespoons. Bring the water to the boil in a small
saucepan, remove from the heat, add the sugar and salt
and stir until dissolved. Add the ginger and let the solution
cool to room temperature. Stir in the lemon juice.

Using a funnel, pour the liquid into a clean 2 litre capacity
(70 fl oz/8 cup) jar or plastic bottle with a lid. Do not
strain out the ginger. Top up with water, leaving about
5 cm (2 in) of space at the top. Taste the liquid, and add
a little more lemon juice or sugar, if liked. Add the yeast,
secure the cap or lid and shake the bottle to distribute and
dissolve the yeast.

Let the ginger beer sit in a cool, dark place for 48 hours,
until carbonated. Pop the lid after 24 hours to relieve a
little pressure and check for carbonation (small bubbles
will form on the surface and you will hear gas escape when
you open the bottle).

Strain the ginger beer through a sieve into sterilised
glass flip-top bottles and store in the fridge overnight or
for up to 2 weeks. The refrigeration will slow down the
carbonation process so the bottles don't explode.

To serve, open the bottles over the sink in case of
over-carbonation, and pour into glasses filled with ice.

tip

*Champagne yeast is available from brewers' stores
and online. It is a clean, neutral-tasting yeast that
produces more bubbles than other types of yeast.*

FOR BETTER OR FOR WORSE

Suzanne, now twenty-one, was tucked upstairs in her mother's Balmain home. Denis was still around, and Suzanne had left Robert in London so he could make his way, partly overland, back to Sydney. She had scored a job at *Woman's Day* with Margaret, cooking by her mother's side in the test kitchen, developing recipes and joining her on photo shoots for the ongoing catalogue of cookbooks.

My father took a bus to India en route to Sydney. But fighting between Pakistan and India disrupted the journey. In Thailand he came down with the local version of Delhi belly, the dreaded stomach bug, and he dealt with corruption while trying to negotiate passages on rickety boats through the Indonesian archipelago. He was delayed longer than Suzanne had hoped, and it being 1971 and this being my father, the beleaguered traveller didn't just dial in from the hotel. He was moving from youth hostel to worse, spending as little as possible, even in Asia. Finally he arrived in Darwin, then hitched his way into Sydney.

Late one evening, Suzanne was at her lowest and had gone to bed early. Denis, meanwhile, had driven up to the Balmain shops to buy a packet of cigarettes. The phone rang: it was Denis calling from a public phone box.

'Is Suzanne there, Margaret?'

'No, she's gone to bed.'

'Get her up, and tell her to go downstairs immediately.'

Margaret woke her sleepy daughter, who shrugged it off as one of Denis' practical jokes.

'You'd better come down,' her mother said.

A few minutes later Denis descended the sandstone steps from the front gate, trailed by a tired and familiar figure. My mum shot into his arms. Dad had hitched all the way from Darwin to the bottom of Darling Street, Balmain. Hitchhikers were not a common sight on this working-class street and Denis had taken pity on the complete stranger, offering him a lift. When my dad told him the address Denis did a double take.

'Well, that's precisely where I'm going.'

Robert and Suzanne married a year later, in May. As her own mother had done before her, she wanted to cater the wedding herself. 'We considered ourselves a bit bohemian,' my mum tells me.

Suzanne made her mother write out every one of the invitations by hand –

'instead of buying those packets of silver wedding invitations with bells on the front'.

Suzanne and Robert married in a tiny church in Balmain, and then the entire wedding moved down to Margaret's home on the water.

'It was fairly natural for us to have the wedding at home and cater it ourselves,' Mum says. 'There was Mum and Jeanie, who was a good cook, plus me back from the Cordon Bleu, and a couple of staff from *Woman's Day* came to help.'

Dad adds: 'Plus the alternatives for weddings were pretty grim, we felt. There were these sort of clubs that catered to weddings.'

'Yes, like a Hellenic club or a type of RSL place,' says Mum. 'You would get chicken in a basket. It's almost fried, but probably roasted chicken, with chips in a little wicker basket lined with paper napkins. It sounds worse than it was, though. Chicken was a big deal because, in the 1960s, chicken was expensive compared to other roasts. We had a lot of meat about but chickens were only starting to be produced in vast numbers.'

That's why we hear stories of roast chicken for Christmas in the good old days. As mass production of chickens, otherwise known as battery chickens, started to occur in the late 1970s and 1980s in Australia, the birds became more available.

'But it also started to lose its flavour,' my mum says. 'Chicken always used to be free-range. It was a big deal but it was always good chicken in the 1960s and when I was a girl.'

So when coronation chicken appeared at the Doonan–Gibbs wedding, it was impressive. 'It wasn't so well known as it is now,' Mum says. 'Some of my English friends now pooh-pooh the dish: "Oh yeah, the old coronation chicken at your wedding, of course." But it was rather special and different. I used the Rosemary Hume recipe from the Cordon Bleu, we made the mayonnaise ourselves and did the whole thing from scratch. Properly made, it's very beautiful.'

And Margaret made 'the most beautiful dish', my mum says. 'I often think about it: crepes Louise. The handmade, almost transparently thin crepes were filled with seafood, mostly crab. A bit of béchamel sauce with wine in it, and seafood. They were rolled into cigars and baked in little copper gratin dishes, and came up bubbling. They were passed around on bread-and-butter plates with forks.'

They also served a fillet of beef, 'which was very cheap compared to the prices today'. It was served slightly chilled, and cut into one-centimetre-thick slices, rare. And it came with salad.

'The only kind of lettuce available was iceberg, and we had very ordinary tomatoes. We have gone backwards with chicken since then, with exceptions, of course, but forward with tomatoes and lettuce.'

Also served with the fillet of beef were whole baby potatoes, skin on.

'I remember being down in the kitchen on my wedding day, scrubbing potatoes that were going to be steamed with mint. I had my hair all done up and wore an apron over my white dress. The car was waiting by the front gate to take me to the church. Mum came into the kitchen and said, "For heaven's sake, Suzie, put down that potato."'

And then there was something really special: a side of smoked salmon. In 1972 we weren't yet farming salmon in Tasmania on any scale, so Margaret arranged to have the fish sent over from Scotland.

'It didn't come sliced, but whole, so you had to slice it yourself,' Mum tells me. 'Auntie Jean got very possessive with the salmon and wouldn't allow people to hack it. She had a terrible fight with Rob's friend McKinnon, who she thought was hacking it. We had it with bread and butter.'

My mum bursts out laughing: bread and butter.

Another huge luxury was asparagus, which was very hard to get. They were not like they are now, apparently. 'You had to go over them carefully because they were always filled with sand. They grow under the ground and then they sprout up, but sand was always tucked under the little leaves, or whatever that is. They are of the lily family, you know.'

I love how my mum talks about food, the way things were. Our conversations about food are always backed by her extraordinary knowledge, after more than forty years in the industry. She moved from the Cordon Bleu to *Woman's Day*, then joined *New Idea*, *Home Beautiful*; she was the food director at *Australian Table* magazine which later became *BBC Good Food* magazine. She also wrote twenty-something cookbooks, and has just finished another, at sixty-four.

She was so busy scrubbing potatoes until the eleventh hour, she didn't think of packing a bag for their honeymoon, in a place called Black Head.

'Someone offered us a house up past Forster,' Mum explains.

For going away, the bride wore the white knee-high leather boots that she had been married in, and a camel cashmere coat she had brought back from London.

'It had a belt with a buckle but you didn't use the buckle, you tied it around you; it was very cool.'

But she wore no knickers and left for the trip with no other clothing options for her entire honeymoon. My mum. Someone from *Woman's Day* packed the couple a hamper: a pork and veal terrine with bacon wrapped around it, some bread, olives, lemon sable biscuits: 'everything handmade'.

I think about their wedding often, and their marriage. Love is one thing, but if that comes without respecting each other's differences, accepting and even treasuring them, it's not enough. I want to come home and feel safe, loved, calm and excited, all at once. I want the inspiration and the madness but also to know that despite some terrific row, some maddening upset, we're going to come out the other side. It's asking too much, until you find it. The ups and downs of my grandmother's marriages terrify me; I don't want that. The hurt and the terrible sadness, the wondering, I can do without. We can't all find a kindred spirit right off, and in my grandmother's case it took three major partnerships to get there. I know others never do.

My grandmother did teach me, though, that the best relationship you can ever have is the one with yourself. That's a love affair worth pursuing.

HAVE PEN, WILL TRAVEL

What I was not ready for, and Bingley will never be ready for, was the natto. The Japanese love natto. It's a gloopy pile of something in a small bowl. Looked simple enough: a plop of tiny soybeans. As the waitress handed me this concoction for breakfast, in our hotel deep in the snow in a Japanese prefecture called Hakuba, she signalled to stir it with my chopsticks, kind of whip it up. From a lumpy condiment it turned into an unbelievably slimy, glutinous, stringy goop. It got more sticky the more you whipped it, and I worked it into a contorted lather. It tastes a bit like soy sauce, but with spider's web. The taste of the natto isn't bad, if you can get past the texture. Bingley has meanwhile put down his knife and fork (tourist), leans over his own breakfast, and is looking wide-eyed into my bowl, face distorted in horror.

There's no elegant way to eat the stuff. I lift a few beans on my chopsticks to my mouth and a viscous trail of the mucous follows, a web from mouth to bowl. When I put the chopsticks down, the long strands form another path. It sticks to my chin and my chopsticks, I twist it around one stick like a savoury lumpy fairy floss and still these horrible strings form. I choke them down, a couple at a time, all the while smiling at Bingley, who's looking smug with his fatty porky American sausages, his 'western' breakfast choice. I wipe away the remnants of the web and dissolve in gratitude when the waitress brings another layer of the Japanese breakfast marathon to the table. I shift the beloved natto aside, putting it down to national taste that nobody foreign quite gets, just as Australians have Vegemite, and beetroot on our burgers.

Travelling gives you a glimpse into other countries' weirdness. I like that. And also into your travel companion's oddness. Bingley learned early on that I'm the type of person who gets the traditional, local version of breakfast in the hotel. When we shuffle from our room down the lift to the hotel restaurant in Hong Kong, he heads towards croissants, yoghurt and fruit, a ham and spinach omelette, and I go the other way. We meet at the table, me with my steamed buns filled with strange wobbly things, chilli sauce for dipping, a bowl of congee topped with tiny fried prawns and onions. I figure that if you're going to try out another country's breakfast, you may as well do it in the safety of a decent hotel. He thinks it's too much ambition with your morning espresso.

Being able to write, or finding people willing to pay me to write, gives me the chance to travel. I can't believe my luck. I know there was hard work, too; it continues to be hard work. But I know I got here with the hand of others. I'd got the job writing at the *Evening Standard* on my own, but I managed to break into the food industry because one extraordinary Australian book publisher, Julie Gibbs – the surname a coincidence – gave me the chance to join my mother and write my first cookbook, *The Thrifty Kitchen*. I'd been to hundreds of food shoots and helped work on hundreds of recipes, but being able to make decisions – actually choose the recipes, write the recipes myself, attend shoots and have a say in things – that was the luck of heritage and hard work, as well as the kindness of strangers. And then the benevolence of food writers Simon Thomsen and Jill Dupleix, who had faith in my blogging scribbles or saw some talent in my words, but who went a step further and actually did something about it. They recommended me for articles, and to editors who then put me onto various food guides and my by-line inside their magazines. In the competitive business of food, this is huge. It changed my life.

Bingley hired some navy-blue European thing for us to get to Barcelona from Bilbao. It was the middle of summer and after a quick walk around the Guggenheim in Bilbao, we ordered a plate of dark jamón, plus a glass of something sparkling, and his beer. The jamón was hand-cut and I'd never tasted anything like it – rich with sweet oil and laid out in thin slices on the plate. Within a couple of hours of arriving in Spain, I ate one of the best things I've ever had; that's either an extraordinary case of luck, or it boded well for food in this country…

We drove into Barcelona – then the usual bag drop, shower, shave, hair wash, makeup reapply, a summer dress slipped over my pale Sydney winter shoulders – and we headed straight out to a little tapas place overrun with people our age. We perched on stools and leaned over our beers, waited for the various bravas, pintxos and croquetas to arrive. First, though, the octopus. A slightly warmed plate arrived with pieces of octopus, large cut-up segments of the larger tentacles, and it had been slowly braised, a hint of wine or vinegar, so the meat was soft and slightly jellied at the edges near the skin. It came in a little dish with pieces of just-done potatoes and a dollop of saffron alioli on top (see recipe on page 267). Bingley and I swooned, wiping our bread around the plate to mop up all remaining juices. More octopus, more beer came. I ordered a salad, 'for health'. Soft little butter leaves from the inside of the lettuce came spread out on a large plate. They had deep-fried smoked chickpeas doused in paprika, so they turned crispy on the outside, nutty and fragrant inside. A slab of grilled rare tuna had been torn into large pieces and scattered over the salad, so the pretty pink rare insides could be admired by those of us who cared. We cared, so much. Bingley dipped his bread into the bowl again, soaking up the creamy spiced dressing and herbs through the salad (see recipe on page 268). Our first night in Barcelona, our second in Spain, set the tone for the rest of our trip.

We walked back to the hotel in the summer air, still light even though it was past ten o'clock. I looked up at Bingley and couldn't believe my luck. My mad and funny companion, his beautiful reassuring face and occasionally ridiculous imagination. He drove me mad, sometimes. Mostly, he made me happy. I would write a story about the night, about the food, and add it to my list of where to go in this food destination. But right now, I could live it.

OCTOPUS, POTATO *and* CAPER SALAD WITH SAFFRON ALIOLI

See story on page 265

SERVES 6
PREPARATION 20 minutes
COOKING 1 hour

1 celery stalk, chopped
1 carrot, chopped
1 brown onion, halved
2 fresh bay leaves
75 g (2¾ oz/½ bunch) flat-leaf
    (Italian) parsley, leaves finely
    chopped, stalks reserved
1–1.2 kg (2 lb 4 oz–2 lb 12 oz)
    octopus, cleaned
800 g (1 lb 12 oz) all-purpose
    potatoes (such as desiree),
    peeled and cut into 2–3 cm
    (¾–1¼ in) cubes
2 tablespoons extra virgin
    olive oil
45 g (1¾ oz/¼ cup) drained
    capers, rinsed and patted
    dry with paper towel
80 ml (2½ fl oz/⅓ cup)
    lemon juice
sea salt and freshly ground
    black pepper
lemon wedges, to serve

Saffron alioli
1 pinch of saffron threads
1½ tablespoons lemon juice
2 garlic cloves, sliced
2 teaspoons sea salt
1 free-range egg yolk
125 ml (4 fl oz/½ cup) extra
    virgin olive oil
freshly ground black pepper

For the saffron alioli, soak the saffron threads in the lemon juice for 1–2 minutes to infuse.

Grind the garlic in a mortar and pestle with the salt. Add the egg yolk, and stir in a circular motion to combine well. One drop at a time, and then in a very slow stream, stir in the olive oil until the mixture is thick, stirring constantly. Be careful not to add the oil too quickly or it will not form the right consistency – the slower the better.

Stir in the lemon and saffron and season with pepper. Set aside until ready to serve.

Combine the celery, carrot, onion, bay leaves and parsley stalks in a large saucepan with 2 litres (70 fl oz/8 cups) of water. Bring to the boil, then add the octopus, cover and reduce the heat to medium–low. Cook for 40 minutes to 1 hour, or until the octopus is tender. Remove from the heat, leave the lid on, and allow the octopus to cool completely in the stock.

Meanwhile, steam the potato over lightly salted water for 10–12 minutes, or until tender. Set aside to cool.

In a small frying pan, heat half the oil over medium–high heat and fry the drained capers, stirring frequently, for 5–8 minutes, or until crispy. Drain on paper towel.

Drain the cooled octopus and cut into 2 cm (¾ in) slices. Combine in a bowl with the remaining olive oil, lemon juice, chopped parsley, potato and capers. Toss well and season with salt and pepper, then serve with the saffron alioli and lemon wedges.

SPANISH CHOPPED SALAD WITH TUNA *and* CHORIZO

See story on page 265

SERVES 4
PREPARATION 15 minutes
COOKING 10 minutes

1 x 425 g (15 oz) tin
  organic chickpeas, drained,
  rinsed and patted dry
3 tablespoons extra virgin
  olive oil
2 teaspoons hot paprika (or
  sweet, if you prefer)
sea salt and freshly ground
  black pepper
60 g (2¼ oz) dried chorizo,
  cut into lardons
300 g (10½ oz) yellowfin tuna
1 large head butter lettuce
  or 3 baby cos (romaine),
  chopped into 3 cm (1¼ in)
  chunks
2–3 radicchio leaves, torn
1 spring onion (scallion),
  white part only, finely sliced
  on the diagonal
1 roasted capsicum (pepper),
  cut into strips (see page 24)
1 handful flat-leaf (Italian)
  parsley leaves, chopped
2 tablespoons
  sliced almonds, toasted

Spicy Spanish dressing
1 tablespoon hot
  smoked paprika
60 ml (2 fl oz/¼ cup)
  lemon juice
2 tinned anchovies,
  finely chopped
3 tablespoons olive oil, plus
  extra, if needed
freshly ground black pepper

For the spicy Spanish dressing, combine all the ingredients except the pepper in a jar and shake well until thick. Add a little more olive oil, if liked, shaking between each taste, and season with pepper. Set aside and shake well again before serving.

Preheat the oven to 200°C (400°F) and line a baking tray with baking paper.

Put the chickpeas, 2 tablespoons of the oil, the paprika and ½ teaspoon of sea salt in a bowl and toss together to coat. Spread onto the prepared tray and bake for 20 minutes, or until crispy and golden. Set aside to cool.

Heat a small frying pan over high heat, fry the chorizo until golden and crisp and set aside.

Season the tuna with salt and pepper and coat with the remaining olive oil. Heat a frying pan until very hot and cook the tuna for 2–3 minutes each side, or until seared on the outside but still quite rare on the inside. Set aside.

In a medium bowl, toss together the lettuce, radicchio, chorizo, spring onion and 1–2 tablespoons of the dressing. Transfer to a serving plate. Break the tuna into pieces over the salad and garnish with roasted capsicum, parsley, chickpeas and toasted almonds. Drizzle over a little more dressing to taste, then serve.

tip

To toast the almonds, cook them in a dry frying pan, tossing them around until just golden.

IN SICKNESS AND IN HEALTH

There's something 'treaty' about being in Grandma's bed when you're eight years old. The sheets are crisp and clean and it's a massive big bed; plus the ceiling is painted pale blue with clouds about a hundred feet above your head. So when your parents are away in America and she says you can sleep in her bed in the day because you're home sick from school, you're going to take that offer. You're going to jump – sniffling and mopey, dragging a box of tissues over the duvet to put next to the Vicks Vaporub on the bedside table – at the chance.

From Grandma's bed a VHS marathon played out on a 40 cm–wide television. *Annie*, obviously, the 1982 classic with Albert Finney as Daddy Warbucks. *The Sound of Music* then, because Michael's love of musicals rubbed off on my sister and me and I couldn't really see the point of a movie if the characters didn't stop mid-sentence to sing. And then I listened to the gulls on Goat Island in the middle of the harbour and watched the clouds in the ceiling until the sheets turned smelly in my feverish sweating, wriggling dreams. It was night-time when I woke up, disorientated. Grandma had been pressing me to eat all day and I didn't want anything; not the grilled cheese on toast idea, not the porridge idea, not the plain rice. But French onion soup: 'Yes, please, Grandma.'

She leaned in, gave me a squeeze and a kiss on the forehead, and then left. I fell back asleep.

Grandma's version of onion soup involves seven cups of homemade beef stock. She picked up the pick-me-up in *The Garrulous Gourmet* book she had bought for her sister Jean in 1952, but after years of making the recipe for *Women's Day* and then *New Idea*, for us, for herself, she improved on it. Introducing extra virgin olive oil with the butter to sauté the sliced onions at the beginning not only increases the health benefits, but also stops the butter burning. Just a little flour gives the stock a viscosity without thickening it, and without allowing it to be too light and fresh either. The flour has to be cooked properly in the beginning, or the soup ends up tasting like raw flour, the raw flavour permeating the lot, just as the onions also will, if they're not properly reduced and close to caramelised before the stock is added. Lots and lots of pepper: essential.

When Grandma came back into the room, she carried a little classic French gratinée bowl on a plate, on a tray. The fragrant soup was sealed at the top with a round slice of sourdough baguette, soaked with broth and topped with grilled, toasted Swiss gruyère. Almost the best bit of the soup is when the crispy grilled-cheese bits cling to the bowl at the sides and you get to scratch them off when the soup is done.

'It's hot, darling, let it sit a moment.'

I rolled over, sat up, leaned into the bowl to smell it on my bedside table.

When I woke up, the bowl was gone, it was morning, and Grandma opened the wooden blinds to let in the sunshine. I didn't get the soup. And so, years later, I still crave it when I am sick. I think of all the trouble she went to, making this elaborate homemade brew to heal. Maybe all I needed was the smell of the rich brown broth next to me, and the comfort of knowing that Grandma would make it for me.

The smell of Tiger Balm, though, to me, is real sickness. That's how you know when it's really, really bad. Suddenly, in 1988, when I was eleven, it infiltrated our lives. All I knew was that we were going to Brisbane, to Expo, with Grandma and Michael. Louise and I did great splashing competition bombs into the pool at the resort, we drank pink lemonade *in* the pool, and at Expo we learned that Switzerland had snow, that Japan had an excellent red dot in the middle of its flag, and that in Ireland people drink 'a lot' of black beer. I was dripping wet in swimmers and ran back to the hotel room to get my goggles. I opened the door between our room and Grandma and Michael's room and he was in bed, propped up with pillows. The room was warm and thick with the smell of Tiger Balm, which Grandma rubbed into his legs and chest a few times a day.

In 1980, eight years earlier, Michael had visited Sydney for work and contacted Margaret, inviting her and Denis out to dinner.

'It will just be me,' she said. 'Denis and I separated.'

Silence on the other end of the phone. Relief.

'I was unattached,' she says now, 'and I wasn't about to tell Michael to bugger off.'

They spent the next eight years in sync, each independent and busy but attached, in love.

He was planning another trip for them to take together in 1988, while Margaret finished another book. He had a persistent cough and pains in his legs. He saw the doctor and was fine, he told her, but would take more tests. One day she opened a big envelope containing a medical report, and her eyes caught the word 'carcinoma'. She approached Michael.

'Isn't that cancer?'

'Yes.'

She joined him on visits to the doctor, for more X-rays and tests, more analyses. One day she gathered the courage to ask the terrible question: How long?

'Sixteen weeks.'

Home again, having declined chemotherapy, Michael sat with Grandma on the sofa, holding hands.

'What do you want to do with your time?' she asked.

'Curl up and die.'

'No, you don't,' she said. 'You want to take that trip to New York, London, Paris, Provence. See your old friends. See a few shows.'

So they did. Plus Expo, with the girls.

Sixteen weeks later, on 6 October, 1988, Michael died. It was my grandmother's sixty-fourth birthday.

RSVP

I love the concept of worlds colliding: people from different parts of your life coming together, fusing awkwardly for a moment, while the mutual party bubbles and combusts. I love the messiness of collided people – it's uncomfortable and adorable.

After a couple of decades languishing in the deep freeze of gastro fashion, dinner parties made a comeback. They always seem like a good idea at the time. It starts with dreaming of fairy lights and bubbles in glasses, seeing your friends rub shoulders over flickering tea lights, with your boss. Around the fourth course of a six-course meal, as the boeuf bourguignon and the gently braised artichokes come to the table, you imagine your munificence bringing happiness to your careful selection of brilliant guests.

But while we're all cooking at home now, and sharing our culinary repertoire with our nearest and dearest, hosting a dinner party remains an art form few of us have mastered. From deflated soufflés to tipped-over croquembouche, everyone has their own dinner party catastrophe to tell. Worst of all are the ones where the guests never get to eat, the ones where the host realises on the afternoon of the dinner party that the 36-hour slow-cooked lamb – currently just a shoulder in a bag in the fridge – is not going to be ready.

If paying attention to my grandmother's soirées and my parents' extraordinary feasts has taught me anything, it's to do as much of the preparation in advance. Otherwise, it's this: hungry guests pawing at the nut bowl and popping into the kitchen, four glasses of wine in, asking if they can do anything. You forge ahead with mutilating a quail's carcass or deboning a pork belly. One guest peers over the pile of unwashed, unpeeled, unchopped, unsautéed vegetables on the bench, pours you a glass of wine, says it sure looks delicious and nips back out to join the starved, increasingly tipsy masses on the sofa – at least being hungry is something they can bond over. I know this from experience.

I have the ultimate plan-ahead recipe. Everything is done ahead. One duck, or a few duck breasts are minced ahead, either by the butcher, or in a hand-mincer at home. And with this rich mince, you create a ragu with onions and celery, leek and garlic, plus a dollop of tomato paste, sage and cherry tomatoes. You want long, slow cooking, and this can be done days beforehand. The hand-rolled pici, that palm-length pasta made only from semolina and water, is made in advance and then left to dry a little. As with most ragu sauces, the whole thing is better after a day or two; it turns rich and all the flavours fuse together. When the guests arrive, all that's needed is a bit of a reheat, the pasta cooked al dente, and guests can serve themselves at the table (see recipe on page 277).

Three weeks out, I sent out an email invitation to twelve friends. I made an effort with a letterpress-look e-card: half really special, half a bit lame. My besties, Meg and Jess, got back to me immediately. I was forced to phone those who obviously regarded RSVP as a fancy sign off, rather than a polite request. I'd tag it onto the end of our conversations nonchalantly.

'Oh, yeah, and are you coming to the thing?'

A week before the event, I pre-ordered a slab of pork belly, and the beef brisket for the sliders. I did a menu plan and Bingley tested a recipe for spiced tuna crostini, little corn tortillas topped with smashed avocado, chargrilled corn and jalapenos, a sliver of raw tuna on top with a zigzag of spiced Kewpie mayonnaise. He talked about those crostini a lot, whether they should be toasted to a crisp, which beer we should have, a Mexican beer? I pre-ordered enough little brioche for two each – they'd come in a large flat single-layer box so as not to wreck the glaze on top. I drove out to a supercentre to pick up four packets of paper lanterns, bright pops of colour for the balcony. I ordered peaches to grill on the barbecue: I had a peach amaretti almond crumble in mind.

Rhubarb was in season, so I bought a bouquet of that. I'd roast the stalks and toss that with fresh raspberries. I flick through one of my grandma's old cookbooks, past chocolate roulade and lemon soufflés.

'Crème brûlée,' I say to Bingley, 'with the roasted rhubarb. How does that sound?'

He nods.

'But with ginger.'

Ginger gives it a lovely kick, and infused into the cream, it becomes aromatic and soothing somehow (see recipe on page 278).

A few days before the gathering the phone rang. My friend Beth, the only one I'd not spoken to about the soirée, said she realised her sister's birthday was on the same night; she was so sorry, she couldn't believe she didn't notice, but let's catch up the following week and also *sorry*.

I picked up the cryovacked meat, which would last well in the fridge.

A couple of days before the dinner party, we rang another couple, good friends with children. It was one of those phone conversations on loudspeaker in the car, staccato and confusing, kids screaming.

'So, guys, we're a bit…' Bill's on loudspeaker.

His voice is overruled as a bevy of Harleys overtakes us on the highway, a thunderous clapping of black that sucks sound and sense from the car and replaces it with vibrations through your bones and teeth.

'…Is that cool? Sorry.'

We filled in the gaps.

'Yeah, we understand, that's cool,' Bingley said. 'See you soon anyway. Take it easy mate.'

We did understand. Life with children was different from ours. All good intentions and yearnings to go out didn't stop a child's flu or a bung nose forfeiting everything. But, well, damn it. We counted on one hand who would be coming. Meg and Andrew, Jess and Jay, a couple of others.

'Oh, well, at least it will be a lovely chilled night,' the chirpy one said.

'No comment,' I said.

'Non répondez s'il vous plaît,' he cackled to himself. I looked over at his silly face, watching the road, proud of his own joke. At least he was going to be there.

For the party, I make crackers using Australian extra virgin olive oil – that fresh, latest-harvest stuff – drizzling it into a very simple dough that's so soft, so packed with water, that you almost think it will never make a cracker. It's the water content in the dough that makes it crack, and I like to roll it out on the same kitchen paper it's going to bake on, throw some quinoa seeds in there to pretty it up. I roast a couple of eggplants and scoop out the silken flesh, give it a couple of turns with lemon and tahini, and call it a dip (see recipe on page 281).

But it's not about how much was spent or how complicated the menu, where the prosciutto was sourced. It's about the unforeseen magic that happens when the best-laid plans derail and the socially impoverished can come together and, importantly, eat before midnight.

When it finally happens, in the end, you're always glad for who did turn up. Because the best ones always do. Or the ones most in sync with you right now always do. Others are out at clubs or holding a baby bottle under their chin while they use both hands to do up the baby's nappy. So they can't answer the phone anyway. For me those best ones have always been Meg, Jess, and my sister Louise. All of my friends are hugely important to me, and more so in recent years. But it's these three women with whom I end up curled into the sofa after a night of drinking and eating and sending the babies to bed. It's these women who overwhelm me with their strength. My mother, father and my grandmother did that for me, taught me to look for that. It's strength I'm looking for, that I'm drawn to, that I'm working to emulate and learn from.

It's lightness, too, that we need from our friends, and that they need from us. My parents and my grandmother taught me that, too. It was Meg I told the other day that I bought a pair of comfortable underpants, like the granny ones – because why would you tell anyone else that?

'I want some!' she said. 'Why do we have our kidneys out there for the world to see every time we shut the boot?'

And the wine dripped out my nose from laughing.

When I told Meg I was writing a book that kind of whipped up Grandma's stories and my stories, she smiled and said: 'Excellent. Can you please call it "Stiff Peaks"?'

These are the friends for a lifetime, no matter whether you're eating boeuf bourguignon or a cheese sandwich.

PICI with DUCK RAGU

See story on page 273

SERVES 4–6
PREPARATION 1 hour
15 minutes, plus
20 minutes resting
COOKING 2 hours

1 x 1.8 kg (4 lb) duck,
   deboned, skin removed
2 tablespoons extra virgin
   olive oil
1 onion, chopped
1 carrot, chopped
2 celery stalks, chopped
½ leek, chopped
3 garlic cloves, chopped
2 tablespoons tomato paste
   (concentrated purée)
20 g (¾ oz/½ bunch) sage,
   leaves chopped
2 whole cloves, ground in
   a mortar and pestle
250 ml (9 fl oz/1 cup)
   white wine
1 x 400 g (14 oz) tin cherry
   or chopped tomatoes
freshly grated Parmigiano
   Reggiano cheese, to serve

Pici
400 g (14 oz) fine semolina
200 ml (7 fl oz) warm water

Remove and discard any excess fat from the duck, then grind the meat in a mincer or food processor until still quite chunky (see Tip, below). Set aside.

Heat the oil in a large heavy-based saucepan over medium–high heat, add the onion, carrot, celery, leek and garlic and cook for 8–10 minutes, or until tender.

Add the tomato paste and cook, stirring for 3–5 minutes, or until the paste darkens. Add the duck meat, sage and ground cloves, stir well and cook for 5 minutes, then pour in the wine and simmer for 10 minutes, until reduced. Stir in the tomatoes, cover and simmer over low heat for 1½–2 hours, adding extra water to the pan, if needed

Meanwhile, for the pici, combine the semolina and water in a large bowl and mix well, then knead in the bowl or on a work surface for 8–10 minutes, or until smooth and elastic. Wrap in plastic wrap and let rest for 20 minutes.

Roll the dough into a long cigar shape, about 2 cm (¾ in) thick, and cut into 4 cm (1½ in) lengths. With floured hands, roll the lengths out on a board until about 3 mm (⅛ in) thick and anywhere from 10–20 cm (4–8 in) long (they'll resemble rustic-looking spaghetti). Keep the remaining dough covered so it doesn't dry out. Dust the pici with semolina and let them rest in the fridge, loosely covered, until needed.

Cook the pici in boiling salted water for 4–5 minutes, or until just al dente. Towards the end of cooking, spoon 125 ml (4 fl oz/½ cup) of the pasta cooking water into the ragu and let the sauce simmer for 2 minutes. Drain the pici and add it to the sauce, stirring to combine.

Serve in shallow bowls with freshly grated Parmigiano.

tip

This recipe is better with hand-minced (ground) free-range duck, using both the dark and breast meat. Your butcher may be willing to debone and mince a whole duck for you, or you can mince the meat by hand with a sharp knife or in a mincer, or in batches in a food processor (be careful not to overprocess it – chunky is much better than mushy). Alternatively, use 750 g (1 lb 10 oz) bought minced duck.

GINGER CRÈME BRÛLÉE *with* ROASTED RHUBARB

See story on page 274

MAKES 4 x 250 ml
(9 fl oz/1 cup) brûlées
PREPARATION 20 minutes
COOKING 1 hour 50 minutes
Start this recipe 1 day before

650 ml (22½ fl oz) thin
   (pouring) cream
200 ml (7 fl oz) milk
1 tablespoon ground ginger
1 vanilla bean, seeds scraped
13 free-range egg yolks
110 g (3¾ oz/½ cup) caster
   (superfine) sugar
demerara sugar, for sprinkling

Roasted rhubarb
450 g (1 lb/1 bunch) rhubarb,
   leaves removed,
   stalks chopped
200 g (7 oz) caster
   (superfine) sugar
juice of 1 orange
1 vanilla bean, halved
   lengthways, seeds scraped
125 g (4½ oz/1 cup) raspberries

Preheat the oven to 110°C (225°F). Place four 250 ml (9 fl oz/1 cup) ceramic ramekins in a deep-sided roasting tin so they are not touching.

Combine the cream, milk, ginger and vanilla seeds in a medium heavy-based saucepan over medium heat. Bring to the boil, then remove from the heat and set aside to infuse and cool for 10 minutes.

In a mixing bowl, whisk together the egg yolks and sugar. Pour the cooled cream mixture into the egg mixture. Whisk gently to combine, then strain through a fine-mesh sieve into a jug. Pour the custard into the ramekins, then pour enough boiling water into the roasting tin to come halfway up the sides of the ramekins.

Bake for 1 hour 45 minutes, or until the custard is just set but still wobbly in the centre. Remove the ramekins from the tin and refrigerate until cold, or overnight if possible.

For the roasted rhubarb, preheat the oven to 200°C (400°F).

Toss the rhubarb in a bowl with the sugar, orange juice and vanilla seeds to coat well. Transfer to a roasting tin that will accommodate the rhubarb in one layer. Roast for 8–10 minutes, or until tender, then transfer to a bowl. Toss gently with the raspberries and set aside to cool.

To serve, sprinkle the custards evenly with demerara sugar. Using a kitchen blowtorch, *brûler* (burn) the tops in an even circular motion to form a shiny glaze, which will harden as it cools. Alternatively, put the ramekins on a baking tray and place under the grill (broiler) on the highest setting until browned, watching constantly to make sure the tops don't burn.

Serve the brûlées with some roasted rhubarb spooned over the top.

CHARRED EGGPLANT DIP *with* OLIVE OIL QUINOA CRACKERS

See story on page 275

SERVES 4–6
PREPARATION 30 minutes, plus 1 hour resting
COOKING 30 minutes

2 large eggplants (aubergines)
1 garlic clove, finely chopped
1 tablespoon tahini
juice of 1 lemon
sea salt and freshly ground
   black pepper
1 spring onion
   (scallion), chopped
2 tablespoons extra virgin olive
   oil, plus extra for drizzling
plain yoghurt, to serve
2 teaspoons thinly sliced mint

Olive oil quinoa crackers
260 g (9¼ oz/1¾ cups) plain
   (all-purpose) flour
2 tablespoons black quinoa,
   well washed and dried on
   paper towel
1 teaspoon sea salt
125 ml (4 fl oz/½ cup) extra
   virgin olive oil

For the olive oil quinoa crackers, preheat the oven to 170°C (325°F). Line a baking tray with baking paper.

In a bowl, combine the flour, quinoa and half the salt. Make a well in the centre and pour in the oil and 185 ml (6 fl oz/¾ cup) of water, mixing with one hand as you go. Mix gently until you have a soft, wet, pliable dough.

Turn the dough out onto a well-floured work surface. Pinch off walnut-sized pieces of dough and roll out on baking paper into paper-thin rounds – they will be quite delicate. Carefully transfer to the prepared tray and sprinkle with the remaining salt.

Bake for 30 minutes, or until lightly browned. This may take less time, depending on how thin the crackers are, so watch them carefully. Remove from the oven and transfer to a wire rack to cool. Store in an airtight container for up to 1 week.

Hold the whole eggplants over a medium flame on a gas stove or barbecue, turning every so often, for about 15–20 minutes, or until the skin is charred all over and the flesh is tender. Halve and put in a colander, cut-side down, for 30 minutes, to drain a little.

Scoop out the flesh from half the eggplants and blend in a food processor with the garlic, tahini and lemon juice. Season with salt and pepper. Scoop out the remaining flesh, mash with a fork, then fold into the blended eggplant with the spring onion and olive oil.

Serve in a shallow bowl, dollop over the plain yoghurt, scatter with mint and drizzle with more olive oil. Serve with quinoa crackers.

LIFE, DEATH AND BEEF TEA

'Going on is a family trait,' Margaret says.

This comes from a woman who at ninety does yoga once a week. An instructor named Brad comes to her house, lays down a mat for her in the sunroom, and stretches her into various positions. In one, she tells me, she lies on her back, and Brad leans into her foot, which presses, right-angled at the knee, into his chest. Another, Grandma on her knees, circling her arms from her side up to the sky, is the older-person's version of salute to the sun. Brad reminds her to do her bra up at the back of her body, arms reaching behind her. If she always does it, he says, she will always be able to. She was interviewed about her weekly escapades with Brad recently, when a radio jock asked her how she stayed fit.

'Well, yes, I do stay fit,' she told the nation live on air. 'I always do my Karma Sutra.'

She has a knack for shock on live radio, especially when it comes to talking about her yoga. Another time, when she was eighty-seven, the host welcomed her and asked her how she was. She moaned in reply.

'Oh dear, Margaret, what's wrong?'

'Oh well,' she said. 'I have a pain in my groin. And it's not at all for the usual reason.'

She fully intends to do what her hardy Scottish relatives have always done: keep going. Her father, Alexander, didn't retire until he was eighty-five. Her sister Jean, an equally clever sibling, who was startling and cutting in her wit, and who became her closest sister over the years, retired at eighty. And at eighty-nine, Margaret wrote a book called *Baking*, which came out soon after yet another rendition of the *Encyclopedia of Food and Cookery*. Nobody knows exactly what number she's at, book-wise, but if you count the *Woman's Day* cookbooks and the collection with *New Idea* magazine, it's probably reaching a few hundred.

The Fulton family does have a knack for 'going on', despite the pummelling that life sometimes offers. When Alexander retired, he came to Sydney, oscillating between his various children's homes. At eighty-six, he was 'run over by a car', as Grandma puts it, and broke a leg. Within four months he was walking again so, at eighty-seven, he used the proceeds of the accident insurance to 'tread the paths Lord Byron trod'.

'But Dad, you don't speak Greek,' Margaret wailed at the time.

And then she realised he didn't hear that well either – in English or any other language – so what did it matter? This is the whisky lover who, when asked if he would like a cup of tea, would reply in his thick Scottish accent: 'Oh, yes, love, a wee dram.'

And he did, he followed in the footsteps of the British poet – avoiding the Greek War of Independence by a couple of centuries and skipping the part with the deadly fever – but with all the romance and hopefully all the excess of his literary compatriot. He returned with a head filled with colourful adventures, plus a Celtic brooch from Scotland, a cameo from Italy, and an olive-wood bowl from Ibiza.

Nearly a decade later, when he was ninety-five, he died – as his wife had years earlier – in Margaret's arms. He was staying with Jean in the Sydney suburb of Lindfield at the time, and Margaret got it into her head that he needed some beef tea to cheer him up. The recipe appears in *Mrs Beeton's Book of Household Management*, published in 1893, as a Victorian broth to be given to 'invalids to whom flavourings and seasonings are not allowed'. She drove to Lindfield with the broth, but he turned it away.

'How about a whisky then?' she offered.

Yes, he would have that, thank you, Margaret. He took a sip of whisky, smiled and looked up at his youngest daughter.

'I can see angels and hear beautiful music.'

Then he closed his eyes. It was the greatest loss.

Margaret found her sister Jean and the doctor in the living room and passed on the news. Jean poured her sister a whisky from the same bottle, which Margaret promptly spat out.

'What was that?' Margaret asked.

'Whisky,' said Jean.

'It was terrible.'

'It was cheap.'

'No wonder Dad died. Anyone would die after drinking that. What's it called? Clan McFuck'em?'

Her outburst turned the room to laughter. It helped relieve their pain. It was a perfect send-off for their darling father.

Jean wasn't for early retirement either. At sixty she became the food writer on a new national magazine, *Woman's World*. She wrote a book called *Good, Cheap Cooking* when she was sixty-five and then tried to retire at seventy. Two days into her golden years she was offered a job as a cookbook editor, which she did for the next ten years. At eighty, while still working, she was diagnosed with breast cancer and Parkinson's disease. Only then did she retire for good. A few years on, she broke her hip and when Margaret was heading out to visit her in hospital, a publisher called, trying to contact Jean. Apparently Jean was the only person who could handle the complex book. Grandma, nearly ten years younger than her closest sibling, felt buoyed that you could still be needed professionally at eighty-four.

'What keeps you going?' I asked Grandma recently.

'Whisky!'

We had a giggle, then she expanded. 'I think I have a panic attack when I know the bottle we have open is the last one. There has to be another after that. It's the way of the Scots.'

My uncle Graham, of the lamb's tongues fame – my father's elder brother – brings her a bottle of single malt every time he comes to Australia from New Zealand, several times a year. So she usually has a bottle after the bottle after the open bottle. She has a wee dram an evening or two a week.

'Really, it's knowing I've had a good life,' she corrects herself. 'And now it's keeping fit and things like getting my face on a stamp. These are all fun things that keep you alive.'

She means it figuratively, because what the Fulton clan is looking for is a mind that stays alert, happy and enthralled, not just a heart that is beating.

I pull an envelope out of my bag and hand it to her. She opens it.

'Ooh! Golly.'

She stands up and puts the card on her shelves, propped against other precious things.

'And this, too, Grandma. I want you to be there at my wedding, cheering me on from the front row.'

A few days later she gave me a card with a drawing of a man on the front. Above his head it reads: 'Anatomy of love' and then all around him, little words point to different parts of the body. To the stomach, points 'self-control', to the heart, 'love' and 'compassion', to the head, 'joy', 'wisdom' and 'faith'. To the legs, point 'humility' and 'commitment', and so on. The card is right up her alley, humour-wise, and mine too.

Inside she writes: 'To dearest Kate and that wonderful [Bingley]/Every happiness/Keep this card to check body parts – it's just as well to know how and why everything works – just another of life's mysteries/xxxx 100'.

RECOVERY FOOD

I'm interviewing Grandma for a story in the *The Sydney Morning Herald* on bereavement casseroles. In the midst of grief and shock, I say, we all send out those well-intentioned but poorly executed offerings that mainly provide a bit of comic relief for the recipient.

'Yes,' she says. 'It must be chicken soup.'

So Grandma tells me a story about chicken soup.

'I remember when a woman was having a baby in the corner house. There was a lot of screaming going on and then the police came because people were worried,' she says. 'What the woman was doing was having a baby in a water bath and there were a lot of hippies down there visiting.

'I had been making chicken soup – I had this big pot of it. At any rate, when the yelling stopped and the police left and we discovered what was really happening, I took the soup down and everyone pounced on it. I wanted to say leave some for...I couldn't even say the girl's name because I didn't know it. But you see, it's strange how it works.'

It's a delicate balance of thoughtfulness and practicality, she tells me. 'You've got to really think of what would bring people back.'

She means back from the throes of illness, but maybe more than that.

'Colourful foods and spicy foods are stimulating and it's not a time you want to be stimulated. That's why the chicken soup is my favourite, because again, it's pale and you don't do the things like brown the meat, like you would for a casserole, so it hasn't got that savoury smell. It has got a lovely reassuring smell.'

Grandma makes her 'Jewish penicillin' with risoni pasta, or with sticks of thin spaghetti, broken into short pieces. I use her exact recipe but add brown rice instead, another nutritious element that I find much more digestible (see recipe on page 288).

She doesn't always stick to her own advice, however. When my mother gave birth to me in Sydney's Royal Hospital for Women in Paddington, my father called Grandma and said she could come to visit now, if she liked. Margaret made the usual 'Can I bring anything' offer and Dad said that would be lovely, specifics not required because this is Margaret Fulton, and she's supposed to know what to do with food.

Grandma turned up to meet me for the first time, her only daughter's first child, and her first grandchild. She raised her celebratory bounty in the air when she walked in the room: a bottle of French champagne and three dozen Sydney rock oysters. Mum turned white at the sight of the fresh oysters: it was a little too close to the bone. So Dad and Grandma sat by the hospital window and squeezed lemon over plates of oysters to have with chilled champagne. I like to think this meal rubbed off on me, somehow emanating into the room in which I took my first breaths.

We, as a family, are fascinated by tales of food poisoning. Once, when my sister and I were about seven and nine, my mother was travelling overseas and so Dad looked after us, cooking all our meals and packing us off to school, tucking us in at night and taking us to the park, the beach on weekends, making pancakes piled high with strawberries on Saturday morning. Then he became ill. Maybe it was something he ate. My sister and I had no idea what to do, and let him sweat it out one night in bed. I remember his rolling on top of the sheets, or lying perfectly still and staring listlessly at the ceiling, waiting for the next wave of illness, when he'd have to rush to the bathroom.

Louise and I stood at the end of the bed.

'Dad, you have to eat something,' one of us said. 'How about some boiled rice?' Louise said.

He peeked through his eyelids and nodded. My sister and I ran downstairs and got out the packet of basmati, a saucepan, and then each of us stood aside.

'Aren't you making the rice?' she said.

'I don't know how to do rice,' I said. '*You* recommended it.'

I put the saucepan on the stovetop and Louise poured in about a cup of grains, then filled it about halfway with water from the tap. When it started to bubble she stirred it, just as we did with our own porridge every morning. Seemed fine. But as she stirred it got thicker, and the grains began to meld together, gloopier and stickier the more she worked at them.

Dad sat up in bed, and looked at the bowl in front of him. He nudged a spoonful out of the muck with his spoon.

'Do you know what?' he started, nodding a little.

We leaned in to hear his praise and thanks.

'I think that might be the worst thing I've ever eaten.'

Above left: Kate's parents, Robert and Suzanne, in London, March 1970, on Suzanne's 20th birthday; above right: Suzanne and Robert on their wedding day, May 1972; below left: Kate at the kitchen bench in Annandale; below right: Kate's sixth birthday.

CLEANSING CHICKEN *and* BROWN RICE SOUP

See story on page 285

SERVES 4
PREPARATION 35 minutes
COOKING 4 hours

2 tablespoons extra virgin
   olive oil
2 garlic cloves, peeled and
   finely sliced
25 g (1 oz/¼ bunch) coriander,
   leaves picked, stalks and
   roots finely chopped
1 leek, trimmed, cut into
   1.5 cm (⅝ in) thick rounds
sea salt and freshly ground
   black pepper
465 g (1 lb 1 oz/2½ cups)
   cooked brown rice
2 spring onions (scallions),
   cut into 3 mm (⅛ in) slices
   on the diagonal
2 fresh jalapeno chillies,
   coarsely chopped
3 radishes, finely sliced
lime wedges, to serve

Chicken stock

1 x 1.5 kg (3 lb 5 oz) free-range
   or organic chicken
5–6 black peppercorns
2 celery stalks, chopped
1 large onion, peeled and
   coarsely chopped
2 carrots, peeled and
   coarsely chopped
2 sprigs thyme
4 sprigs flat-leaf (Italian)
   parsley (including stalks)
1 fresh bay leaf

tip

For the chicken stock, put the chicken, breast-side down, into a large stockpot with the remaining ingredients. Add 3–3.5 litres (101–118 fl oz/12–14 cups) of cold water to come about three-quarters of the way up the sides of the pot and bring to the boil over high heat. Reduce to the lowest heat possible and skim any foam from the surface using a large spoon (this removes any impurities). Simmer for 35–45 minutes, or until the chicken is tender.

Transfer the chicken to a large board using tongs, taking care to drain it well over the pot. When cool enough to handle, remove the breast meat and refrigerate until needed. Transfer the carcass back to the pot with the stock and simmer for a further 30 minutes. Remove the carcass, pick off all the meat and reserve, then transfer the bones, fat and skin back to the pot and simmer for 2 hours.

Shred all the chicken meat with your fingers. Reserve 175–350 g (6–12 oz/1–2 cups) of the chicken meat, and store the remainder in the fridge for another use (it will keep for up to 3 days).

Remove any large bones from the broth and discard, then strain through a fine-mesh sieve into a large jug or clean saucepan. Reserve 1.5 litres (52 fl oz/6 cups) of the stock, and store the remainder in airtight containers for another use (it will keep in the fridge for up to 1 week, or the freezer for up to 1 month).

Heat the oil in a medium saucepan over medium–low heat and sauté the garlic, coriander stalks and roots, and leek for 5 minutes. Add the reserved 1.5 litres (52 fl oz/ 6 cups) stock and simmer for 20 minutes, or until the leek is cooked. Add the chicken meat and simmer for about 5 minutes, or until heated through. Season to taste.

Spoon the rice into serving bowls and divide the chicken meat between the bowls. Ladle the chicken broth over the top and garnish with spring onions, jalapenos and radishes. Serve with lime wedges.

If you want a clear stock, skim any foam and fats from the surface as it cooks. This improves the clarity and also reduces the fat content of the stock. And don't stir the stock while it's cooking – this will infuse the fats and impurities into it further (you want them out!).

NEW ORLEANS

When it is good, though, food can nurture, it can 'bring people back', as Grandma says. When Michael died, food helped bring her back. Not a few bowls of chicken soup or a bereavement casserole, but the food on a recovery tour that she took with her daughter to New Orleans with Tabasco, the company. It was a media trip, and Charmaine and Reuben Solomon were also there, along with a smattering of other food writers and editors – about twenty people in all. There's nothing like a dash of hot sauce to shake you from the blues.

'It wasn't an area of food that I knew about and not really one that she knew about either,' says Mum.

My mother learned that Creole food came from the French living in Louisiana, where they adopted the concept of roux.

'It's very big in Creole cooking. You can buy it there in jars. To me, going to the Cordon Bleu, it was one of those things you make carefully in a saucepan in the kitchen. It wasn't part of my education in food and it wasn't part of Mum's. But there it was – a lump of flour and butter you just scooped out of the jar and added to the saucepan with your liquid. It was well browned already so you didn't have to worry about that. This is the mainstay of many of their dishes.'

When Mum told me this story, Dad walked in halfway and I caught him up:

'Mum's telling me how you could buy roux in jars in New Orleans.'

'Kangaroo?' said Dad.

I love him.

Margaret and Suzanne met Reuben and Charmaine in local bars.

'We'd go to bars and have beers and shrimp. Reuben was going for the jazz and we were going for the fun, and the food.'

In one of these bars my mother learned for the first time about sweet corn fritters.

'They've become a staple now, but this is where I first saw them. It was just fresh sweet corn. Sometimes they also used maize, like polenta, in it. They beat it into a batter with lots of herbs and you'd have them with beer.'

Margaret had been to New Orleans before, with Michael. It was here she picked up her family-famous crab cakes, also one of Michael's favourite dishes. I love the idea of these sweet corn fritters, with crab pulled fresh and tossed into the mix, lots of herbs. I make a light buttermilk batter to hold it together. Small spoonfuls of the mixture – dropped into hot oil, so the fresh corn starts to crisp up on the outside – is my ultimate beer snack, with hot sauce, obviously (see recipe on page 298).

The mother–daughter duo ordered po' boys all over New Orleans.

'All the bars had them,' says Mum of the sandwich, which is stuffed with lettuce, a slab of tomato, and fried spiced oysters. 'They also had other kinds of boys, like shrimp. They were in all the run-of-the-mill places, where the locals went.'

Oysters are doused in a batter of buttermilk, flour and egg, rolled in a dry mix of polenta and cayenne pepper, then deep-fried. The batter forms a crust on the outside and inside the oysters are creamy and soft. They're eaten hot in the roll, with crunchy greens. I do mine with watercress for an extra peppery kick, and a zigzag of spiced mayo (see recipe on page 296).

Margaret and Suzanne stayed in a boutique hotel in the middle of the French quarter; they couldn't believe their luck. By day they would join Tabasco on the tour, doing tastings. They visited Avery Island, where the chillies for Tabasco were once all grown. They learned that the island is a sanctuary for egrets, which were slaughtered by plume hunters in the thousands in the 1890s to cater for the fashion of feathered hats. And by night they went to bars and, one evening, had a 'crawfish boil'.

'The crayfish are boiled up with potatoes and cobs of corn, drained, then the whole lot is turned out on the table in front of you. They're like yabbies, and you put bibs on and there would be sauces and melted butter. It's a bit of a rough-and-ready kind of meal and you eat with your hands. We loved it,' my mum tells me.

They visited a grand old house of the cotton days for a Tabasco lunch. Mum felt as though she had stepped into a scene from *Gone with the Wind*.

'The tree branches were hanging, with lichen on them, you know,' she gestures with her hands. 'There were black waiters, with gorgeous, very dark skin. But it was all so foreign to me. They stood there in this garden in white coats, holding trays. It took me aback.'

The pair was offered trays of Tabasco-spiked Bloody Marys and champagne, or daiquiris, and Suzanne loved the celery sticking out the top of the glasses. There was a large buffet in the garden, on the green grass, and guests helped themselves to the Creole food, 'the food for the rich in this area'. There was something called 'blackened fish', where the fish is marinated in smoked spices that permeate the flesh and turn it black. Suzanne discovered spoon bread too; a bit like a savoury corn pudding with bacon and sour cream cooked into it. And there was more familiar food: prawn cocktails done the old-fashioned way in stemmed glasses, cob salads, fresh prawns with buttermilk dressing.

'Mum and I kept pinching each other: "Isn't this amazing?"' Suzanne says now.

I like to think this is the moment that Grandma was 'brought back', as she puts it.

I'm a bit jealous about these crawfish boils, and the Bloody Marys on the green lawn and the prawn cocktails. So I invented a version of it, using Australia's own large, local prawns. I slice the prawns right through the middle with their shells still on, cleavering right through the head, because inside there is culinary gold. In a bowl I whip together softened butter and hot sauce, a dollop of tomato paste, and brush the raw meat inside the prawns with the butter, then grill them on the barbecue. It's an Australian tilt on that trip they had, I think. I asked Mum what she thought of the dish, and she pulled the just-done meat from the prawn with her fork, charred and buttery, a thrill of spice and tomato.

'I love it,' she said (see recipe on page 295). 'That's like a kind of Bloody Mary butter.'

GRILLED KING PRAWNS WITH BLOODY MARY BUTTER *and* GREEN OIL

See story on page 292

SERVES 4
PREPARATION 30 minutes
COOKING 10 minutes

12 large raw king
 prawns (shrimp)
1 handful watercress sprigs
lime wedges, to serve

Bloody Mary butter

60 g (2¼ oz) butter, softened
1 garlic clove,
 very finely chopped
2 teaspoons Tabasco
 or hot sauce
1 teaspoon sweet paprika
1 tablespoon tomato paste
 (concentrated purée)
1 teaspoon
 Worcestershire sauce
pinch of sea salt

Green oil

250 g (9 oz/2 large bunches)
 curly parsley, leaves picked
60 ml (2 fl oz/¼ cup) extra
 virgin olive oil
sea salt

For the green oil, bring a medium saucepan of salted water to the boil and have ready an ice-water bath. Add the parsley leaves to the boiling water, cook for 20 seconds until bright green, then drain and quickly transfer to the ice bath to stop the cooking process. Drain, then put the parsley in a food processor or blender and blend until smooth.

Pour the parsley purée into a muslin- (cheesecloth-) lined sieve placed over a jug or bowl and allow the juice to drain into the bowl for 5 minutes. Squeeze the puréed leaves gently to extract more juice, then discard. Add the olive oil to the parsley juice, season with salt and whisk together. Set aside.

For the Bloody Mary butter, combine all the ingredients in a bowl and mix well.

Using a sharp knife, cut the prawns and heads in half lengthways, taking care not to cut all the way through – they should still be joined along the centre back. Open cut the prawns and remove the gastrointestinal tract.

Using a pastry brush, brush the prawn meat with half the Bloody Mary butter.

Heat a barbecue or chargrill pan to high and cook the prawns, meat-side down, for 1 minute. Turn them over, brush with the remaining butter, and cook for a further 30 seconds, until just cooked.

To serve, arrange the prawns on a serving platter, drizzle with the green oil and scatter with watercress sprigs. Offer lime wedges for squeezing.

tip

You can make the green oil in advance and store in a jar or airtight container in the fridge for up to 1 week.

NEW ORLEANS PO' BOYS

See story on page 291

SERVES 4
PREPARATION 30 minutes
COOKING 10 minutes

1 free-range egg
125 ml (4 fl oz/½ cup)
    buttermilk
2 teaspoons sea salt
freshly ground black pepper
150 g (5½ oz/1 cup) plain
    (all-purpose) flour
250 g (9 oz/1⅓ cups) fine
    polenta (cornmeal)
2 teaspoons cayenne pepper
1 litre (35 fl oz/4 cups) rice
    bran oil
4 x 12–15 cm (4½–6 in) long
    soft bread rolls
12 fresh oysters, shucked
1 handful watercress, leaves
    and tender sprigs picked
1 tablespoon lemon juice
2 teaspoons olive oil
Tabasco sauce, to serve
lime halves, to serve

Spiced mayo
120 g (4¼ oz/½ cup) Japanese
    mayonnaise (such as Kewpie)
1 chipotle pepper in adobo
    sauce, chopped
juice of ½ lime

For the spiced mayo, combine all the ingredients in a small bowl and whisk to combine. Set aside until needed.

Place the egg, buttermilk, ½ teaspoon of the salt and pepper to taste in a bowl and whisk together. In another shallow bowl, combine the flour and a pinch of pepper. In a third shallow bowl, combine the polenta, remaining salt and the cayenne pepper.

Preheat the oven to 220°C (425°F).

Working in batches of three or four, dust the oysters in the seasoned flour, shaking off any excess, dip in the buttermilk mixture, letting any excess drip off, then dust in the polenta. Transfer to a clean baking tray.

Heat the oil in a large, deep saucepan or wok over high heat to 190°C (375°F).

While the oil is heating, prepare the rolls. Cut each one halfway through from the top, place on a baking tray and bake for a few minutes, or until warm and a little crunchy on the outside. Remove from the oven to a serving plate, and drizzle 1 teaspoon of the spiced mayo inside each of the rolls.

Toss the watercress in a bowl with lemon juice, olive oil and a pinch of salt. Divide between the rolls.

To cook the oysters, gently drop them, one by one, into the oil, in batches of about three or four. Deep-fry for 45–60 seconds, or until golden on all sides, turning them occasionally with tongs. Transfer to a plate lined with paper towel. Check the temperature of the oil between batches, keeping it at 190°C (375°F).

Divide the oysters between the rolls and drizzle with a little more spiced mayo to serve. Offer Tabasco sauce and lime halves on the table.

tip

Chipotle peppers in adobo are available from good grocers and delicatessens.

CRAB and CORN FRITTERS

See story on page 291

MAKES 40–45
PREPARATION 20 minutes, plus 30 minutes cooling
COOKING 30 minutes

3 tablespoons extra virgin olive oil
20 g (¾ oz) unsalted butter
1–2 large sweetcorn, kernels stripped, to give about 400 g (14 oz/2 cups)
1 teaspoon dried chilli flakes
3 spring onions (scallions), sliced
sea salt and freshly ground black pepper
250 g (9 oz) cooked crab meat, picked over to remove any shell
30 g (1 oz/¾ cup) chopped coriander (cilantro)
75 g (2¾ oz/½ cup) plain (all-purpose) flour
40 g (1½ oz/¼ cup) fine polenta (cornmeal)
1 teaspoon baking powder
185 ml (6 fl oz/¾ cup) buttermilk
2 free-range eggs, separated
1 litre (35 fl oz/4 cups) vegetable or rice bran oil
hot sauce, to serve
lime cheeks, to serve

Heat the oil and butter in a saucepan over medium heat, add the corn kernels, chilli flakes and spring onion and sauté for 3–4 minutes, or until tender. Season with salt and pepper to taste and transfer to a bowl to cool to room temperature.

When the corn mixture is cool, add the crab meat, coriander, flour, polenta, baking powder, buttermilk and egg yolks, and fold together until well combined.

Whisk the egg whites with a pinch of sea salt until firm peaks form, then take a large spoonful and fold it into the corn mixture. Fold in the remaining egg white.

Heat the oil in a wok or small saucepan. Working in batches of three or four, slide heaped teaspoons of the corn mixture carefully into the hot oil, turning with tongs to cook on all sides. They will puff and turn golden when cooked. Transfer to a plate lined with paper towel.

Season with sea salt and serve immediately with hot sauce and lime cheeks.

tip

You can buy vacuum-sealed, pre-picked crab meat from most good fishmongers and fish markets, and, if it's fresh and good-quality, then it will work well here. But avoid those canned versions: the crab meat won't provide the same taste or texture. The best option, of course, is to hand-pick the cooked crabs yourself. I love the texture of Australian blue swimmer crabmeat, and it's a good sustainable choice, too.

GROWING UP FOODIE

There's now generation four of the Fultons: Grandma, my mother, my sister and me – and now Harry. He's a thigh-high four-and-a-half-year-old and just the thought of him makes me well up with love. I can't believe he is real. He has thick hair like his mother and legs like his father, and he's as bossy and independent as the best of us in the Fulton clan. For a while he called me Annie but now he's perfected it: Aunty Tate (close enough).

Last Christmas he walked into the living room at my parents' place and approached Margaret, his great-grandmother, who, after all the present opening and tossing of wrapping paper into great piles, was making a bouquet of ribbons. Every year she does it, bending down to collect all the knotted strips, or we pass them to her when one of us opens a gift, and from the would-be colourful junk she ties them into bow upon bow, knot over knot, ending up with a stunning bouquet. Harry's onto the tradition; he already knows the bouquet at the end is worth more than all the gifts put together. She passes him the bundle.

'Thank you, GG,' he says, his abbreviation of great-grandma.

Harry is brimming with health and energy, and that's down to my sister's rigorous routine with his food. Plus the genes, obviously. She grew up a foodie too and after a brief stint in the law she moved into food as well. More targeted and absolute than me, she focused on children, specifically babies and toddlers. She did a nutrition degree, thus honing those skills even more to focus on children's culinary health. It's a win for Harry, who for the past four years has been nourished with iron-rich meat, calcium-rich this-and-that, vitamins B, C and zinc in his leafy greens and blueberries, a chocolate zucchini cake for his birthday.

'When I grow up,' I joke with my sister, 'and I have a baby, I'm definitely going to come to you for help.'

One day I will, or hope to. Meanwhile, there's Harry – the perfect, hilarious boy.

I grew up, like thousands of other Australians, with parents who cooked. I was not the only one whose grandmother went to the markets and bought trays of tomatoes in season, or bartered backyard beans for front-lawn radishes over the fence.

In my teens, my peers were happy to eat burritos, and not the good kind. An abiding interest in food was something for snobs and at school my poached chicken sandwiches with watercress, flaked almonds and homemade mayonnaise were considered odd and fussy. I took my mother's chicken and pistachio dolmades in to school and my friends thought they looked weird, until they realised they were delicious.

In my twenties, bothering about food was like being into golf; it was stuffy and got in the way of what everyone really wanted to do: drink. Now, food is cool. Even better: extraordinary, real food, made using quality ingredients is cool. What I love about modern discerning epicurean fashionistas is that they've turned a fusty hobby – eating amazing food – into a youth-culture phenomenon. Kids today: they'll go for a sichuan jellyfish and cucumber salad, a couple of beers, and call it a great night out. They join a vast Australian population that cares more now about food – the way it's grown and how it's cooked – than it ever has.

The other day I was writing a recipe for stollen for a food magazine. I macerated the fruit and called my mother to borrow some citrus peel. An hour later she called me back with a recipe she had written for one of my grandmother's cookbooks in the 1970s. I made my stollen, then I made her stollen as a comparison. I carted two containers of the German fruitcake over to my mother's house, so she could make an informed comparison. I found her in the kitchen with my dad and Grandma. They half-looked up at me, distracted by something much more important right now. Mum had two stollen in the oven and was slicing into another. My grandmother leaned into the loaf, poked the side with her finger, then pulled out four little plates. I put my loaf on the bench, with the others. Three generations lined up at the kitchen bench.

Grandma told us a story about the time she had stollen in Norway with an ambassador for Germany.

'Never let the truth get in the way of a good story,' Dad said, giving her a gentle nudge.

She spread the butter on thick. And Dad and I had a dig at her, the woman who once said she likes enough butter on her bread 'so I can see my teeth marks in it'.

We debated and wondered: more yeast, less marzipan, no glacé cherries, currants are better than raisins, snow sugar is better than icing sugar, can you make two loaves with the same dough, 'more butter please'.

Icing sugar and citrus peel were scattered and dusted over the bench. It has always been like this, and I wish it always could be.

THANKS

I feel so incredibly lucky and so grateful. There are a great many people who made this book what it is, and indeed without whom it frankly would not have happened.

My grandmother, the smart, strong, savvy and superb Margaret Fulton, how can I ever thank you enough? You not only gave up many, many hours to sit and chat with me as I painstakingly muck-raked your entire life, and asked you to relive and spill on the most painful and joyous bits, but you did it with more grace and ease than I could have ever hoped for. I wonder sometimes whether I wrote this book just so I could sit with you over never-ending cups of tea and the odd wee dram of whisky. Even without this book at the end of all the interviews and stories, I am grateful for this time with you. I hope it's a reminder to us all that previous generations have so much to share, so many stories to tell, so much wisdom and quirk, and tales often much more wild than our own. If only we'd take the time to hear them. I will always be thankful I listened to you. Grandma, thank you for everything – the powerful steps you took, the courage, the strength, the high standards and hilarity, the extraordinary love.

If all the world's a stage, Grandma has enjoyed the best lighting in our family. But that doesn't mean that the best supporting actors, my darling Mum and Dad, were not equally important both in the making of this book and in the making of me. Suzanne and Robert Gibbs, the magnificent duo, thank you. Your tireless work behind the scenes, all my life, has not only given me fodder for my book, but it also allows me to do what I do, and gives me the energy and passion with which to do it. You did this, and I owe you everything. Thank you, too, to the freaking stunning Louise Fulton Keats, my clever, loving, inspiring sister. Thank God for you. And Jannie Brown, the Gibbs clan's best firend, thank you for the constant generosity, the sage advice and all the laughs. You are so important and loved.

My new husband – whether I call you Bingley, the Brunette, the Boy, no matter – you are the bubbles in my champagne, my constant companion, my inspiration and my future. I love you.

To my strong, beautiful, intelligent girls. Meg, Jess, Jodi – what would I do without you? Thank you for making me laugh every day, you are perfect to me. And Polly… my brave and inspiring friend. I miss you every day.

Big love and thanks to the people who made this book. To Murdoch Books for welcoming my first manuscript that isn't solely a collection of recipes. To my publisher, Jane Morrow, for believing that the story is worth telling, for reminding me how the lives of two women can hopefully entertain, and that the story of one certain woman might still inspire. To my editorial manager, Virginia Birch, for your incredible support and impeccable decision-making, for knowing when to cut me short and when to let me roam free. Thank you. To the illustrious editor Georgina Bitcon, your eagle eyes have saved me many future blushes, and made the book a much better read.

To Kirby Armstrong for making it all so beautiful. Thank you for your artistic flair and unique cleverness with fonts and layout and working my elaborate concepts into something that will work in an actual book. To Michelle Noerianto, the extraordinary stylist, your endless skill during our photoshoots, your meticulous fashioning of plates and ingredients – do you know how remarkable you are? To Rob Palmer, thank you for your clever way with light and dark, things on a plate, endless smiles and skill behind a camera. And Tina McLeish, you can handle the heat in the kitchen. But more than that, you can handle the author in the kitchen. Thank you for your organisation, high standards and cooking wizardry.

GENERAL INDEX

MF = Margaret Fulton

RECIPE INDEX

Page numbers in italics refer to photographs.

Published in 2015 by Murdoch Books,
an imprint of Allen & Unwin

Murdoch Books Australia
83 Alexander Street
Crows Nest NSW 2065
Phone: +61 (0) 2 8425 0100
Fax: +61 (0) 2 9906 2218
murdochbooks.com.au
info@murdochbooks.com.au

Murdoch Books UK
Erico House, 6th Floor
93–99 Upper Richmond Road
Putney, London SW15 2TG
Phone: +44 (0) 20 8785 5995
murdochbooks.co.uk
info@murdochbooks.co.uk

For Corporate Orders & Custom Publishing contact
Noel Hammond, National Business Development
Manager, Murdoch Books Australia

Publisher: Jane Morrow
Editorial Manager: Virginia Birch
Design Manager: Hugh Ford
Editor: Georgina Bitcon
Designer: Kirby Armstrong
Food Photographer: Rob Palmer
Stylist: Michelle Noerianto
Home Economist: Tina McLeish
Production Manager: Mary Bjelobrk
Paper art by Sonia Rentsch

Text © Kate Gibbs 2015
The moral rights of the author have been asserted
Design © Murdoch Books 2015
Photography © Rob Palmer, except for the following:
picture on page 1 © Kristian Taylor-Wood; pictures on
pages 4–5, 6, 33, 99, 105, 141, 167, 293, 302–303 and 311
© Luisa Brimble; pictures on pages 2, 8, 91, 123, 174, 197,
243 and 287 from the Gibbs and Fulton family archives.

A cataloguing-in-publication entry is available from the
catalogue of the National Library of Australia at nla.gov.au.

ISBN 978 1 74331 027 4 Australia
ISBN 978 1 7433 6 324 9 UK

A catalogue record for this book is available from the
British Library.

Colour reproduction by Splitting Image Colour Studio
Pty Ltd, Clayton, Victoria
Printed by 1010 Printing International Limited, China

IMPORTANT: Those who might be at risk from the
effects of salmonella poisoning (the elderly, pregnant
women, young children and those suffering from immune
deficiency diseases) should consult their doctor with any
concerns about eating raw eggs.

OVEN GUIDE: You may find cooking times vary
depending on the oven you are using. For fan-forced
ovens, as a general rule, set the oven temperature to 20°C
(35°F) lower than indicated in the recipe.

MEASURES GUIDE: We have used 20 ml
(4 teaspoon) tablespoon measures. If you are using a
15 ml (3 teaspoon) tablespoon, add an extra teaspoon
of the ingredient for each tablespoon specified.